RITUAL AS REMEDY

"Mara Branscombe welcomes us into ritual as a doorway to the sacred in our everyday lives and reminds us of our inherent connection to the great mother through the cycles of the earth. She sprinkles poetry amid a carefully crafted road map shaped by her years on the path of love, inviting us to dance with our shadows and awaken the mystic within each of us, guided by the elements and aligned with the moon. This is potent medicine as we rise to tend to the cries of our embodied world."

— **MIRABAI STARR,** teacher, speaker, and author of
Wild Mercy and *Caravan of No Despair*

"A sacred alchemy of healing is found within the pages of *Ritual as Remedy*. Mara Branscombe weaves ancient teachings into powerful and accessible rituals that remind us that nothing is mundane and that each moment holds the possibility for renewal."

— **TRACEE STANLEY,** founder of Empowered Life Circle and
Sankalpa Shakti Yoga School, author of *Radiant Rest,*
and creator of *Empowered Life Self-Inquiry Oracle*

"*Ritual as Remedy* lays a path to rediscover the sacred in our everyday lives. It invites us to use the power of ritual to see the beauty, wonder, and vibrancy that lies before us. Each ritual weaves a way back home to true self, transforming the quality of our entire life."

— **MICHELE KAMBOLIS, Ph.D.** (mind-body medicine),
clinical counselor, and author of *When Women Rise*

"Mara's purposeful, steady instruction invites us to heal, transform, and connect to what matters most. *Ritual as Remedy* is an embodied, wise, and wondrous guidebook for our times."

— **ELENA BROWER,** yoga and meditation teacher, mentor, artist, and author of *Practice You, Being You,* and *Art of Attention*

"Mara is an intuitive writer with a special ability to see what's below the surface. She has a unique understanding of rituals and how to weave them into your life in ways that are meaningful and magical. A beautiful read for anyone seeking to grow more joy using soul care."

— **SAMANTHA SKELLY,** entrepreneur, motivational speaker, and author of *Hungry for Happiness*

"*Ritual as Remedy* emanates warmth and wisdom. Mara Branscombe provides a clear and vital path to retrieve and enliven our inherent soul intelligence through nurturing rituals designed to illuminate our own inner worlds of wonder and self-healing. The prose, invitations, and rituals overflow with a heartfelt authenticity that harmonizes the reader with his or her own soul, as if a tone is ringing through the words calling each heart to open, trust, and nurture the process of unfolding. I highly recommend this book! It is a wondrous journey, offering rituals as medicine to cultivate the most true and soulful version of ourselves."

— **ELIZABETH E. MEACHAM, Ph.D.,** environmental philosopher, teacher, healer, and author of *Earth Spirit Dreaming*

"History reveals centuries of spiritual practices through ritual and ceremony in every culture. It is important to evolve our understanding of Earth energy and heal the collective karma. We are on the precipice of major change and this gem, *Ritual as Remedy,* is the ticket!"

— **SONJA GRACE,** mystic, healer, artist, and author of *Spirit Traveler, Odin and the Nine Realms Oracle,* and *Dancing with Raven and Bear*

RITUAL

AS

REMEDY

EMBODIED PRACTICES
FOR SOUL CARE

MARA BRANSCOMBE

FINDHORN PRESS

Findhorn Press
One Park Street
Rochester, Vermont 05767
www.findhornpress.com

Text stock is SFI certified

Findhorn Press is a division of Inner Traditions International

Disclaimer
The information in this book is given in good faith and intended for
information only. Neither author nor publisher can be held liable by
any person for any loss or damage whatsoever which may arise from
the use of this book or any of the information therein.

Cataloging-in-Publication data for this title is available from the Library of Congress

ISBN 978-1-64411-424-7 (print)
ISBN 978-1-64411-425-4 (ebook)

Printed and bound in the United States by Lake Book Manufacturing Inc.
The text stock is SFI certified. The Sustainable Forestry Initiative® program
promotes sustainable forest management.

10 9 8 7 6 5 4 3 2 1

Edited by Jane Ellen Combelic
Illustrations by Laura Mowbray
Text design and layout by Anna-Kristina Larsson
This book was typeset in Garamond and Gill Sans.

To send correspondence to the author of this book, mail a first-class letter
to the author c/o Inner Traditions • Bear & Company, One Park Street,
Rochester, VT 05767, USA and we will forward the communication,
or contact the author directly at **www.marabranscombe.com**

I dedicate this book to my beloved daughters—
my forever teachers, Desa Rose and Phoenix.

May you bravely dance with the light and the darkness
in all of life's adventures, may your loving hearts be free,
and may you trust that this precious life is yours to create.
Anything is possible.

Contents

Move through your days as a lighthouse for your own soul.
Be it simple and quiet or loud and wild, trust that by being
authentically you, your channel of goodness, compassion, and
truth will ripple far and wide. You will touch the hearts of others
so deeply, their lives and your own will alter for the better. Learn,
live, and evolve into this technology of love as the ultimate source
of your embodied consciousness and freedom.

INTRODUCTION

The impulse to write this book of embodied rituals, practices, prose, and formulas comes from 28 years of life experiences, trainings, academic studies, and body–mind practices that deeply shifted my life. The intuitive call to share this body of work through the medium of emotional, physical, intellectual, creative, and spiritual channels began to speak louder than anything else—I knew it was time.

As the global Covid-19 pandemic swirled its way through the world, it ushered in societal, political, and emotional life-altering change on all levels. In response to this great shift of consciousness came a potent and humble pull to share self-guided practices for inner peace, balance, and intuitive counsel.

Inside these pages you will find embodied practices, supporting tools, technologies, and earth-based resources to help you feel connected, alive, heart-centered, and ultimately empowered to live out your dreams.

Truly, the heart intention of this book is to generate your own ability to live this precious life with your highest self on board. The book's essence rushed through me, loud and clear. To "support the collective" was the vision I received. It is an honor to go on this journey with you, to share resources and grow the body of your own inner mystic, healer, and intuitive guide within.

Personally, the deepening of the years of training in various mind–body practices—meditation, yoga, breathing techniques, pagan moon rituals, shamanic ceremonies, various forms of dance, studying philosophical, historical, and spiritual practices of traditions around the world—cultivated a lasting imprint inside me. An embodiment that I could no longer ignore.

The impulse to express it in writing was like potent alchemy. It felt as if a great-grandmother landed herself inside my studio encouraging me to express the rituals, practices, and teachings that have supported, shaped, and generated the path before me. And like a river, the words and worlds began to flow—sometimes fast, sometimes slow. I have been blessed with the most generous, inspiring, and wise teachers—too many to name here— and to each guide, family member, and kindred spirit that has graced my path, I bow in gratitude for all I have received. My background in feminist studies, cultural history, and world religions, along with my dedication to the path of yoga, meditation, art, dance, teaching, and my love of ceremony are woven into the fabric of this book.

Imagine the journey of life like a spiral. At times we are inside the center of the spiral, where we find ourselves in the gestating, visioning, planting, or new beginnings cycle. Sometimes we are more expansive, coming to the end of the spiral as we may be completing a specific chapter or cycle. Whatever stage you are currently at in your life, create space in your day-to-day living to trust your process and acknowledge the "divine timings" when they arrive. When we truly dwell in the present moment, set our intentions with clarity, and release our attachment to the outcome or the "final product," we can witness our life as a living ritual. Not everything happens at once, and when we hold true to our personal process, live inside the current of reciprocity of equal giving to receiving, we are living inside the essence of our true potential.

Cast your visions and prayers out into the world. Create daily rituals to magnetize the energy of what you want in your life while at the same time releasing the outcome. When we can let go of our attachment to the final outcome, we begin to radically accept the universal laws in which we live. Sometimes the universe brings us something a little different than what we asked for, but it was meant to come to us.

Once you begin this wildly creative journey, you will unearth an intuitive response pathway, and your own inner guide will be nourished. Embodiment of mind to heart to body to spirit comes alive when we do the work and commit to expressing the highest essence within. See yourself for who you are at your highest, not for who you are not. The mystic within will come alive; the healer, teacher, poet, student, architect, sculptor, midwife, shape-shifter, water protector, steward of the earth, gardener, activist, ceremonialist, peaceful warrior, and the fire dancer. These shape-shifting archetypes will not only support you in your everyday life but will allow you to take flight and reclaim the inner visionary inside you.

Continue to dive deep into your own healing. Live your life as a sacred ritual, share your gifts with your community, and integrate your soulful practices so that you may lead others in this meaningful way. The world needs humanity to step up now, to be the best version of ourselves possible.

Together, may we rise, strengthen our inner sense of self, and share our personal stories and rituals with our communities. May we speak with truth, listen with compassion, and train our eye to see the beauty in all things. May we remember that we are not alone and we are supported. May we give and receive equally and inspire others to live with an awakened awareness so that our actions, our voice, and our thoughts can and will make a difference in the world.

RITUAL AS
THE REMEDY

Rituals are like mirrors that we can hold up to reflect our lives' journeys. The ceremonial process allows us to step out of time and experience something beyond the mundane, revealing the sacred turning points in our lives and guiding us deeper into our souls' calling.

Chapter 1

Ritual as the Remedy
Awakening the Inner Mystic in You

WHY RITUAL?

Throughout history, the power of ritual has been at the heart of both ancient and modern civilizations. Within secular and religious cultures, humanity has embraced the deepening of the self, community, and spiritual awakening through the power of ritual. From intricate organized traditions to simply stating your gratitudes each morning, rituals provide rhythm and repetition; a framework to enter a state of being that's free of the confusion and chaos of our lives.

A ritual can be anything that is done with intention. It can be done alone or in a group, and can be formulaic or intuitive. We can gather and celebrate the turning points in the wheel of the year as the seasons shift, we can share holiday meals or birthdays with intention, we can celebrate the outer expansion of the full moon or the internal expression of the new moon. We can prepare a ritual for a young woman who is coming of age with her menstrual cycle or a blessing ceremony for a mother who is ready to give birth. We can create a personal ritual by lighting a candle and stating our intentions out loud as we come to the end of a project or a relationship, or when we release an old way of being and open ourselves to the next phase in our lives.

Rituals give us direct access to our healing, reflect our emotions, and show us how we can access inner transformation and awaken our intuitive power. Rituals serve as sanctuaries from which we can contemplate the pivotal moments in our lives. Mindful, intentional, and ceremonial experiences can reflect back to us both the "truths" and the "untruths" we find in our life stories.

Over time and with practice, it is the "inner state" that transforms negative, toxic, or limiting thoughts and behaviors into glimmers of understanding (peace) and transformation, and a feeling of oneness or "unity consciousness" ignites within. This is the power of ritual: to engage and infuse life with present moment awareness, gain inspiration from our current experiences, and align with a deeper connection towards the sacred, individually and collectively.

THE REMEDY: WAKING UP TO CONNECTION

Mass consumption, materialism, and the onslaught of media influence in today's world are contributing to the rise of anxiety, depression, confusion, and overstimulation. So many people feel estranged from the religious structures in which they were raised, and they are no longer served by their foundations and traditions. This has created separation, and for some, a feeling of loss, disconnect, and a lack of purpose and connection with the earth and her healing rhythms. The planet is at a precarious tipping point right now. Mother Earth is calling to us to change our ways in order to preserve and protect her resources. Her divine feminine energetic pull is reminding us to step up and be earth keepers for future generations. She is opening her arms to us, inviting us to praise her, to celebrate her, and to honor her cycles and rhythms. For many of us, immersing ourselves in earth-based spirituality is the call of the modern church; the awakening of the modern mystic inside of us.

Could it be that small daily rituals can be our guide to connect to our best selves, to our most essential selves, to our intuitive power, to strengthening our inner bodies and minds so that we can self-heal and self-direct the life we choose?

I believe yes.

I wholeheartedly believe in this very simple philosophy:

Your life is shaped by what you feed your energy body.
Your thoughts, actions, words, and beliefs become your reality.

Your thought patterns, the words you speak, your attachments and your habits—both unconscious and conscious—all become the soil in which your system grows. The work of the modern mystic is to be the gardener of your own energy body: create healthy soil, plant your seeds intentionally, water and weed your inner garden, and tend to the sacred alchemy of life all around you.

I believe that small, daily rituals are a remedy to feeling disconnected in our overly connected world. When we awaken the impulse to become our own guides, we can connect to our full potential; our most essential selves. This is where our intuitive power lies, and through it we can strengthen our inner bodies and minds so that we can self-direct the life we choose.

Ritual can take many forms. For some, it takes place on the yoga mat or the meditation cushion. For others, it is spending time in nature, being physically active, or engaging in artistic endeavors.

Through self-guided rituals you allow your mind to release the vibration of negativity or doubt and create a spark within. This spark filters from your mind down into your heart, and your intuitive and creative nature becomes enlivened. Small rituals can be quite different from going to a yoga practice or sitting in meditation. Creating an altar, sipping tea, lighting a candle, journaling, praying, or chanting out loud are all examples of how the experience can become more textured, creative, fulfilling, intimate, and liberating.

The next time you find yourself in a place of doubt, fear, stress, or imbalance, ask yourself, "Am I feeding this situation?" This is a golden moment to shift your awareness back to gratitude, breath, nature's gifts, and trust in divine timing. Slowly, you will begin the process of shifting your default drive from feeding toxic energy in your life to fueling your life with truth, positivity, and compassion.

The daily task of the modern mystic is to bear witness to what thoughts, feelings, actions, and words you are feeding into your being. To become aware of what no longer serves you, and to truly accept what is going on inside of you—the positive, the negative, all of it. What is so important here is not to repress, push down, or bypass the core of your emotions, but to be constantly working with this material as a catalyst to activate a healing experience for yourself.

The average brain thinks thousands upon thousands of thoughts every day, and research has suggested that about 70% of them are on the negative spectrum. This means that the average person is living in a constant state of toxic thinking, and if left unattended, you will carry this energetic weight with you in your physical, emotional, mental, and spiritual life.

What would your life feel like if you started to dismantle the toxic thoughts or limiting paradigms in your life?

Can you get a sense of the feeling connected to this freedom?

Awareness is key, and this is where rituals can support the shedding of toxic thoughts and behaviors. By entering into a mindful state you can open up pathways, doors, and portals into a positive, conscious, and mystical way of living.

The need for ritual is a primal and human instinct; a compelling impulse to unite with something beyond the mundane world towards the infinite. Ritual brings forth a web of archetypal understanding and allows us to grow towards paradigms such as unity, continuity, connectivity, transformational states, and higher consciousness.

When we awaken the power to self-guide through ritual, we get intimate with the great mystery that life brings. A door opens beyond the mundane of everyday life to the sacredness that exists within us and in the cosmos all around us.

Once you give yourself permission to live a spiritual life in the form of a human body, the divine timings, the omens, the helping and compassionate spirits, the creator, the angels, the gods and goddesses (whatever your personal belief is), the spiritual energies awaken and journey alongside you to support you in fulfilling your wildest dreams.

You begin to see, sense, observe, and feel how you can attune to the signs and symbols around you; you can open up to the alchemy of spirit sending you messages. You begin to understand how and when to let go of toxic energies, overcome fear and anxiety, strengthen your personal boundaries, and do the work it takes to stay in alignment with your own personal mission in life.

THE ANCIENT TEACHINGS
AS YOUR INNER COMPASS

For thousands of years, the mystics of ancient cultures have followed the rhythms of the sun, the moon, the stars, the planets, and the seasons, not only for survival, but also for spiritual connection. Every 29.5 days the moon completes its cycle from new to full to new moon once again, and every day the sun rises in the east and sets in the west. Annually, the earth orbits around the sun on a tilted axis, giving us the shift in the seasons: spring equinox, summer solstice, fall equinox, and winter solstice. The sun is symbolic of the sacred masculine force, while the earth and the moon are symbolic of the divine feminine force. These forces of energy come together to create the whole of life around us. Earth-centric wisdom has taught us to understand that we are all connected; plant, animal, mineral, human, and beyond. We are all born of stardust and the richness of the earth's alchemy.

The properties of the five elements, air, fire, water, earth, and ether, created the source of all life and are alive inside all of us. Everywhere around us we see the elements at work. We are part of this force; the very essence that creates life force or "prana" (energy) also dwells inside of us. It can become a part of how our mind works, expand our capacity to love ourselves and others, inspire a creative and grounded daily existence, and deepen our understanding of how to work with our emotions to fully express ourselves in the world.

Throughout the rituals in this book, we will work with the five elements and the four seasons of the year to connect to nature and ourselves. We will be guided by the structure of the pagan wheel of the year, which draws from an "earth-based" spirituality and is symbolic of integrating the alchemy of your personal surroundings into a force field that is rich in rhythm, ritual, and elemental celebration. The wheel follows a circular pattern highlighting the four quarter points of spring, summer, autumn, and winter, along with four more cross-quarter days that mark the halfway point within each season. The seasons are in direct relationship with the five elements: air, fire, water, earth, and ether.

The symbolism of each point on the wheel offers endless wisdom and ritual inspiration. The relationship between the wheel of the year, the four directions, the five elements, and the cycles of the moon provides a rhythm and an inner compass or structure that can support us on our journey through life.

Through nature's lens, we receive the living wisdom teachings that are equally simple and complex, ancient and contemporary. Embracing the wonders of the natural world while observing the abundance and beauty alive inside the elements will purify our minds, cleanse our bodies, and free our spirits towards lasting joy and peace. This practice becomes a transformational daily ritual.

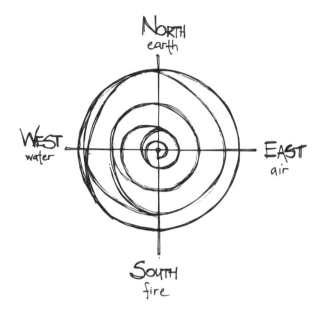

THE WHEEL OF THE YEAR AND ELEMENTAL SYMBOLISM

Throughout history, the wheel of the year has inspired many different forms and interpretations. Diverse cultures and traditions have their own versions of the wheel, with elements connected to different directions and seasons. Discovering how you personally connect to the wheel is up to you. The path of the modern mystic is to create structure, rhythm, and ritual practices that are meaningful to you.

The rituals in this book are based on my own personal interpretation of the wheel of the year.

EAST

The place of the rising sun, where we welcome in the element of pure, fresh, sweet morning air. We honor the spring equinox, new beginnings, fertility, the return of the light, and the energy of our heart; our capacity to love and to be compassionate. Air is associated with the realm of thought, breathing, heart awakening, learning, knowledge, harmony, communication, and all things connected to our mental capacity and our breath.

SOUTH

Symbolizes the element of fire, the power of the sun, and the transformational growth that comes with the force of light. We honor the summer solstice, the wild growth of seed to fruit, wonderment and child-like playfulness; we celebrate our renewed energy from the sun. Symbolically, the south supports the shedding of old narratives and limiting core beliefs as we release these layers and attune to our healthy ego and esteemed self. Fire represents change and transformation. It's symbolic of willpower, freedom, passion, vision, love, and strength.

WEST

The resting place of the setting sun, where we open up to the element of water for flow, creativity, and renewal. We honor the fall equinox, the abundance of the harvest, and are reminded of the life–death–rebirth cycle in all things. Water represents the emotional realm, symbolic of healing, dreaming, flowing, the subconscious, and everything internal and cleansing.

NORTH

In this direction we greet our great mother and open up to the element of earth for grounding and abundance. We honor the winter solstice, the shortest day and the longest night of the year; a time of rest, hibernation, and inward reflection. Our grounded, calm, balanced energy and our ability to face our fears with a willingness to transform them is key to attuning to this element. The earth is stable, solid, and dependable, and is symbolic of abundance, sustenance, grounding, and physical manifestation.

ETHER

The center of the wheel symbolizes the vital life force that holds everything together. Also known as the soul element, it is the essential energy of spirit that creates and enables life in all forms. It is the divine life force that holds air, fire, water, and earth, along with the stars, the moon, the sun, and all of the planets to coexist and interact with each other. This universal life force or "unity consciousness" energy holds the container for the realms of spirit, where mysterious or unseen realms exist. Here, at the center of the wheel, lies the source of our own inner mystic; it lives above us, below us, before us and behind us, as well as within us.

Use the guide on the previous page to serve you time and time again as you engage in your own rituals and lead others to do the same. Stay curious about how you can invite more energy, peace, flow, balance, passion, clarity, and connection into your life by accessing the power of the elements. Source from nature whenever you can to stay grounded and inspired. Open to every moment of your life as a walking, living, breathing ritual.

THE PROCESS IS THE JOURNEY

When we welcome in the attitude that everything that exists can be broken down into one or more of the five elements, we reinforce the belief that all things in life are connected. There are no mistakes, no accidents; we begin to imbue a spiritual gratitude that supports us to observe where imbalanced energy lives and where divine timing dwells, which in turn allows us to grow our intuitive or gut instincts. When we live in this energy of gratitude, it doesn't mean that we need to be grateful for everything all the time, rather, it allows us to be more aware, present, and discerning. Wherever we find ourselves in our lives, during good times or bad, we are able to stabilize our energy and activate the truest intentions that align with our souls' purpose.

Imagine the journey of your life as a spiral. At times, we are at the center of the spiral where we find ourselves in the gestating, visioning, planting, or new beginnings cycle. Sometimes we are more expansive and external, coming to the end of the spiral as we complete a specific chapter or cycle.

Whatever stage you are currently at in your life, create space in your day-to-day living to trust your process and acknowledge the "divine timings" when they arrive. When we truly dwell in the present moment, set our intentions with clarity, and release our attachment to the outcome or the "final product," we can witness our life as a "living ritual." Not everything happens at once. When we are true to our personal process, live inside the current of reciprocity, we are truly living inside the essence of our authentic potential.

The world needs us to step up now, to raise our own energetic field of kindness, compassion, and heart-centered living. As the Hopi blessing states, "May you walk in beauty." This can become a lifeline as we navigate our modern times of political unrest, technological overload, societal pressures of high productivity, and the lack of focus on community.

Now is the time, more than ever, to train our inner eye to see the beauty around us; to attune to our compassionate hearts, our conscious minds, and our clear, precise calls to action. By strengthening our inner sense of self and sharing our personal connection to rituals, whether they are ancestral or adopted, we can inspire our communities and future generations to effect lasting, positive change: emotionally, physically, mentally, and spiritually.

Rituals to Connect with the Elements

Throughout this guidebook, you will find meditations, visualizations, breath work, elemental rituals to inspire connection, practices to expand your mind–body intuitive channels, poetic prose to inspire your personal alchemy, and journal prompts to awaken present-moment awareness, healing, and soul activation.

Read through each ritual practice first to get a sense of it, gather the supplies needed, then follow along, taking time between each step to feel the healing, welcoming changes in your body and mind. Always have your journal to write notes.

1. Five Steps to Begin a Daily Ritual

Many of us already engage in daily rituals through yoga, meditation, exercise, communing with nature, following personal faiths, practicing daily gratitudes, or following the rhythms of the earth, sun, moon and stars. Whichever rituals you choose, keep following and studying the path that inspires you. Share your gifts with your community, and integrate the practices so you may guide yourself and others in this meaningful way.

Use these five simple steps to get started. Write them down in your journal to get you committed and focused on your daily self-care rituals.

1 Set a simple intention. For example: "Today, I am opening up to Grace…" Look inside yourself to find what you would like to manifest or shift.

2 Start with a simple assignment; one small step. For example: call in three gratitudes each morning.

3 Use a power symbol to inspire you. It could be anything: an image from nature, a deity, a crystal, etc.

4 Honor the ritual. Remind yourself to do it every morning; do not allow anything to get in your way. Allow your soul work to weave into the fabric of your daily life.

5 Release the outcome. True transformation takes time; release the need for instant outcome. Observe how your energy shifts when engaged in mindful rituals.

2. Clear Your Energy Field and Connect with the Elements

Intention

To let go of everyday stress and ignite a connection with the five elements for clear energy, renewal, and mind–body–spirit integration.

1 Find a comfortable seat and close your eyes.

2 Visualize yourself in a place in nature that you love, one that allows you to feel calm and at ease. Picture the landscape all around you and get a sense of the energy that allows the plants, the trees, and the flowers to grow. Welcome the grounded energy of the earth into your body. Focus on the lower half of your body; imagine yourself becoming truly connected and embraced by the warmth of Mother Earth.

3 Take six deep, full breaths to connect to the earth.

4 Now, welcome in the element of water. Perhaps you can imagine the sounds of water nearby and visualize the flow inside the water. Welcome the flow of water inside yourself; into your hips, your pelvis, and your abdomen.

5 Take six full breaths in and out as you welcome the flow and ease of energy in your body and in your life.

6 Go to the element of fire, visualize a candle flame. See the bright colors of the flame, and welcome this energy of passion into your solar plexus.

7 Take six full, deep breaths. With each breath, allow the flame of the candle to grow brighter. Swirl the colors throughout your body and your mind.

8 Visualize the element of air. Imagine the sky. Are there clouds, or is the sky bright and clear? Is the wind soft or strong? Imagine any heavy emotional energy inside your heart clearing away. Imagine the element of air now bringing fresh and clear energy into your whole body.

9 Take six full, deep breaths to welcome the release that comes with air.

10 Visualize the element of ether. Bring your awareness to the force of energy all around you. Imagine the alchemy of vital life essence that creates everything in existence. Visualize the energy of the stars from which you came long ago; the matrix of the inside of a flower that was once stardust, and the cells of rich fertile soil that birthed this earth and human life. This is all a part of you. Imagine the element of ether, the mystery of the divine, swirling around you; inside you, connecting you to the divine spiritual essence of life.

11 Take six full, deep breaths as you fill yourself with this alive and expansive energy.

12 Return now to your breath, into the space in which you are currently sitting, and reflect on any shifts you feel or sense from within.

13 Witness any changes in perspective or attitude, and welcome this fresh energy as you move throughout your day.

14 Call forth a positive "I am, I will" statement that resonates with you. For example, if I am ready to activate both fire and earth energy into my day, it may come out like this: "I am a blazing fire of grounded energy. Today I will ignite my balanced, radiant self in all ways."

15 Repeat this statement three times and write it down. Weave it throughout your day when you need a reminder.

3. Journal Prompts

- Which element, earth, air, fire, water, or ether, most resonated with you in the previous meditation?
- Did you experience any sensations in your body?
- How does your grounded, earthy self show up to support you in your life?

- What brings you to a state of balanced energy?
- What brings you to a state of overwhelm?
- What brings you into a state of joy?
- Describe how each element supports you in the best version of you. Then imagine it in its purest form and receive this positive energy. Remind yourself daily how to access this energy when you feel tired, stressed, imbalanced, anxious, or fearful. Welcome your ability to change your state and upgrade your vibration and energy field by accessing the power of the elements.

Build altars
Light candles
Create time for the quietude
of your mind to get spacious
Welcome in the unknown
Dive into the mystery of life's grandest questions
Touch the earth
Kiss the sky
Be a channel for spirit
to move through your sacred body
Trust
Every single day

INTO THE
HEART TEMPLE

Like a huntress on her path towards opening and
adorning her heart temple, you are the tracker, fierce yet soft.
Bow humbly, forgive often, and do not fear new beginnings. Tend
all your gardens, seek the vision seeds, and plant them deep in
the earth. Kiss your prayers with an alchemy that attracts
the divinity of a wild, untamable love.

May your intentions be steeped in radical acceptance, non-
judgment, and a worldly perspective that celebrates the mystery
of the unknown. And beyond all, may you embody an anchored
channel that heals, expands, and allows others to source their
own healing through your radiant heart capacity.

Chapter 2

Into the Heart Temple
Living Wild, Loving Free

DANCING WITH THE SHADOW SELF

As we have all experienced, life brings initiations: wounds, shame, blame, addictions, traumas, attachments, breakups, celebrations, breakthroughs, breakdowns; the list goes on. While we can't control what happens to us in life, we can control how we respond. By activating steady, mind- and heart-fueled practices to awaken to the present moment, we open the channels to align and live out the best versions of who we are.

When we begin to investigate our life experiences as "material" to reflect back to us the ways in which we can self-direct our healing process, we begin the journey of meeting our shadow self rather than running away from it. Our fears, our broken sense of self; the "I am not good enough," the "I will never find love," mixed with our anxieties, stressors, and repressed feelings, become the materials through which we heal. No longer do we run away from them. We bring awareness to them, we name them, we arrange them all before us, and we begin to sculpt, massage, dismantle, decode, unveil, uncover, and strip away our desire to hold on to them so tightly.

We become the architect, the choreographer, and the shape-shifter. We use the shadow self as present-moment material to transform. This becomes the work. This becomes the path towards integrated awareness, no longer bypassing the core of the issue or the depth of the trauma—the anxiety, grief, fear, rage, or depression.

The presence of an embodied, ritualistic way of living will be your guide on this journey. This is no part-time gig, and it is not an easy path. When we are able to rewire our thought patterns and our triggered protective reactions, we get to the heart of the matter. We begin to understand more intimately how we can practice daily self-care rituals to ground, release, invite, forgive, integrate, and to do the work required to live the best life possible. Your life as a living, breathing, creative, messy, present, compassionate, forgiving, and awake creation. This is how to deepen our experience in life, fulfill our dreams and love wildly.

You get to choose, you get to do the work, you get to make the rules, you get to be your own guide on this journey.

Are you up for it? Let's journey.

THE PRACTICE OF COMPASSION AND UNSHAKEABLE SELF-LOVE

The practice of self-love is the healing balm of our times.

Pause for a moment. Place your hands on your heart, take three deep, full breaths as you hold the intention to meet your whole body from a place of love. On each exhale, let go of the self-talk and actions that are holding you back from standing strong in your ability to fully accept and love yourself. By loving ourselves with unshakeable composure daily, we can fully show up and be loving and compassionate towards others in our lives. When this kind of radical self-love becomes the main channel of energy, we begin to shed the self-judgments, the "I am not good enough" or "I am not worthy" paradigms, and the heart center aligns, anchors, and magnetizes.

When anxiety, stress, fatigue, and unhealthy motivations and actions arise, they take over our lives without us even realizing it. All of a sudden, we find ourselves in a heated, triggered moment, and we begin to say, do, and act out in ways that are not aligned with our capacity to be a source of love and connection. We begin to live out the past or project into the future, and this separates our attention like a raging river blocked up by a dam. We go into fight or flight, sink or swim, rage or cry, and we begin to swirl into the eddy of the river.

Again, take a moment, *pause*, and breathe deeply. Know and trust that the work of the contemporary mystic is to remain rooted in the present moment, to feel fully, repressing nothing, to listen to the signs and signals of the physical, mental, emotional, spiritual, and intuitive whispers coming though.

To be compassionate is to be accepting and forgiving of each individual's differences. It is also to be accepting and forgiving of your own personal judgments, actions, and differences. When your mind begins to loop in a negative track, a signal is sent to your heart to close, which then creates an energetic pull on the body that detracts positive energy and attracts negative energy. When we are able to catch our internal mind chatter in a state of judgment or negativity instead of allowing it to continue, we can make a choice to pause, breathe, and ask ourselves, "what value does this thought and feeling serve the greater good in me or others?" This kind of presence becomes a catalyst for transformation to occur. The mind realizes that this kind of low vibration judgment is of no use, the heart softens, and the channels of heart–mind–body open.

When we awaken to our heart center as our spiritual teacher and commit to honoring our personal soul-care work, we hold space to mend our heart wounds, both past and present, and we access a higher vibration and capacity to love. Our self-love becomes unshakeable and wildly magnetic. We are able to align with present-moment sensations without compromise, allowing us to see, feel, and sense where our energy gets pulled. We attune to the conditions in which our heart closes, opens, becomes numb, pounds, races, and feels more anchored and at peace in our day-to-day lives. This work brings us to a place where we can recover more quickly from the heartbreaks and heartaches, from the "I am not enough" mentality.

Mind–body practices such as yoga, tai chi, meditation, breath techniques, nature inspiration, and visualizations can keep us steady and awake, and they have the capacity to set the foundation to live life through the lens of our spiritual hearts—to live wildly and love freely. Our unique capacity to love and to heal becomes a temple within our soul. The journey—working with grief, trauma, sadness, even past-life pain— becomes the process and the adventure.

Each cycle, relationship, and life experience create the navigation points within our hearts' compass. When we intentionally move our energy, clear our minds of toxic residue, and practice compassion towards ourselves and others, we magnetize the vibration of an evolved love.

NEW BEGINNINGS: TODAY IS A NEW DAY

We are always in a state of healing, each one of us, every day.

Our body intelligence encourages our internal ecosystem towards a state of wholeness for optimal functioning.

Today is a new day and it holds the capacity for wide-open potential and possibility. Take a pause and a deep breath in and out. Let's repeat that line. Today is a new day and it holds the capacity for wide-open potential and possibility. The current of healing and loving wildly and living freely requires us to hold space for new beginnings; for new forms of compassion and forgiveness to come through us. We are born with this pure state of inquiry. As our ego forms and our life experience takes its own unique shape, we begin to play out a version of our self that seeks approval of others or compartmentalizes ways of loving and not loving in order to stay safe. How we can embrace a radical intention of self-love?

When our mind plays tricks on us, as it does, we interrupt the healing by choosing conflicting thoughts, actions, and words over being present with our wholeness. When we become connected with our essential, higher self, we grow, heal, expand, and deepen our intuitive nature. As technology advances, we need to advance and commit to grounding practices for inner strength, compassion, and enduring self-love. As society grows more complex, we need to remember our soul's mission every day. Recalibrate through present-moment awareness and the power of daily rituals. Meet our energy fields where they are, unearth and bring light to current stressors or triggers. Learn how to honor where we currently are, change our state through mind–body practices, and move on to living life with a heart full of joy and freedom at the core of our being.

Every time we activate self-care rituals in an intentional way, a healing takes place. Sometimes the healing is quiet and subtle, other times wildly transformative.

Celebrate your radiance and raise your energy by reclaiming self-love. If your self-love practice stays consistent every day, you are holding space for transformation to occur before your own eyes. The daily rituals you activate can shift you from one state of being to another. They can release a long-time negative pattern of shame, blame, self-doubt, self-loathing, anxiety, fear— into reclaiming and loving your sovereign self. Let this light in. Your guides will support you; they will acknowledge your work. You will feel supported, connected, and increasingly conscious of unity within your soul.

THE ELEMENT OF AIR:
BREATHING AS A PURIFICATION PROCESS

Air is what is breathing you, what is giving you life. By bringing awareness to your breath (how you breathe, when your breath is short from stress, how your breath is after exercise or a great night's sleep, etc.), you will begin to form a reverence for your breath and the element of air that will bring a greater perspective into your life. When we become aware of what affects the tone, rhythm, and quality of our breath, we begin to listen more fully in the moment. You might say to yourself, I feel my breath is restricted, tighter, or shorter—how can I take a deep, long breath in and a deep, long breath out and let go of whatever I am holding on to in this moment?

The moment we were born we merged with the element of air with the first breath we took. Our tiny lungs opened and expanded to gift us with this life. Imagine yourself right now, emerging from the womb, taking your first breath, greeting the world with your purest essence in its full capacity. This unique essence is your gift to the world. May you recall, fuel, and breathe into your soul essence every day. May you no longer forget. May you hold, rinse, polish, and share your unique gifts with the world. Sometimes it's like a quiet revolution inside your heart. Other times, like a fierce mama lion's roar. Honor your journey every day. Breathe deeply, with compassion, and remember your pure love heart medicine is the remedy of our times.

The element of air is the bridge between the water of our mother's womb and the great spark of fire initiated during the birthing process. When we came down to earth through our mother's body as a channel, we instantly merged with the alchemy of all five elements: earth, air, fire, water, and ether. We are born of this nature, each of us unique in alchemical make-up, yet as a collective, we hold this elemental essence inside us. Integrating the element of air and acknowledging the direction of east, which gives birth to the sun each morning, is to honor all of the winged ones that grace our skies and grant us perspective as we greet the earth, the sun, and the waters with deep respect and reverence. Every day we receive the healing energy of illumination through the elements as we open our perspective to the mystery and grandness of life.

The element of air is associated with breath, and in Sanskrit this is known as "prana," which translates as the physical, mental, and spiritual energy or power. In Chinese medicine traditions it is known as "qi," which translates as the vital life-force energy that flows through each organ and system of the body. At the core, the Eastern and indigenous teachings teach that the more you develop the breath, the more powerful life force you will experience. The winds of change, the limitless sky above, and the essence of infinite space all around us hold the mystery of the great unknown. There is so much more to life than we can see or know. Air teaches us how to shift energies within our own mind and heart capacity. Air is symbolic of the realm of thought, learning, knowledge, harmony, communication, and all things connected to the channels between the heart and the mind. Begin to open yourself as a bridge or a channel between the heart and the mind. What you feed your mind has a direct relationship to your heart and how you love yourself and others, and how you feed your heart has a direct relationship with the workings of your mind.

Just as the shape-shifting clouds in the sky, we too can open the energy channel that moves from heart to mind and mind to heart. Our intellect and heart wisdom, or our capacity to practice wild, unconditional self-love and compassion, when in alignment with our vital life force, can merge into a sacred union informed by the expansive nature of the winds around us.

When we hold or constrict our breath, we tighten and constrict the flow of air inside us. Our thoughts may become muddled or chaotic, our heart may beat faster, and the channels between heart and mind may become severed. Take a deep, full breath in right now and a deep, full breath out. Welcome in another deep, full breath cycle and bring it into the back of your body, then again below you, on either side of you, and lastly, visualize your breath all around you. When we can drop into the body and get dimensional with our breath, we get attuned to the present moment and open the body as a channel to feel, see, sense, hear, and bridge our own primal life force with that of the divine.

When we can let go of our regular programming or social conditioning (or when we can move beyond placing our full attention only on the mundane aspects of life) and engage in life's inner knowing, we can shift our stagnant energy by becoming aware of the element of air. How we breathe changes us. Our perspective changes when we see from a bird's-eye view.

Take a moment right now and visualize a great bird in flight, a high flyer. Take in a fresh perspective of your life from an entirely different angle. What messages on your current life journey can you receive through this bird's-eye perspective? Is there a way you are pushing or projecting or forcing that may not be working? Welcome in the powerful element of air to let go of the old ways and begin anew. Air brings fresh beginnings. As you receive the healing of this new viewpoint, what does your heart want to speak? Is there a vision or a healing for yourself or others? See with the eyes of your heart; feel air supporting you in every direction, and welcome in the heart visionary for guidance beyond the mind's interpretation. Drop your mind into your heart and let it speak to you from this axis.

Be the high flyer, breathing deeply, shifting perspective, and flowing with the winds of change as they come ripping through your body. Sometimes the winds are stormy and fierce, other times gentle. Greet them all as guests and material to work with. This will become your healing journey. Welcome all the messengers, whether they be the old friend who calls, the eagle soaring above you, the powerful dream, the thought you had that manifested into reality, or the stormy skies inside your heart. This is your capacity to live a spiritual life in the form of a human body. You get to be the huntress, the warrior, the high flyer, the tracker of the energies and experiences that are currently presenting in your life.

Air is not static; it weaves and bends and shape-shifts. When we awaken to working with the power of air, we choose to be adaptable, to sense which direction it is coming from, to face it head-on, to clear past projections and social constructs. We meet her power like the goddess she is, opening our ability to live with compassion for all beings, to tend to the gardens of self-love or soul-love, to dance with adversity, to let go of our firm grip, to unearth the ways we have repressed our grief, to touch down deeper into loving every ounce of who we are. Ultimately we step out of time and space to align with the call of our own heart guide.

Hear the call. It's time. Welcome the compassionate energies seeping through your windows, waking you up from the slumber of life's mundane happenings. Trust in the journey and hold space for the sacredness of the shape-shifter inside you, every single day.

LAY IT ALL DOWN: WORKING WITH GRIEF AS A CATALYST FOR TRANSFORMATION

The one constant in life is change. Like the element of air that surrounds, supports, and generates such epic life-force energy, may we stay awake to the winds of change within our own being. The element of air, associated with the heart center, is a vast, unconditional teacher of love, loss, compassion, and forgiveness. To experience the loss of a loved one is a deep, soul-wrenching pain. To experience physical or mental illness can flip our world so far upside down and away from what we once knew as our truth that deep sorrow sets in. To feel the grief of lost opportunities, expectations, and confusion about individual purpose can take a grip on our soul and create not only inertia but debilitating suffering every day. Change can be so difficult. And the grieving process takes time. As we journey through life, our experience of grief will vary based on what has happened to us and our loved ones. When we begin to weave together rituals to support our grief, when we name it, call it forward like a teacher, unpack, uncover, and unearth every part of it without trying to figure it all out, we begin to listen to the outpouring of our heart's deepest griefs and longings. We begin to heal.

Could it be that the essence of grief is the essence of love? The longing of our heart's call with nowhere to go, no one to touch or reach towards? Can you hold space in this moment to feel and open to the pain of your own suffering? Can you open yourself in this moment to gather your inner self and acknowledge and be present with the truth of your own loss? Can you open yourself to soften so that you can face life and death and loss and sorrow? Can you locate where this might live inside your body? Can you become present with the sensations, the visuals, the body sensations, the mind talk as they arise? Your pain and your grief do not make you wrong, bad, or unworthy. Acknowledging that your suffering and your pain exist allows you to work with it and not be completely taken over by it. Breathe into these sentiments:

I accept my sorrow yet I am not my sorrow.

I accept my grief, sorrow, and pain, and yet understand that this does not limit the vastness and boundlessness of my heart's capacity to love.

I understand that my present-moment awareness of breath, body, heart, and mind will awaken me to the great depths that arise from loss.

I accept my capacity to love alongside my capacity to mourn.

My heart's rhythm is the alchemy that will move me into the next cycle of my healing—my living, my loss, and my loving embraced fully.

We can work with our grief as a catalyst for the transformation of our mind, body, and heart by holding space for the grief to move through us with the wind, with the water, with the fire, and with the earth. Laying down our sorrows when we no longer need to hold them becomes the catalyst for inner transformation. Allow the process of grieving and feeling to cycle through you and through your day-to-day living in rituals such as a breath exercise, a nature altar, a daily meditation, a journal session, or a creative pursuit. The practice of this kind of presence steeped inside soul care will, over time, become the healing elixir and the impulse for shape-shifting within. Try pouring your words out on paper, communing with nature, praying out loud to a lost loved one, communicating with the energies of the unseen realms (spirit guides, creator, goddess, god, angels, etc.; whatever belief you may have). Open yourself to ask for and receive support through the medium of this intentionality. The body becomes a channel. Your spirit becomes the vessel. The salt of your tears are the medicine through which the energy shifts.

Your broken heart slowly begins to mend over time, and the force of compassion swirls into your mind like a wild windstorm. And every day you go back to praying out loud, in the bath, to the trees, to the waters, the mountains, the flowers, to the teapot, to the fire, to your supporting guides, to the divine nature and goodness of all of this that lives in you. You are the visionary. May the eyes of your heart come alive as you tend your grief and longing until one day it shifts. Give in to the shift of the winds of change before you, behind you, and welcome your heart visionary, all around you.

How do you love today, sweet one?
Take my hand, walk me to the river,
wash my hands clean of my own dis-ease.
Lay me down beside you, mountain waters
caressing my naked body.
Deep blue skies shape-shifting, clearing, limitless creations.
A messenger whispered, "lay it all down here."
It coursed through my bones and out of my hands.
The unbearable grief, the collective pain,
the firm grip on the uncontrollable.
Alas, it ripped out of me like a fierce storm.
Heart pounding, my bones spoke.

A new language surfaced.
And I awoke, inside my own vessel.
A love song emerged like a symphony of the skies,
An invitation I could no longer refuse.

PLANT YOUR VISION SEEDS AND WATCH THEM GROW: THE PROMISE OF SPRING

Each morning as the sun rises in the east, the majestic glow infused with life force brings a fresh perspective. Each day a new beginning can emerge. When we train our eye to witness the beauty around us in every moment, we begin to align with a life force that brings inner strength, inquiry, awe, and an opening of mind–heart–body into a powerful alchemy.

When we train ourselves not to open our phone first thing in the morning but rather to sit in silence, witnessing the shift of light, ushering in a new day with reverence and possibility, we become connected to our inner rhythms, and we come home to ourselves. There will always be busy times, but if we do not create time for the silence and the stillness, for merging with the forces of the natural world, then we miss this opportunity for personal growth and a reclaiming of our essential nature and unique life journey.

Ideas can come in a flash, a download, a fast glimmer of energy; sometimes fleeting, sometimes lasting. Yet, when we can sit intentionally and hold space for the ideas to become seeds we are planting in the garden, we can hold space for the cyclical nature of our own personal growth. As we open to greeting the sun each morning in the east, we align with the element of air, the bringer of life. Here we can honor and celebrate the spring equinox with its life-giving force. The soil is churned, the seeds get planted, the spring rains come, and the earth cradles the seed until it's ready to root and sprout. To be held by the warmer winds and the promise of spring is to hold your life's greatest dreams in a way that they become possible. We learn to follow a cyclical course with patience, trusting in the universal and cosmic sequential order that lives inside all of life. We brave the storms, we grow resilient, and when the time is right, we burst through the earth into the real world manifest. Give yourself permission to see your life's goals as seeds you are planting and tending to—daily, monthly, yearly.

Can you get a sense of holding your own visions in this way? Your heart and life path visions are like sacred seeds to source, gather, plant, and grow. As you cycle through your life, this knowledge of the growth cycle allows you to see what is missing, what else is needed, and to truly tend to your personal visions so they can blossom into fullness. With this consciousness of the seed cycle, one gets to see more clearly where the old patterns, past narratives, or limiting beliefs emerge. And here we can call out the untruths. When we name the untruths, we interrupt a behavior that would otherwise become a block in the vision seeds. Our reality is created by our beliefs and our feelings. When we dig deeper and get truly curious about why our hearts call to us in a certain way, we begin the journey of attuning with our own heart visionary.

The tools and technologies of the mystics have brought forward techniques harnessing breath, mind–body practices, prayer, and ritual. When we feed our body with clear and clean breath, its energetic capacity grows. If we forget to feed our visions and our hearts, our capacity to feel love, compassion, and joy will diminish. Our intentions become the purest aspect of how we live our life. When we can begin our mornings by greeting the sun, sitting in meditation and ushering in a new day, one that we have never experienced before, we become a channel for our own intuition to grow. We can consciously awaken to the power and possibility of our energy field and attract what we actually want in our life and what we were destined for. But we must get very clear on what that is. If intention is not cultivated, the vision gets muddled.

HEART DEVOTION: A LIFELINE TO THE DIVINE

Devotion is your lifeline to the divine. As the ancients recall, we came from the stars, and we were transformed down through to the cells in the earth. We morphed over millions of years and arrived as a human species earth-side. We are born of both stardust and the microbes of the earth; we are products of this alchemy. Through this lens we can open more fully to embrace mystery, the unknown, and the cosmic, spiritual nature of life.

The whispers of life's calling come like seeds throughout our lifetime. When we create space for silence, stillness, prayer, and meditation, we discover the gift of deep and radical self-inquiry. From here, we can choose to connect with our guides, our teachers, our ancestors, angels, goddesses, gods; the deities that call to you, the ones that resonate with you. As you give yourself permission to trust in your personal evolution, you create pathways to have a cosmic experience in the form of a human body. You will, over time and with devotion, begin to feel yourself supported and held by the grace of spirit.

Now, more than ever, we must do the inner work required to allow the energy of spirit and the positive alignment of intentions to present itself to us. Thus we awaken to the flow of spirit's call. It's time to answer the call by making space to hear it. This may mean taking time to rest and being less productive, becoming more intentional, observational, and relational with others. We begin to imbibe the cosmic forces of energy and nature that are everywhere around us.

Can you open yourself up every morning to be intentional, to gather your inner self, and to call forward the support you are ready and willing to receive in your life? A simple and highly effective prayer can be spoken out loud like this:

> *I am ready and willing to receive support at this time.*
> *To my supporting and compassionate guides, I am listening,*
> *I am present, I am open and willing to receive support. I am ready*
> *and willing to be a vessel of compassion and loving energy.*
> *Send me a sign, a messenger, and let me know I am*
> *on the right path at this time in my life.*

When you pray like this, you step out of your own personal perspective and attachment to your feelings, needs, wants, and desires. You leave space to be supported. You open yourself up to another kind of energetic force, one that is unseen and spacious. This devotion and trust in spirit and the unseen realms holds you in your highest self and allows you to cultivate your intuition while magnetizing your inner radiance.

When life becomes challenging and overwhelming, which it does and it will, find quiet, nature-infused moments to soothe your fragmented and confused parts. Be the warrior of the sacred; see it in everything, like a whole new world about to begin. Give yourself permission to stay curious, open, and resourceful. If your thoughts become negative, catch them as soon as you can, and practice self-compassion. Soften your gaze, pause, breathe, and speak to yourself: "Here I am again."

Redirect your thoughts, open to your heart capacity, soften your body, breathe fresh air into your words, and just for a moment, encourage yourself to let go completely. Fill your body as a channel of pure air ready to shape-shift into your wholeness, and commit to live and dance with devotion towards your higher self. Let in the divine. Let in the mystery. Open yourself to being supported by something grander than the mundane world before you. Call forward helping and compassionate guides. And just for a flash, like a bolt of lightning or sweet summer breeze, you can access support from the higher powers. If you believe this, trust this, and communicate with your prayers and your whole being, you will begin to sense, see, and feel the energy of spirit moving with you. Spirit will come to you, grant you messages through the dreamtime and the real time; through the beauty of still waters, rushing waterfalls, majestic cloud formations, the radiance of the sun, and the pure air we get to breathe.

Create space in your life to pause. Let the pause be sacred. Allow the murky and messy bits to pour through you. This is the cycle of spirit. Give yourself permission to trust in your personal reckoning. Extend your awareness of devotion beyond your personal needs. This is your lifeline to the divine. This is your heart temple calling you home. Let this light in. Your guides will support you; they will acknowledge your work. You will feel supported and connected. A consciousness of unity within your soul will begin to awaken.

Be the huntress of the sacred.
Gather wood. Carry water. Plant seeds.
Weave to remember.
Mystery occurs quietly,
in small, hidden worlds.
Light your fires.
Like a whole new world ready to emerge.
Step into the unknown.
And love,
like you have never loved before.

Rituals to Connect, Open, and Anchor Your Heart's Capacity

Attune to the power of self-love through the ritualistic process of altar creation, breath work, prayer, meditation, mantra and visualization. Awaken and generate lasting transformation by purifying heart, body, and mind. Receive the perspective required to ignite the heart visionary within while connecting to the powerful element of air.

1. Morning Ritual: Anchor Inside the Heart Visionary

Intention
To infuse your day with gratitude, clarity, and compassion.

1. Begin each morning by quietly greeting the rising sun in the east, attune to the element of air. Be mindful of how it breathes life into you.
2. Light a candle and acknowledge three or more things that you are grateful for. You may want to write them down or speak them aloud.
3. Sit in silent meditation for three to five minutes. You may welcome in the support of the mineral world and hold a healing crystal in each hand.
4. Visualize your day going the way you would like it go; mentally rehearse. If you can see it, you will align your energy body towards a higher vibrational field.
5. Bring your awareness to your inhale as a state of receiving and your exhale as a state of giving. Slow down your breath for a count of six, inhale six to receive, exhale six to give good energy out. Repeat six times.
6. Align with the energy of the rising sun. Visualize the energy of your heart. What does it need for it to be full and free? What seeds are you ready to plant at this time?

7 Place both hands on your heart and give thanks for another day of life on this planet.

8 Journal any positive images, symbols, gratitudes, or messages that came to you. Weave them into your day.

2. Breath of Heart Practice

Intention
To awaken your heart's capacity and ignite self-love.

Supplies
For this ritual you will need a candle and a comfortable and quiet place to sit or lie down uninterrupted for ten minutes. Feel free to put on some soothing music if it supports your relaxation.

1 Light your candle and state your intention to cleanse, clear, or support the growth of your capacity to love yourself unconditionally.

2 Close your eyes and begin to take deep, intentional breaths, eventually slowing down your breath to a count of six on both the inhale and the exhale. Go through eight rounds of this counted breath exercise.

3 Begin to visualize your actual heart space, your lungs, and your shoulders. If there is heaviness, numbness, sadness or darkness, allow it to flow out of you on the exhale. Connect to a color you love, and let it swirl and cleanse your heart space both on the inhale and the exhale.

4 Now align with a virtue or an essence you are calling in to support the growth of your ability to self-love, self-heal, and self-guide from your heart.

5 It may come to you in the form of words, sounds, or symbols. I invite you to express this out loud, as if you are speaking, singing, praying; listening to exactly what your heart needs from you to grow.

6 Place your left hand on your heart and your right hand on top of that hand. Soften completely. Feel any emotion that comes through. Let it all flow. Begin to tap your right hand on top of your left in this rhythm: 1–2, 1–2–3, 1–2, 1–2–3, 1–2, 1–2–3. Continue counting the beat if you find it supportive. Go for as long as you can as you relax your body.

7 Come into complete stillness and welcome in the element of *air*. Visualize the cleanest, purest air surrounding you. Inhale for four to

six seconds, hold the breath for four to six seconds, exhale for four to six seconds, hold for four to six seconds, and then repeat. As you hold your breath, welcome radical self-love, streaming through your whole body. Go for at least two minutes and stay as long as you want.

8 Visualize an anchor inside your heart that will allow space for opening, grounding, growth, and strong boundaries. Merge this anchored energy now into your spine, and down into the earth. Once you feel your heart anchor rooting downwards, visualize it rising like a channel back up your spine, through your mind, and out the crown of your head. Your spine becomes a channel of compassion.

9 Keep visualizing your heart is in your spine and observe any sensations, visuals, and symbols that may arise.

10 Complete this ritual by standing tall with your feet hip-width apart. Sweep your arms high over your head on the inhale, bend your knees, and swing your arms down by your sides as you curve your spine so your heart falls towards your knees on your exhale. Swing your arms back up on the inhale and exhale as you swing arms down and curl your spine. Repeat these arm swings eight times. Stand tall and find stillness.

11 Visualize your heart capacity now living inside your spine. Open your whole body as a vessel of *joy*. Ground it to the earth, give it up to the sky, extend it like the sunrise, and greet your day with this wildly expansive and magnetic energy.

3. Awakened Heart Meditation and Mantra

Intention

To expand your heart, receive support, and align with a healing mantra.

1 Rise with the sun or visualize the sunrise before you. Find yourself in a comfortable seat and receive the colors of the sunrise like a transmission into your bones, organs, blood, and inside the chambers of your heart.

2 Welcome the essence of "illumination" throughout your body, and give thanks for getting to live another day on this blessed earth.

3 Open yourself to receiving support from the winds of change today. Visualize yourself as a compassionate channel in which you can be

in service to your vision, your communities, your family, and your heart's calling.

4 Place your hands on your heart. Get soft and comfortable in your whole being.

5 Attune to your breath, sense the expansive nature of the wide-open sky and receive pure air into the chambers of your heart for cleansing and purifying.

6 Visualize a flower that is meaningful to you, and imagine the flower blooming inside your chest, lungs, and heart area. Give the flower life through your breath. Imagine your breath raising the flower to its highest frequency.

7 Allow yourself to connect with the vibration or tone of your heart. Feed it with your cleansing breath and your positive light energy.

8 Open to feeling no separation between you, your heart, and the element of air. Air is what is breathing you, what is giving you life. Open your body now as a channel of illumination, a vessel for the energetic and spiritual alchemy of embodiment. Open your awareness to receiving insights.

9 Ask for guidance from your supporting guides, messengers, angels, etc., and find the right wording that works for you. For example: "I am ready and open to receive support from my helping spirits today. I am ready to give and flow with the positive energies around me to live in balance, joy, and connection."

10 Listen for any messages from your guides. Observe if there are any calls to action. They may come in a flash or as a wave of energy. Listen, observe, take it in, perhaps write it down. Be curious about it.

11 Seal your heart meditation with three cleansing breaths, and call forth three blessings. Visualize each blessing landing inside your heart, lungs, chest, and shoulders. As they land there, notice the feeling. Now release them as if you are giving blessings out to the world from your heart. This is a powerful practice—the reciprocal essence of receiving and giving.

12 Finish your meditation with this simple heart mantra:

I love myself,
I love myself wholly,
I love myself unconditionally.
I am a channel of love, I am, I am.

13 Repeat three to six times.

4. Wild Heart Activation:
Self-Love as the Ultimate Healing Balm

Intention
To awaken, clear, and rejuvenate the energies of your heart.

Purpose
To expand your ability to self-heal, self-guide, and redirect your heart towards a state of healing and wholeness.

This activation can be created inside your home or outside at a park, beach, forest, ocean, lake, or mountain—wherever you feel called. I often create both an indoor and an outdoor altar and love the different elements and symbolism they can bring out.

Altar Materials

Gather items from nature that represent the five elements: earth, air, fire, water, and ether. Have a candle, herbs, essential oils, or incense to clean the energy field, a rattle, chimes, a singing bowl, or a musical instrument. You can also use your hands to clap or clink two stones together to create a rhythm.

I like to gather items that have fallen from trees or plants: pinecones, branches, seeds, petals, etc., or I gather items from my garden. If you want to pick items from nature, ask permission from the item first; get a sense of whether this object is needed or not.

If you do not have access to nature, buying a fresh, ethically sourced bouquet or herb combination works perfectly. Gather items that are attractive to you and that represent your personal intention for the Wild Heart Activation. The possibilities are endless; when you release your mind, you create from your heart and your intuition.

The process of gathering, sorting, organizing, and creating your altar is deeply nourishing, creative, and symbolic. The items selected, the way they are arranged, the colors, textures, tones, and words selected: they will bring you closer to sensing, feeling, and seeing the core of your soul. The unconscious self begins to merge or bridge with the conscious self. The literal meets the non-literal, the inner critic softens, and the mind–body–spirit begins to dance together more freely. Often, there is a profound and healing message that comes through. Sometimes it is a word like "peace" or "freedom," and sometimes a message like this comes through: "May I feed my inner fire through deep soul nourishment daily."

Sometimes an affirmation comes to you: "Today I love myself radically. I am madly in love with myself." Or "I am releasing the pain in my heart today. I choose to rest, to surrender, to not have to figure anything out and trust that is what is needed."

Create your altar by placing items in an intentional way, as follows:

Air > East

Welcome purification and cleansing of your capacity to love. Greet your heart visionary, and visualize seeing your life from a bird's-eye view; open to seeing from a new perspective. Welcome new beginnings and your ability to be guided by your awakened heart.

Fire > South

What aspects of you are ready to transform at this time? What generates passion inside you? What old stories or habits are you ready to shift at this time? What depletes your inner fire? Welcome transformation on all levels.

Water > West

Welcome flow—creativity, luminosity, and healing. In what ways can you commit to self-care, self-love, and a deeper level of compassion towards yourself and others? Where can you be more fluid, patient, and flexible? Is there something you are trying to control that is out of your control? Where is the letting go right now in your life?

Earth > North

Welcome your grounded self. Open to a balanced state of equal giving and receiving. Plant your roots. Welcome your family lineage and your ancestors. Visualize the nutrient-rich soil of Mother Earth; open to her alchemy of abundance, exponential growth, exquisite beauty, and the way in which seedlings must be nourished with the right conditions in order to grow. What seeds are you currently planting within?

Ether > Center

Place an item to anchor the center of the circle to represent your highest self in relation to all plants, minerals, animals, and humans. Connect beyond to the energies of the earth and the skies: stars, sun, and moon. Open up to stepping out of the mundane and allow your helping and compassionate spirits to come forward. Welcome them into your ritual. Your center altar item could be a candle or an ethically sourced crystal, stone, more flowers, an image, a poem or prayer.

Once your altar is complete, sit peacefully, attune to your breath, and observe, listen, and feel into the colors, shapes, patterns, or symbols of your creation.

1 Open yourself like a beam of light to receive messages, insights, visions, and perspective shifts. Feel the warmth in your heart.
2 Place your hands inside your altar and begin to soften all parts of yourself. Allow yourself to become fully present and receptive.
3 Take long deep breaths and slow down your breath to a count of six on the inhale and six on the exhale. Recall your core intention to awaken, clear, and rejuvenate the energies of your heart.
4 Begin to speak, pray, or sing out loud. Share and release the exact state of your heart, as if you are speaking directly to spirit: to the goddess or god, the creator, to specific deities, whatever your belief is; speak to these energies directly. Pray out loud. Then work with this energy and begin to call out how you are ready to show up for yourself. How you are ready to love yourself more fully. Become a conduit for love to move through you in a way that is new, full, and completely present.
5 If you have a singing bowl, a rattle, or a musical instrument, it may feel right to play, sing, speak, pray, or dance the energy that wants to be expressed. Start by directing your energy straight to your altar and observe it. You may witness a perspective shift. Take this perspective shift into your body now.
6 If it feels comfortable, activate your body as a free vessel of heart energy and dance it out, sing it out, play an instrument, go wild—let your heart lead you. You may feel called to put on a track of simple, rhythmic percussion music. Either lying down, sitting or standing, close your eyes and begin to step out of time and space. Leave the mundane, the ordinary behind.
7 Visualize yourself entering a portal into the realm of spirit. Nature imagery may guide you there. Open your whole being to receive a message, a healing, or a clearing with the support of helping spirits.

Welcome your guides, open yourself to receive their positive affirmations and encouragement on your path. Go for as long as it feels right.

8 You may also choose to go into a silent meditation and allow your imagery to clear your heart of blockages. An animal messenger, a compassionate spirit guide, or another guiding image may come to you to support your healing process at this time.

9 You are gathering a higher frequency of unconditional love and compassion to re-energize your heart.

10 Slowly come to a still point. Ground yourself before your altar. Send your rooted nature down into the belly of Mother Earth.

11 Are there any guiding words you want to write down and place in your altar, or any energies you are ready and willing to release at this time in your life?

12 When you are done, close the ritual sacred space. This can be done silently or out loud:

- Honor all of your teachers: past, present, and future.
- Honor the air for its inspiration to gain perspective, to see the bigger picture.
- Honor the fire for its life-giving passion, transformative nature, and magnetic light force.
- Honor the water for its healing, fluid, and creative ways.
- Honor the earth for its abundant and grounded ways.
- Honor your spirit and ether for its universal life-force energy.
- Honor any guides that may have come to you for insight and inspiration in the journey: plant, mineral, animal, or spirit form. Seal in any gifts, messages, symbols, or guiding words received here.
- Honor the energies of the moon, sun, stars, and the sacred spirits all around us.
- Feel, trust, and respond to the cosmic web in which we all contribute to raising the consciousness of all.

13 Repeat the "I love myself" mantra or your personal prayer three times.

If inspired, go straight into a free-flow journal session, draw, or write a poem about your wild heart activation experience.

Tending to Your Altar

For seven days after your ritual, tend to your altar.

If indoors, light the candle each day. If outdoors, visit your altar for seven days if you can. Sit with it, nourish any sacred items with your breath, and allow it to come alive with your radiance.

Observe any changes you may see inside yourself or even in your altar.

Feed your altar creation with anything else that will raise the vibration, for example fresh herbs, flowers, candles, stones, words, love letters, poems, or affirmations. Keep coming back to feeding your heart with the most nourishing soil; water it with your energy, keep it alive, notice when new seeds, ideas, or visions come to you, and plant them deep inside the chambers of your heart.

After seven days, dismantle your altar in an intentional way. Nature items may return to the earth or be offered to the lakes, rivers, oceans, etc. As you go through this process, welcome the healing of your hands and your heart; extend this healing to your altar items and the natural world.

5. Sky Vision: A Visualization and Meditation to Shift Perspective

Intention
To shed negativity and welcome in renewal.

Purpose
Reclaim the essence of gratitude and compassion,
reveal the location of healing within the body, and acknowledge
the guides ready to support you currently.

1 Sit or lie down. Get comfortable and place one hand on your heart and one hand on your lower abdomen.
2 Soften your gaze and relax your shoulders and all the muscles in your face. With each inhale, focus on filling yourself with pure, clean, and clear compassionate energy. On each exhale, focus on letting go of the fears, the anxieties, the pain, the sadness. Feel as if it's being pulled out of you with love, in the name of loving and living with joy as your birthright.
3 Call forward eleven things you are grateful for in this moment. One after the other, without thinking too much about them, see your

gratitudes flash before you and let them permeate the cells of your body, heart, and mind.

4 Bring your awareness to your spine and visualize it as a channel for your capacity to love and to become deeply integrated. Inhale from the base of your spine and travel up to your heart; exhale from your heart and send your awareness back down your spine. Receive a color or an energetic quality and put that awareness into the quality of your breath. If you can see it, you can feel it; this is the practice of deeper embodiment and energetic transformation. Repeat the spinal breath pattern six times.

5 Send your roots down into the earth; anchor yourself again. If you can see your roots, you will be anchored and always have a place to return to.

6 Now open to your *sky vision*. Find an imaginal way to get up into the sky. Climb a tree, fly a plane, receive a ride from a winged guide, shape-shift; get there somehow. Don't think about it. Visualize it. See yourself from a bird's-eye view. See your surroundings. See the energetic qualities of your life all around you. See what is heavy, what is light, where the complicated parts are, where and what brings you joy and into a state of radical self-love. As you open to seeing from your *sky vision* realm, you may begin to understand, sense, or feel the energy behind the current state of your life.

7 Go one step further and be your own healer, your own guide, and begin to shape-shift energetic qualities that no longer serve you in your life. Where there is pain and darkness, pull it out, give it to the earth, and reclaim space for new energy to emerge. You may see how you are reacting to certain relationships or patterns and behaviors in your own being. Work to shift, transform, and pull apart the emotion that lives behind those actions as if you were sorting, sifting, weaving, mending, or patching your inner contents.

8 There may be a loving and compassion guide or teacher that wants to support you on this journey at this time in your life. They may have a message for you. Stay open to receive this. Embrace this. You are supported now and continue to open your awareness to being held, embraced, and supported in this way.

9 Come back into your body fully.

10 Place both hands on your heart. Come back to a state of gratitude. Breathe three deep breaths into your roots, breathe three deep breaths into your spine, and three deep breaths into your mind.

11 Journal about your experience.

6. Prayer for Your Awakened Heart

*Today, may I see from the eyes of my heart and ignite my inner
visionary. Like the sun that rises each morning, I embrace a radiance
that fuels love and compassion for all beings. Knowing that each day
I get to live in this life is a blessing, I listen fully, let go often, and love
fiercely. As I attune to the eastern skies, I open to my winged
perceiver, the deep knowing inside me: self-love is the path
to healing, joy, and living my fullest life.*

When you begin your day with a core belief that self-love is the path to a
joyful existence, you trust that whatever life brings you, you can call on the
divine spirit within and your guides all around you. Take life breath by breath,
moment by moment, day by day. Pray to, with, for, and from your heart's
calling to radically and fully love every ounce of your being.

Practice to write your own poem or prayer. Weave in the energy of the
rising sun, the blessing of a new day; welcome compassion, self-love and
truth, and allow any shadows to come forward so that you can free them.
Draw any symbols or images that support your prayer, and write down any
guiding words or an affirmation that will ignite your path of illumination.

7. Decree: Temple of My Heart

I am the light of my heart.

*I am listening, releasing, and wildly loving the very core of my being.
I am eagle, hawk, hummingbird, raven, sparrow, owl, butterfly.
I am the winged perceiver, the high flyer, the heart visionary.
I embrace the aches, the pains, and the sorrows
that run through me like a river.*

*I trust that when the time is right and my heart speaks of release,
the stormy winds will rush towards me and cleanse me of my
heart's gripping armor.*

*I rinse my body as a channel with self-love even on
the days when I deem myself unlovable.*

*I take my heart back inside my spirit, rebuilding so I may widen its reach.
My spirit infuses my bones with a holy serum so I may feel the truths,
shed the untruths, and become alive with compassion and kindness
each day that I am living.*

*My vessel is receptive to the pure, unconditional love that is being offered by my
loved ones. I am supported fully by my helping and guiding spirits.*

*I am the ancient bones of my ancestry. My heart remembers; I listen.
I am basking in the mystery of life.
Like the high-flying eagle soaring through the skies,
I see from this vast perspective.*

*Today, I choose to see from the eyes of my heart.
I am expansive, luminous, and free.
I am here, heart blown open.*

Now it's your turn to write a decree for your heart. Write freely without judging or censoring, as if you are writing a commitment to spirit about how you are ready to live inside your heart visionary.

8. Journal Prompts

- Where and what inside of you is in need of healing right now?
- At this time in your life, what seeds are you planting? What ideas, visions, and intentions would you like to plant for your future self to manifest?
- Write a love letter or a poem from your heart visionary to yourself, a loved one, your community, an ancestor, or a family member that has crossed over. Go for your first impulse, do not censor, and let your heart sing through the creative process. You do not need to send this letter; that's optional. The process of writing it will clear your heart so it can love more fully on all levels.

- What areas in your life are you ready to see from another perspective?
- Write down three things that you love about yourself. Whenever your mind goes to a lack of self-love, let these three attributes be a guiding force. Welcome in the practice of *self-love*.
- Write out the top three practices that you can activate on a daily basis to bring you into a loving, compassionate, and kind relationship with yourself.

Come home
sweet one.
Your softness
is your strength.
Your dance is only yours.
Your song, like nectar –
let it seep into the marrow of your bones.
Rest now, sweet one.
Come home.
The temple doors are open.

INNER POWER
ACTIVATOR

Be a midwife to your own becoming.
Allow the wild silky parts of your soul to dance, scream, cry, and sing.
Channel the uneasy pieces into sculptures that adorn the earth.
Feed the complexities of your mind with simple universal truths.
Light the fires inside your medicine cave.
The guides await your return, the birthing of a self reclaimed.
Loon call, wolf howl, eagle soar, cricket song, shooting star, waterfall.
Be rose, snake, fireweed, butterfly, cedar tree, sunflower.
This goodness, this beauty, this truth.
This is your birthright.

Chapter 3

Inner Power Activator
Fuel Your Fire, Activate Your Visions

ACTIVATING INNER POWER: THE JOURNEY

Life is a series of events and experiences that shape our sense of character, our lived experience, how we define ourselves, express ourselves. It determines what motivates us, the roles we play, the rules we follow or break, the way we move, the way we hear, listen, feel, sense, and speak. When we experience trauma, shame, guilt, abandonment, and anxiety—to name a few—our body–mind response forms protection patterns to stay safe. These patterns become embedded into our cellular memory, triggering our parasympathetic nervous system into a constant state of fight or flight.

In our lifetime, there may have been little space for safety and vulnerability. The freedom of emotional, creative, physical and intellectual expression may have been repressed through learned behaviors in our environment. When we were children, we may have learned coping strategies to receive the attention, love, care, and support we naturally desired and needed. Through our teenage, young adult, and later years we may have experienced relationships—whether with ourself or others—that triggered reactionary coping mechanisms: longing, gripping, trying to fix, heal, mend, and make things right. We may even have put our own self on the line, becoming the martyr, the victim, the perpetrator, the fixer, the one who escaped, or the one who got abandoned time and time again.

Habitual emotional patterns are formed based on our past experiences. When they are left unattended they become the habits that unconsciously rule our lives. These patterns can eventually manifest as anxiety, addictions, paranoia, phobias, and self-defeating or self-sabotaging behaviors. When we become aware of and accept these patterns, we can take personal responsibility and choose to shift the "limiting beliefs" to ultimately reprogram our minds. (And our lives!)

Through mindful, compassionate, conscious, and supported tactics we can begin to clear away toxic thought patterns and replace them with truthful, higher vibrational thoughts. Consciousness and awareness of the mind is golden here. This is what can transform self-doubt, low self-esteem, injury, and illness into radiant inner health and happiness. Whatever our life story, we begin to go deep into understanding our relationship to our own true self, the workings of the mind, and how we can access our inner power.

When we take a good hard look at our "unconscious rulers"—those things we do to make ourselves feel powerful or in control; behaviors that are reactionary as opposed to authentic and deliberate—we become aware of how we manipulate and control ourselves or others at the expense of not being in true alignment with who we are. When we begin to uncover the falsehoods or the untruths of what drives us to take ownership or power "over" as opposed to power "within," we begin to understand how to tap into our real inner power activator.

WHERE YOUR TRUE POWER LIES

As you raise your awareness around your motivations and desires, you begin to track where your true inner power lies. The call of the inner mystic is to dig deep into the flame of your authenticity and cultivate the unique spark that lights you up from the inside out. This is the space where true power lies. This area in the body lives at the solar plexus, just above the navel in the front and back of the body, and it is what keeps you integrated and esteemed without needing external validation.

When events, experiences, and relationships become challenging—fearful, heartbreaking, stressful—an imbalance can develop in your self-esteem. On the other hand, this can also happen when someone is "overpraised." It can feel like a collapsing of energy. Your creative waterways become stagnant, your heart's capacity for compassionate living and loving becomes numb, and the fire of your self-esteem gets put out. There is no longer a flow between your grounded, fluid self and the illumination in your heart; your ability to wildly love yourself gets lost in space. You may experience a sense of lost identity, inertia, or a lack of motivation to cultivate and live out your dreams. Shame, blame, and victim mentality begin to take over both the conscious and unconscious parts of yourself. This becomes a vicious cycle where a false identity is created based on external factors or motivations, and the ego is then built on this energy. However, this is an unsteady place to form the ego; it is where addiction, stress, anxiety, and depression are born.

You may find yourself living life with a "power-over" mentality in order to maintain a false sense of control. Within our society's past and present, the power-over paradigm is what sexism, patriarchy, violence, racism, and misogyny breed on. Historically, we have been exposed to these deep-rooted paradigms, and because of this, we have inherited trauma that continues to fester until it becomes realized and liberated. In order to stay safe, you may have played small inside this box, this shelter of false safety and limiting belief systems. But once you begin to recognize where these power-over constructs exist in your life, you can decode, disrupt, and dismantle them. You no longer need to feed into the power-over energies. You can set yourself free by cultivating a true sense of identity where your inner power is activated—crystal clear and in alignment with your soul's calling. You can begin to reclaim your personal sovereignty by becoming aware of how you feed the power-over energy; by understanding both the root of your emotions and the truth behind your motivations.

Ask yourself: For whom am I doing this? What kind of praise do I long for? Recognition? Success? Attention? Who do I seek control over? Why does that make me feel good and safe and powerful? What if all of the roles I play out in my life were shattered? Burnt to the ground? Who am I then? Who am I at the seat of my soul? What qualities best describe who I am in my pure essence without praise, control, or power over?

Take a moment to sit with these questions, and perhaps read them a few times. When you can imbue this inner consciousness of pure essence aglow without any attachments, outcomes, and material possessions to identify by and with, then you will have begun to source, reveal, and tap into your true essence. Here, you begin the journey towards hearing the call of your soul purpose while walking the path of the inner mystic.

CHANNEL YOUR INNER POWER

Cultivating inner power comes through awareness of personal motivations and a steady mindful and self-care practice. This means being intentional at all times and truly aligning with what lights you up in life. When we recognize the vicious cycle of roller coaster highs and lows that result from boosting the false sense of ego, we begin to access the inner wisdom that knows how to feed our inner power. The path of the inner mystic is to cultivate a healthy relationship with personal power. Not fearing it, no longer playing small, but anchoring into the present moment and committing to life's opportunities, celebrating others in their true power, and activating a journey of true soul-purpose alignment.

That's when you become the humble warrior, peaceful as the meandering river, strong as Mother Earth, graceful as the sweet summer winds, radiant as the sun. When you are embodied in a true sense of ego, you become an advocate for conscious collective empowerment—not only are you balanced in your own inner power, but you are clean and clear to advocate for the health of the planet, the humans, the animals, the elements, and the unseen realms. You become a source of clean energy. Your call to be in greater service to the planet in this way will generate abundance, joy, balance, soul purpose, and deep-rooted compassion for all beings. You become so charged with love and inner connection that dreams, healing, and prayers come to life within you.

THE ELEMENT OF FIRE: THE PATH OF TRANSFORMATION

Fire represents change and transformation. It's the quickest form of transformation, the second being the breath. Fire symbolizes passion, will, heat, freedom, vision, and inner power. This element is associated with the radiance of the sun; the energy center in the body is located at the solar plexus. It is also associated with passion—that inner fire that glows when you are activated and inspired. The shadow aspect of this energy center is shame and playing out the victim role in life.

When you activate inner power, you begin to form an intimate relationship with a healthy ego. This is the "pure essence" you were born with; the essential or higher self inside you can begin to grow as you nourish the deep well of your esteemed self on a daily basis.

In the pagan wheel of the year, the element of fire sits in the south and is associated with the season of summer. It is also symbolic of our inner child, curiosity, and the sense of wonder and freedom that guides us towards healthy self-esteem.

Fire teaches us how to let go, how to attune to the qualities of anger, passion, shame (past and present), inertia, and low self-esteem. Once we train our brains, our words, our feelings, and our actions to observe the quality of the energies present, we begin to develop boundaries and strengthen from within. When lower vibrational energies come toward us, we can set an intention in a flash and begin to invite in ones of higher vibration. Aligning with the energy of fire will bring profound insights. It will show you how to quickly transform "lack" or "shame" or "I am not enough," "I will never _____," or "I will always _____" statements into positive truths. The first place of discovery on this journey is awareness. The second is letting go, the third is resetting your core intention, and the fourth is follow-through and activation. Herein lies the path of energetic transformation.

What you think, feel, speak, and do affects your world in immeasurable ways. Be attentive to the energies you are inviting into your energy field. Catch yourself in the moment when negativity or limiting core beliefs arise. Forgive yourself. Forgive others. Remember your core intention. Take a deep breath. Soften your exterior and strengthen your interior. Restate your intention, remember your passion, and feed your esteemed radiance in the moment. You are a magnet, a wild fire of light, depth, healing, wisdom, and brilliance. Trust that you are supported. Call forth your compassionate and supportive guides. Listen for the guiding whispers that come through meditation, prayer, dreamtime, and times of flow. Practice the art of patience and divine timing every day of your life, and listen for the guidance, symbols, and call to action that stream from within.

As the match strikes the matchbox and the first flame ignites, give your attention to what fuels your soul. Give yourself permission to be awestruck by the whispers of your soul's calling. All of them: your mending, patching, healing, the humbling, the deep dives, the falling to your knees in prayer. Go to the fire now; let go, be vulnerable, align with the truth of the matter, unveil, de-layer, and toss into the fire every role, assumption, expectation, shame, trauma past or present. Watch it burn. Trust in the process. Witness your mind separating from your story. Give yourself permission to shape-shift and transform. Today is a new day. Every day you awaken with the potential to live inside a new body and a new mind.

SHED LIMITING CORE BELIEFS
TO REWRITE YOUR STORY

Our personal stories are unique to each of us. Life is filled with elements of surprise, questions, and oppositional energy. Sun to moon, day to night, joy to grief, we are all creatures of this capacity. We can never actually know the outcome of any adventure or relationship we choose to engage in, yet each experience leads us towards the next. The opposing forces of nature—water to fire, earth to air—show us dynamic strength found in oppositional energy. In all of life, there is great mystery, cosmic happenings, and divine timings. There are unforgettable spiritual moments that imprint into the matrix of our cells. On the other side there is heartbreak, loss, illness, abuse, shame, guilt, powerlessness, neglect, abandonment, and inter-generational trauma (to name a few). This also lives inside the cellular memory of our DNA. When we open up to truly becoming the witness and unpacking our life events, we begin to understand our life story.

We want to unearth the spirited, positive, and transformational times, as well as the events and experiences that made us retreat, suppress, spiral into shame, and ultimately disappear or disconnect from our true self. The times that made us play too small and the times that made us play too big—where our own egos needed to prove our worth and we became the "people pleaser." The times we agreed and gave our consent knowing full well we didn't want to engage.

Whether we wanted to disappear or were starving for attention to the point of abandoning our own inner power, we must acknowledge everything for the sake of the healing process. These experiences must be uncovered in order for us to understand our relationship to our own willpower, our healthy ego, and the truth of our authenticity. This process is wildly liberating and healing on a soul level. It takes courage, vulnerability, and mindful honesty.

Your life story creates your personal story. It also generates limiting core beliefs—the ones that replay inside your mind, the ones that become unconscious rulers in your life. Understanding this energetic principle is the first step in the process of rewriting your story.

First, listen and actually hear what the limiting core belief is. Then soften, so as to not resist or repress or judge, and instead recognize how the belief may be ruling your life. Track where this story lives inside your body and trace where it comes from. Then discern and dismantle the core belief by connecting to the actual *truth* as opposed to the *untruth* you may be repeating inside your mind. Is the story actually true? Discernment is key here. Your experience of the belief may be true, but the way you are now acting it out in your life, is this true? The way you play small, or act the victim, or hide, or over-power, or react to shame, or exaggerate? Is this way of being necessary anymore or is it a habitual pattern that is unconsciously ruling your life?

The next step is to dismantle the limiting core belief and rewrite it according to the truth of the present moment, then decide what energy you are willing to transform it into and live with. For example, if your limiting core belief is "I am not enough," or "I will never be enough," your work is to track, trace, and dismantle this belief. Practice compassion for yourself and rewrite this statement into something like: "I am wildly abundant, connected, and free," or "I am enough, I carry the light of my full capacity." If your limiting belief is "I am not worthy of love," the rewriting may look like this: "I am a channel of love, light, and universal life force." When you rewrite your core beliefs they must come from an authentic place within you. The shorter the better. Your task is to imprint this positive core belief into your body–mind awareness and speak it inside you every time the limiting core belief tries to take you over.

Once you connect with these deep-rooted beliefs, you begin to live your life with freedom and a healthy connection to your source of power— both inner and outer. You no longer question your ability to free yourself. You can untangle yourself from the old stories that may have taken a firm grip on your life. You can experience freedom. You can transform all of your past experiences and empower who you are today. You are no longer limited by your story—you are empowered by it.

This is the work of the inner mystic; to gather the events and stories that have done their time and to lay them down like precious sculptures upon the earth. You are a channel for the energetic transformation of limiting, painful, toxic, and shameful experiences. Let them burn through you. Like the phoenix, let them burn and fall to ashes upon the ground, only to be regenerated into wisdom seeds of your inner mystic. You will know when to do this. You will no longer question your self-worth, no longer doubt your soul purpose. You will free yourself from the mentality of lack, victim, and scarcity. Once you rewrite your core beliefs based on the essence of your inner power activator, you can dream your authentic life into being.

FEED YOUR FIRE:
TOOLS TO OVERCOME POWERLESSNESS

*We activate inner power through the resonance
of conscious choice birthed by pure inner desire,
a clear mind and a direct call to action.
Letting go of the final outcome is crucial.*

Through awakening to our inner processes, we begin to understand more fully the exact moment where we give our power away or feel powerless. We may experience the state of "inertia," which literally translates as a tendency to do nothing or to remain unchanged. Inertia could be a learned coping pattern to stay protected or disengaged in order to numb ourselves from feeling certain emotional states. Witnessing these coping mechanisms with compassion and curiosity will be key to working on transforming them.

For example, let's unpack the emotion of anger. When we push really hard to get a desired outcome—often steeped in the need to have our own way—this can result in frustrated energy. If things don't go exactly the way we want them to go, we may get angry. When we get triggered in this state and anger takes over, we block our own power. We diffuse our mind–body connections or misuse our own inner power. Ultimately, we give our power away. What follows is most often mental and emotional burnout, and with it goes our compassion, our self-esteem, and our ability to have perspective on the situation. We become overly focused on the problem or the attack, not the solution. This sends our nervous system into imbalance. Our heart races, our minds become unclear, we speak harmful words, and we feed the victim within.

To remedy the forced behavioral patterns in our life, we must look at finding a balance between effort and effortlessness. We pause and breathe before jumping into a reactionary state when faced with a heated moment. One minute of non-action can make all the difference in reclaiming calm, quiet, and effective inner power. The next time we are forcing our agenda on a specific outcome, we check in with mind and body and ask, "Is there an easier way in this moment?" Often when we release our firm grip, we can discern more quickly at what point to let go, and a new stream of energy arrives to bring a fresh perspective. If we can get closer to our mind–body signs and signals that come with anger before they take us over, we can recover more quickly. When we wholeheartedly accept an invitation towards living our lives with a balance of effort and effortlessness, we work intelligently with energy. We become less fatigued and stressed, and we can restore our vital energy.

You are stronger in your releasing than in your constant gripping.
When you let go even a little, you make way for the path of
expansive and effective activation, on all levels.

Let's look at shame. We can track shame back to our experiences as children, young adults, or to the present day. Recalling when we experienced shame can help us begin to understand why we react to specific triggers in our life. This ability to be the "tracker" can lead to a healing process that generates lasting change. Shame comes through when the self-esteem has been weakened. When shame takes over, you collapse at the center of your body. The grounding of your lower body and the rising nature of your upper body become severed, blocking the flow of energy. You become defensive, unable to take direction, feedback, or advice; you play small and convince yourself that you have already failed—so why bother trying? In this moment, your whole system becomes imbalanced. This is a very important energy to recognize the moment it happens.

If your own energy stream becomes muddled by past experiences or future projections, how will you get to the heart of your own pure energy? If you continue to shoot energetic arrows of lack, scarcity, unworthiness, projected failure, fear of your own success, etc., you put yourself in a tiny box. Inside this box, you feed the energetic source of greed, violence, sexism, racism, and patriarchy at the root of the power-over colonial system. You are not only buying into but actively feeding and supporting the very system you may be attempting to liberate yourself from. This cycle is potent. Choosing not to feed it in the moment it arises is pivotal. This becomes an exercise that generates lasting change.

Every challenge, joy, failure, unjust experience and success becomes
a turning point inside life's inner compass. Allow your experiences to
become the intentional material in which your body–mind–heart
heals, shape-shifts, redirects, and remembers the journey home
towards a clear, vast, and recalibrated inner power.

Every time we are presented with a challenge, we have an opportunity to bring our balanced inner power to the table and work with the energy before us. When we can understand its energetic origins, we can see more clearly what triggers us, why we react in this way, and how we can open to learning without getting tossed around in its wildfire effect. With this awareness, we no longer suppress or repress emotions and reactions, but we feel and listen in a way that we can recover more quickly from life's ups and downs while attuning to our own instincts.

Compassionate understanding and non-judgment towards your own process is key. The next time you find yourself being the hypercritical judge, take three deep breaths, let go of your agenda, have compassion for your process, and trust that this is a signal to lay down the negativity and embrace the possibility for change. This heart-fueled acceptance gathers information channels in your body that include past experiences, emotional reactions, mind chatter, present-moment awareness, intuitive flashes, and future desires. These channels can consciously align in a way that connects you back to your inner power activator.

The energetic realm of your embodied, fluid, connected, and awakened self is the humble warrior inside you. That part of you knows how to execute, when to let go, where to activate, who to engage with, and what to call forth. Once your inner mystic has recognized the imbalanced, over-inflated or under-inflated ego, call on the humble warrior. Call yourself out when you begin to dominate others and use controlling tactics to over-power the situation. Receive counsel in the moment, name what the emotion is and where it lives in your body. Honor your mind–body connection.

Call forth your deepest desires, fuel your fire with a steady energy, and trust that you can be both a student and a master of your own energetic field. You can change, shift, transform, let go, and begin again with one single spark of the flame.

Your willpower can be developed through mindful states such as meditation, personal awareness, recognition of negative mental chatter, and clarity around the power of the spoken word. In order to cultivate true inner power, you must discern when you play into the victim role. This becomes the transformational catalyst out of this mentality and into one of deep connectivity, where you will meet the flame of your inner power.

This does not mean, however, that there isn't violence and injustice in the world. You do not simply bypass or repress where you may have been victim to violence, abuse, shame, blame, and traumatic events. There is truth to every experience, and you may need support and counsel to heal.

May you acknowledge and remember: Power is awareness. Power is knowledge. Power is listening. Power is becoming the witness to your own process. Power is releasing the victim mentality. Power is soul care. Power is healing. Power is reclaiming your wholeness, your radiance, your inner beauty, and your truth.

Activating Inner Power:
A Step-by-Step Daily Practice

1 *Awareness* of when you are feeding the inner victim. ("This always happens to me, I will never be good enough, they will always have more than me, I will never be happy," etc.)
2 *Process* the information coming through you: What is your mind saying? Where do you feel it in your body? What words do you speak that reinforce this feeling?
3 Observe the *habitual patterns* that accompany or feed the victim within. Acknowledge them and interrupt the pattern.
4 *Practice compassion.* Soften your body, hold yourself in a loving embrace, take three deep breaths, and let the victim mentality go.
5 *Realize* that this is not you, this is your body–mind response to the habit of playing small within your own inner victim cycle.
6 *Redirect* your senses towards feeling strong within. Find an *"I am, I will"* affirmation. For example, "I am powerful. I will continue to feed my healthy will today."

LASTING TRANSFORMATION

Lasting transformation comes through personal accountability, not by trying to fix or change others. An ignited willpower and positive relationship to our self-esteem becomes most effective when we work strategically and intelligently. We move through our visions, projects, and emotional understandings with greater perspective and grace when we are not pushing too hard to achieve constant productivity. Through perspective and practices such as meditation, time in nature, exercise, and compassionate mind–body states, we open our awareness to listen, make space, and access the essential core of what feeds our inner power. Here we can shift through disappointments, unfortunate timings, and redirections thanks to the combination of letting go and the right call to action (as opposed to buying into life's little dramas). There will always be dramas and disappointments. When we activate our will from a place of clear vision while sensing and enhancing the vibrational field it holds, we can more easily embrace our inner power.

We manifest our future existence through present-moment awareness while discerning and sensing the energetic vibration of the desired impulse. We then organize, strategize, and cast the impulse out wildly into the cosmic field. Think of everything as energy. Become a receptor of energy as if you are the witness of your own energy, the energy of others, and the energy that exists within nature. Attune your senses to the vibration that different energies hold. Is the vibration fluid, sticky, murky, clear, strong, soft, graceful, cold, hot, colorful, dimensional? This approach and curious inner eye will keep you connected and awake to understanding your energy body–mind–heart field and in turn, how to transform it when needed.

Anything is possible. What you feed grows. Connect to the energy at the core of what you want in your life. As you visualize what that energy feels like, you will no longer live out of lack, scarcity, low self-worth, or the constant questioning about your life–soul purpose. Instead, you will be the holder of that container of energy, which will shape-shift and transform as you move through your life.

CLEARING YOUR ENERGY FIELD: THE PATH OF THE MODERN MYSTIC

When your innate desire for goodness and truth becomes larger than any outcome, you connect directly to source and mystery. When you imbue your inner mind–heart field with the acceptance of life's great mysteries, these great wonders become alive to you every single day—the unknowns, the magic, the wonder of seeing through the eyes of a child, nature's most epic beauty, how the trees communicate, how animals migrate and hibernate, how fossils are formed, how mountains move, the solar system and the starry night sky. This mysterious and wondrous attitude—to be always asking, to be curious, to have a thirst for learning—will train your inner being to see with beauty.

You cannot master or control these great mysteries in life. Yet when you can open yourself up to the vibrational fields of earthly and cosmic rhythms, you attune to their potent source of energy. This shifts you out of a focus on lack, scarcity, and powerlessness into a calm, grounded, and vast inner knowing. You become a part of the cycle. You are no longer separate from this rhythmic cosmic vibrational field of energy.

When you get swept up in inner turmoil, indecision, low self-worth, and lack of purpose, you lose your connection to that energy field. You lose your grounding and begin spinning. You may begin to falsely feed your ego and that of others.

In order to clear your energy field you must harness the power of setting healthy boundaries. This could include personal, relationship, career, political, media, spiritual, and energetic boundaries. How much energy do you absorb that does not feel good inside you? Understanding what depletes your energy is key to setting healthy boundaries. Begin by tracking what creates imbalance in your life. This could be anything from food or liquid intake, to conversations, relationships, and habitual patterns, to excess time spent on media, to lack of sleep and toxic thought patterns. When you become aware of these imbalances simply accept that this is so, release judgment, and allow this to become the catalyst to move your energy in a new way. Once you have a sense of this kind of depletion, you will naturally choose to redirect your attention and your actions towards what builds your inner strength.

Committing to daily mindful and soulful rituals is essential in order to keep your energy field clear. The first place to begin clearing your own energy field is to begin a daily mindful ritual. It could be as simple as lighting a candle first thing in the morning, writing down your gratitudes, walking quietly and intentionally in nature, or taking a candle-lit bath; whatever you choose, you must find ways that support you to come home inside yourself. This is "you" time. Think of it as filling up your inner temple with goodness. It's a way to check in and perhaps understand what energy you might be holding onto, what thoughts might be ruling you, or where you may be playing the victim. If you consciously "check-in" like this every day without expecting a certain outcome, you will begin to form an intimate relationship with your inner being, your essential higher self. It will become like a conversation you would have with your best friend, except you will be having it with yourself.

Building a force field of energy all around you comes through steady and daily awareness. It's natural to fall off your rhythm, and sometimes it can be incredibly powerful to do so in order to remember how to get back on the path. The inner mystic in you needs to be expressed fully, no longer hiding in the shadows or putting on the façade that everything is okay all the time. You feel deeply, and through this, you learn how to work with all energies that come into your force field.

Step-by-Step Guide to Clearing Your Energy Field

The following guidelines may support you in strengthening your inner power while clearing your energy field. Use this process when you find yourself at a crossroads, in a transition, or in a place of imbalance or questioning. Before using this practice, find a quiet and calm space within, and get clear on what your intention or question is.

1   *Align* with your intention in the present moment and visualize it in its full manifestation. This may come in the form of an image. Sometimes it comes very quickly, so pay attention. The visions might not be literal, but you receive clues in this way and they contribute to the overall vision.
2   *Connect* to the energy that lives inside the intention. What virtues does your vision hold? Abundance, freedom, balance, joy, peace, excitement, generosity, nurturing, love, compassion, authenticity, artistry? What does this energy feel like inside you? The more you can direct your mind–body awareness to the vibration inside the energy of your core intention, the more you can attune to this energy.
3   *Organize* by gathering, sorting, and sifting through your ideas and visions. Get practical and dream big. Which ideas need to be cleared out of this picture? Focus on clearing the fearful ones that may be blocking your energy. Get crystal clear and organized on all of the pieces of your vision. Writing them down will support your process.
4   *Strategize* to execute your vision. This step is key. Visioning does include practical strategy. The trick is to not play small, but to go for the humble victory. Open to real time, visualize the vision, see it manifested, and gather each piece of the strategy in order to effect the vision.
5   *Let go* of the desired outcome. After you follow the steps above, release the final outcome of your vision. Remember, when we open ourselves up to work with spirit and co-create our life, the universe may have a

slightly different version of what we imagine. We learn and receive so much more when we approach our lives in this way.

Remembering to *"follow the desire, release the outcome"* will connect you more deeply to the vibrational field of your vision.

6 *Evolve* the vision. As you go along, there may be times where you need to re-vision the vision. You grow and evolve every single day. Cultivating a deeper connection to yourself requires personal evolution. What was once burning with desire inside you may no longer hold as much importance. These are all steps along the journey. Your intuition strengthens when you give yourself permission to hear the whispers of your instincts. You then become the channel for the manifestation of your dreams.

7 *Cast* your vision out into the world. Imbue your inner being on a soul level with the energy of your vision and you become a magnet for this energy to come your way. In divine timing you will encounter mentors, colleagues, support systems, a like-minded community. Your intuition increases as your inner power becomes balanced, unshakeable, and wildly magnetic. You receive as much as you give out. And you bear witness to the fullness of your life evolving before you, behind you, and all around you.

IGNITING YOUR DREAMS: SOUL INTEGRATION

The element of fire lives inside each of us. It keeps us warm, connected, passionate, and reminds us that we too as humans are "transformers." This acts as inspiration to spark our own inner fire. We begin to share warmth, love, leadership, and integrated power that can ignite lasting change in the world.

When you do your personal work, you are working for the collective heart. When you take responsibility to heal your own wounds, you are supporting the energy of planetary healing and change. When you activate your pure inner power, you are leading by example through your own humility, focus, vision, and passion.

May you rise, so that others may rise. May you live with passion, connection, joy, inner strength, and grace, so that others may also. When you liberate yourself from what binds you and holds you back, you empower others to do the same. This becomes an energetic, inner-mystical way of living that goes beyond the mundane of ordinary life. You begin to dismantle and transform traditional belief systems. You tap into the unseen realm of spiritual energy and your intuitive nature will grow in ways you never imagined. You begin to receive insights and messages that support the foundation of your own evolution and contribute to your soul purpose.

Connect to the vibrational field of your own authenticity and begin to welcome in this energy wildly, with your whole body and a fully open mind. Feed it clean, clear, unshakeable energy. Remember, what you feed grows. Increase your capacity to internalize the energetic field in which this energy flows, moves, churns, and transforms.

Find the places and spaces in which your soul simply says *yes, I am fully here*. With this comes not only the deep release of stress and unnecessary tension, but also a softening into your internal world—your temple, your inner spirit. Each day becomes a living ritual. Fueled by curiosity, the wonderment of a child, the radical acceptance of letting go of all things you cannot control, you collaborate and co-create your life with spirit.

At the same time, you will meet your own resistance and perhaps the resistance of others, bearing witness to the judgments and criticisms, to the visceral and somatic reactions in your body. You will attune to your nervous system in all of its states, from fight or flight to rest and digest, getting to know it with an evocative intimacy. This kind of intimacy goes beyond what you feel you need from a lover, a partner, a family member, or your friends. As you let go of the need to be seen and to be acknowledged in a way that strokes your egotistical fur, allow the mystical creature you are to emerge. In-source before you out-source. Become the reflection to your own shadows and be the mirror to your own light. Welcome your body–mind–heart wisdom in a way that is soulful.

You are a mystical, magnetic, deep, and wise being. This is your birthright. You were born of this capacity to time-travel through the archetypes of humanity. Child, maiden, mother, crone, father, elder, artist, warrior, inventor, leader, extrovert, introvert—you are all of these energies. When all of these identities inside your personal stories get stripped down to their core—naked, vulnerable, undefinable—then who are you?

You are truth. You are freedom. You are connected to the cosmos all around you. You are living a spiritual existence in the form of a human body. You are igniting your dreams and answering the call of your soul purpose in this lifetime. Imagine every single event, experience, and happening in your life as part of the journey towards soul integration. You are the channel between earth and sky on the vertical access and you are the channel across the horizon line between sunrise and sunset; this points you to the center of your inner compass. This center is right inside of you— your center of gravity.

The flame of your solar plexus ignites, sometimes burning with wild passion, other times only embers glowing. This is your soul's flame calling you home to tend your inner temple. Pray to her, feed him with positive vibrations, notice when she needs to be held, remind him of his worth. No longer fear peeling off the layers and tossing them into the fire. Ablaze! Ignite! Your inner mystic longs to be set aflame.

Rituals to Awaken and Empower Personal Transformation

Work with the element of fire to transform habitual ways no longer serving your highest self. Learn breath techniques, mind–body perspective shifts, and ceremonial practices to clear your energy field and activate your inner power.

1. Fire Breath: Awakening and Empowering from the Inside Out

Practice
Preferable in the morning to mid-afternoon, without any food in the belly.
(Important: If you are pregnant, do not do the fire breath.
Instead, take long inhales to long exhales.)

1 Find a comfortable seat in a chair or sit cross-legged on the floor.
2 Place your left hand on your heart and right hand on your lower abdomen.
3 Take six deep clearing breaths in through your nose and out through your mouth.

4 Breathe in through your nose, holding your breath for six counts while pulling your navel into your spine. As you hold your breath, visualize the flame of a candle inside your solar plexus area. Let it grow and drink in the colors like nectar. Exhale a fire heat and sound out the mouth for six counts.

5 Take a center activation fire breath: fully exhale, take a long inhale through the nose, keeping the mouth closed, and then push short, sharp, and rapid exhalations out the nose. Focus on the exhale, pulling the navel into the spine each time you exhale and letting it naturally bounce back on the inhale. Go for as long as you can maintain the quality of the short, sharp exhales—up to 50 to 60 breaths.

6 Repeat this exercise three times.

7 Come back to a soft inhale and exhale.

2. Tapping the Thymus Gland

This exercise is known to decrease stress levels, enhance your immune system, and awaken positive energy in your self-esteem center.

1 Bring your hands into prayer pose, interlace your fingers, and begin vigorously tapping the area around your thymus gland (located behind your sternum bone).

2 As you are tapping, open your mouth and allow the sound of "Aaaaaaaaaa" to come out. Be loud and proud here. There may be more sounds that want to come through you. This is a healing process. Improvise, move your jaw from side to side, stick out your tongue, cross your eyes, explore a high-pitched sound, then your lowest pitch; completely let go. This will restore your vital energy.

3 Repeat for three to six rounds.

3. Meditation: Clearing Your Energy Field

1 Find a comfortable and quiet place to sit.

2 Visualize a fire before you.

3 Take time to be with your breath, and slow it down to a count of six on the inhale and six on the exhale.

4 Visualize any layers inside you, on you, or around you that you may be ready to throw into the fire. Anything that tires you, stresses you, or creates imbalance in your life. These may appear as words, images, memories, etc.

5 Let them come to the surface as they are ready and offer them to the fire, shedding layers of old narratives one by one.

6 Once this feels complete, take long deep breaths and welcome any symbols, words, flashes of insight, or revelations that come to you.

7 Seal your clearing with gratitudes, an intention, or a vow to hold yourself in your healing process and to feed your inner power daily.

8 Journal about the experience.

4. Inner Power Activation and Altar Creation

It may be supportive to gain insight by asking yourself the following questions:

- How do I currently feel/sense my relationship to my self-esteem?
- Are there any limiting voices present?
- What am I currently feeding my thoughts, feelings, emotions that is of negative or limiting energy?
- What lights me up? What am I most passionate about in life?

Build an altar that represents your relationship with your *inner power*. Honor the elements—air, fire, water, earth, and ether—and anything symbolic of your lunar/feminine and solar/masculine inner power alignment. Refer to Chapter 2 for altar guidelines if needed.

Once your altar is created:

1 Light candles and burn incense or herbal smudge wands to purify your space both inside and out. You can also open the windows to clear the space.

2 Soften your whole being and begin to focus on your inhale for the count of six and exhale for the count of six.

3 Bring awareness to your intention to activate your inner power. Visualize the flame of the candle aglow inside your solar plexus.

4 Visualize any energies of lower vibration leaving you, coming right out of you. See them burning in a large fire before you.

5 Welcome the support of your fully activated esteemed self. Visualize yourself in your highest state of love, light, joy, and confidence.

6 Call on your intuition to speak to you. Call forth your supportive guides: ancestral, animal, mineral, plant, landscape, shapes, symbols, and sensed energies ready to communicate with you. Envision a compassionate energy to work with you at this time—a face, a name, a landscape. Pay attention to any visuals that want to appear.

7 Make one "call to action" and see if there is a remedy to support it. Use the present tense and the words "I am, I will." Keep it short and simple. For example:

*"I am powerful beyond measure. I will meditate daily to
keep my solar plexus activated and strong."*

"I am wildly expansive. I will soar with a vast, open perspective today."

8 Write it out seven times. Repeat each morning for seven days. It may shift; allow it to evolve and see what arises.

5. Body–Mind Exercises to Integrate the Vibrational Fields of Fire and Transformation

Fire Dance

1 Light a candle and put on your favorite track of music.

2 Dance *wildly* for five to ten minutes without stopping. Feel the heat and focus your awareness on feeding your central energy channel—your spine—with the colors you see in the flame of the candle.

3 Allow your exhale to clear out stagnant energy and toxic thoughts and feelings.

4 Allow your inhale to light you up like the wild fire energy you are. Let your radiance grow in this embodied, out of this world, personal dance party.

5 Notice if your voice wants to channel any sounds, words, screams, or gypsy calls. Do not repress anything. Have fun!

The Wood Chopper

1 Stand tall with your legs hip width apart and fingers interlaced so your palms are touching.
2 Visualize a massive piece of wood before you that you need to chop. You can see the wood as a symbol for stuck energy, frustration, inertia, impatience, resistance, lack of focus, etc.
3 Take a big inhale as you sweep your arms and interlaced fingers upward, and on your exhale bend your knees, bend forward, strike your interlaced hands to chop the wood in half before you while loudly saying "ha!"
4 Repeat eight times. Stay focused and support your lower back by generously bending your knees.
5 Ground yourself in a seated position or a squat until you feel calm and balanced.

Esteemed Self Rising

1 Sit in "chair pose" or a squat position, feet hip width apart.
2 Inhale as you put your arms straight out in front of you.
3 Exhale with a loud "ha!" As you do this, stand up and pull your bent arms into your sides, making fists.
4 As you pull this energy in, visualize a fire or the flame of a candle lighting up and growing at your solar plexus.
5 Repeat eight times. Rest and shake out your arms and legs. Repeat as many times as it feels empowering to you.

Warrior: Inner Power Activator

1 Bend your front knee to 90 degrees and plant your back leg out straight, arms out in a T position, in Warrior 2 stance, the yoga pose. Welcome your luminous warrior spirit.
2 Focus a strong yet soft gaze before you. Stay for as long as you can.
3 Become aware of your breath. Visualize your bones made of light, integrating into every crevice of your body. Let it come through you; embrace your inner power.
4 Direct your attention to a specific project or something you desire to feel or be in your life. See yourself already there. See it already manifested. You are already there because it already lives inside you.

5 Change sides and repeat the exercise.

6 Close the ritual by standing tall and visualize your whole body as a stream of luminous energy.

Guided Visualization: Reclaim and Restore Your Vitality

1 Scan back from this present moment to all the times you felt shamed in your life. All the experiences that broke your self-esteem down. Not to dwell on them, but to truly observe them, like a mini-death of sorts.

2 Bring to mind the parts of your essence that became lost or fragmented through your life experience, for example, a painful experience that left you feeling depleted.

3 As you track back in time, visualize your current self compassionately picking up all of your lost parts, the parts of your spirit that left you or shut down for protection. Keep going all the way to childhood; you may even have some memories of being an infant.

4 Focus your attention on weaving these lost parts back into your solar plexus. Visualize the flame of a candle brightening each time a part of you comes home.

5 There may be memories that come unexpectedly. Stay with your breath, continuing to hunt for all positive pieces of yourself. There may be moments where you can forgive yourself or others, and there may be moments of sadness, anger, fear, and doubt. Let it all come. Leave no stone unturned. Trust you are the healer now. You get to choose and reclaim your lost parts.

6 Visualize a cloak or a cape that holds all of your life experiences in right relation and peace inside you now—a celebration of all the shames now liberated, the fears transformed, the what ifs, should haves, could haves. Celebrate your renewal and your integrated esteemed self rising.

7 Once you feel that you have gathered all your lost parts, visualize yourself in a sacred landscape where you build a ceremonial fire. Gather the wood and light it. Give it offerings that are symbolic to your return to your whole self. There may be imprints of anger, grief, fear, and shame. Let it pour out of you and give it to the fire now. There may be words, sounds, shapes, symbols, and colors that want to be expressed. There may be joy, relief, and calm as a newfound sense of freedom—nothing holding you back anymore. Embrace what comes through you; repress nothing. You are supported and

protected and safe in this place. Offer the fire a sacred gift that will seal this newfound sense of inner power and autonomy.

8　Open yourself to receive support and guidance from your compassionate guides and your intuition. Let it swirl deep into the marrow of your bones. Again, there may be a gift given or received here. Open fully while you are in this sacred space to receive insight.

9　Seal this code of inner radiance with any guiding symbols, words, or inspirations; a direct call to action may come forward. A project, a path, a creative pursuit, a relationship, a healing, a forgiveness, or an energetic vibration that serves the greater good in you in service to the world.

6. Empowerment Letter to Your Esteemed Self

Use the template below for personal empowerment and connection to your intuition and your compassionate guides. If you are inspired, write your own poem, prayer, or letter of commitment to your esteemed self, as if you are speaking directly to your inner radiance. If you can see it, you will feel it.

> ### Dear Guides (or Dear Intuition),
> *I open myself fully to receive support from you at this time in my life. I am open, ready, and willing. I will listen and take supportive actions towards my personal healing process.*
>
> *I am empowered, I am anchored. Like fire itself, I am a vessel for rapid transformation. As toxic energies come towards me or through me, I know I am capable of working with them. I gracefully allow the negative pieces to fall away as my inner fire grows brighter. My shimmer extends far and wide.*
>
> *Next time I doubt myself, I will stay open and ask, "What is the lesson here in this situation? Where can I raise my own vibration and stay true to my journey?" I can turn a situation around by stepping into my power, listening, softening my defensive reactions, speaking only my truth, and slaying the patterns of victim-shaming in my life.*
>
> *My radiance has a ripple effect that begins deep inside my inner temple and extends beyond what I know is reachable. I trust these moments as I leap, fly, dive, spin, twirl, and shimmer. All the while, the sacred moves through me, around me, and out of me.*

7. Shed Old Stories and Narratives

Write out your top three limiting core beliefs about yourself, those that most often play in your mind. For example:

- I am not good enough.
- I never get enough sleep.
- I am always stressed and living in chaos.

Take a moment to sit with these beliefs, which may be unconsciously ruling you and potentially holding you back in your life. Each time you repeat this it may be like throwing energetic darts of "lack" or "negativity" into your energy body, your mind, affecting how you show up in the world.

Go further, and see what the origin of each core belief is:

- Where does it come from?
- Who was involved?
- How does it take over/affect different parts of your life and relationships?
- Can you get a sense of how it may be unconsciously holding you back from living your best life?

Now, cross each one out and rewrite as a positive affirmation.

I am not good enough.

I am enough, I am whole, I am living within my full capacity.

I never get enough sleep.

I am attuned to my body and my mind. I am resting when I need to.

I am always stressed, I live in chaos.

I am calm, connected, and activated.

Celebrate and honor your new core beliefs. Recite your "I am" statements each time your mind goes back to your old narratives. Catch yourself in the moment! Be kind and compassionate; laugh at your tricky mind. On a daily basis, welcome the energies of the sun, fire, and light to feed your esteemed self. When we can release the expectation of others doing this for us, we begin to shed false parts of our ego, step out of victim mentality, and take full responsibility for our own power, joy, and freedom.

8. Journal Prompts

- What is your relationship to shame? Anger?
- Where does it arise in your life?
- Can you track it back to childhood/young adulthood or current experiences to find out when you felt shamed or angry and why?
- What stones have you left unturned in your life? What past experiences have you not dealt with? They could be events from the past that you still think about or maybe your "unconscious rulers."
- Write about these experiences to understand them a little more.
- What are you currently outgrowing? What attachments are you releasing?
- What practices support your inner strength?
- Is there a mantra or a positive affirmation that will contribute to your personal growth at this time?

Tend to your temple daily.
No longer play fool to the state of illusion.
Face the lurking fears and see them as alchemical medicine.
Shadows cast a story of unspoken truths.
Lay down the collections of past.
Offer your future longings to the cosmic night sky.
Gather her, collect him.
Surrender to your own tender embrace.
Listen for the still point.
Rest when the cocoon calls.
Break free when your wings unfurl.
Become the sculptor of your treasured pieces.
Your inner mystic longs to be worshiped.

SHAPE-SHIFT

Tend to your inner self the way you tend to your garden.
Feel the call to weed, water, plant, and harvest.
Elemental wisdom surrounds you.
Churn, burn, morph, twist, turn, reach, fall, and begin again.
Your soul arrives through all the dimensions.
Shimmery flash, the heart speaks of an unforgettable alchemy.
Source in its purest form.

Chapter 4

Shape-Shift

Flowing with Your Creative Genius to Manifest Your Dreams

AWAKENING YOUR CREATIVE GENIUS

We are born naturally creative, intuitive, and wildly unique. Our life is a daily, living, creative experiment. Our nine-month gestation period in the womb gave us life, granted us breath, and prepared us to share our gifts with the world. This experience of our creation in the watery womb lives inside our cellular memory.

We are born into this world with a personal mission and a soul vision that will touch the lives of many and become our legacy. However, we may get lost or misguided as life happens and all of our experiences and stories play out. Perhaps a part of our soul or our deeper sense of purpose gets abandoned. But this is the beauty of life: these experiences become our path to finding our way home. It may be our life's journey to remember how to access our creative genius—our resilient, powerful, and intuitive channels—all of which need to be exercised in order to come fully alive, just like a muscle.

Whatever your story is around your own creativity, the bottom line is this: you are highly creative in your own way, and when you can merge with this energy, your life will become more fluid and fulfilled. It's time to shed the layers of projection, failure, and judgment you have accumulated around your creative process. It's time to liberate yourself from the energetic blockages that limit you to mundane daily needs. Your ability to live your life through a creative lens allows you to solve problems and clear your energy channels. You can bring in fresh perspectives that are steeped in beauty, intelligence, hope, love, and freedom.

You are not alone in reverting back to childhood stories when your creativity gets shut down. We all have those stories, and they are painful. They often come with "I am not good enough" or "I am not creative enough." This then transforms into energetic blockages that may now be affecting your career, your relationships, and your inner peace.

There are many ways to live inside the realms of creativity! When we feed our creative channels we naturally connect to our inner impulses. This allows us to awaken our intuition, to rebalance our emotional intelligence, and to become a channel for energy from the spiritual dimensions. We can hear the song of the divine through the paintbrush, through words, through the sound of trees calling in the quiet forest. The way we listen and speak openly and freely is a creative act. The intimacy of sex is also a wildly creative act, especially when we release the desire to place all of our awareness on our own needs. Sex becomes a creative pursuit when we co-create with our partner, when we sense their energy and we meet them there—not only to please them, but to come into an ecstatic dance of energy. Time stands still when we feel the resonance of transcendence through our sexual, sensual, and creative experiences.

When we let the intellect soften and feel the pure source of energy all around us, we can attune to the highly creative and intuitive experiences in our lives. The body is a receptor of energy. It naturally comes alive and is inspired by the force of nature, whether we are conscious of it or not. The sky grants us perspective, the sun's warmth fosters transformation, the water's essence brings us flow and purification, and the earth reminds us of our grounded, abundant nature. Attuning to the elements and resourcing ourselves in nature brings us into a creative and present-moment mindset, allowing us to go deeper into our own creative process.

Start to shift your perspective from the mundane tasks of everyday life to sacred, mindful, and artistic experiences. Your meal takes the shape of a beautiful piece of art, your morning journal pages become a poem, you speak to your loved ones in a new, articulate way. Your commute to work becomes a vehicle for engaging in creative thinking. Your forest hike becomes a way to integrate with the creative source of the elements—the light in the trees, the sound of birds flying, the ripples in a stream. If you let go of your personal agenda, you can immerse yourself in sensations.

The inner life is a creative life. To be contemplative and present in these precious moments is a creative act within. Inside this sphere, our energy becomes fluid, our channels open, our perspective widens, and we may sense the source of rhythmic creation. There the sacred encircles your soul. In the quietude of nature's precious ephemerality, we connect with the truth of our genuine nature and we discover what makes us come alive. This is your soul inviting you to dance and co-create with the force and source of the divine. He whispers in the softest places, she calls to you in the darkest night. Together, the feminine and the masculine energies, the moon and the sun, hold you with a cosmic love. You need never question your worth again; you are liberated from the past and future; you are willing to adorn the inner temple of your creative genius.

THE ELEMENT OF WATER: FLOW, SHAPE-SHIFT, AND ADAPT TO CHANGE

We are always in a state of change. Our breath mirrors the cycle of our innate ability to renew, release, and be fluid in every moment. Our inhalation aligns with our inner expansion, and our exhalation represents our inner contraction from the realms of inner awareness out to expression in life. In essence this is our ability to flow like water. When we bring awareness to this primal flow of expansion and contraction, we connect more deeply to our inner and outer individual process. From a vaster perspective, we begin to see it in the flow of water, the life cycle of flowers, and the waxing and waning of the moon. When we train our eye to see the beauty in the cycles of nature, we develop reverence for the universal law of change: birth, growth, death, transformation, and renewal.

The element of water is symbolic of healing, fluidity, and cleansing. It is associated with our emotions and our internal systems, including the subconscious mind and the body's energetic field. Whereas fire sparks transformation, air provides perspective, and earth grounds us, it is water that facilitates the integration of movement and change. Water, creativity, and our ability to let go allow us to adapt to the state of flow and harness our emotions to access our own embodied, intuitive power.

When you learn to embrace the inner mystic and welcome the message that water brings you, your mind–body channels open and you find yourself in the universal flow of the life force. This becomes a practice, never to be taken for granted or to be misused for purposes of the ego. It becomes a sacred relationship between you and the water.

I love to work with the image of a large stone dropping into a body of water and seeing its ripple effect. Just as we can use the element of water to purify our own energy body, we can also become conscious that the ripple effect of our words, actions, emotions, thoughts, feelings, and energy is cast out far and wide in the world.

In the pagan wheel of the year, the element of water corresponds to the fall equinox and lands in the direction of the west. This is the time when day and night are equal, opening the portal for the darker days of winter. It's a time when we can celebrate what we are harvesting and release what is ready to die out of us and around us. As the life–death–rebirth cycle grants us release and renewal, we are reminded by nature's transformation how we too can align with this alchemical energy and reap our inner harvest.

We can open to the direction of the west, the place of the setting sun, and seek council from the fluid waters, the sky's epic beauty, and the wild abundance of plant life at its fullest expression. We can source this within ourselves as well—our emotional, creative, and intuitive capacity in its fullest expression. Impeccability of our words, our thoughts, and our actions is the work here—no longer repressing emotions, leaving no stone unturned in our lives. Through daily acts of courage, radical acceptance, letting go, and diligence, we can transform our personal and ancestral fear, shame, guilt, blame, and uncertainty.

When you do the work, you can live out the life that is your destiny, and your soul path emerges before your eyes. Yes—it's been waiting for you. You become deeply intimate with your inner source by feeding it on a daily basis with illuminated, steady, and fluid energy.

SHAPE-SHIFT EMOTIONAL PATTERNS

Understanding, harnessing, and working with present-moment emotional information is the source of your creative abundance and emotional intelligence. This is key to living life through a creative, evolutionary lens. There are three key steps that can help you shape-shift old emotional patterns:

1 **Awareness:** What are the reactions, habitual thought patterns, and body sensations inside the emotion?

2 **History:** Where does this emotion come from? Family history, society, life experience, or present moment?

3 **Effect:** How does this emotion affect you?

Once you understand and honor this process, you can acknowledge your emotions and flow with them. Remember that you are like water; this energy will shape-shift when the time is right.

The area of your lower abdomen, lower back, and in a woman, the womb is the container for your emotions, your creative life, your desires and passions, and your ability to generate abundance, and a healthy relationship with your sexuality. This energy center is located from the navel down through the lower abdomen, lower back, pelvis, and sacrum—including the reproductive organs. Here you can track your emotions, your triggers, and your patterns of behavior. You can discern with a very keen inner sense—a gut feeling—what is good, what is truthful, and what is the right action to take. This is where your intuitive nature is born. That's why it's so important to align with the water-infused wisdom that is innate to our human nature. Your lower abdominal space and its container of watery energy also aligns with the pull of the lunar cycle. When you align with the feminine energies and cycles of the moon, you can go within your own energy centers to feel, listen, receive, and respond. You become a channel for your emotions to be expressed rather than repressed. You feed your life with the sweetness that makes you come alive, fully embodied, and connected to all your dimensions.

You can never control outside forces, but you can work with your own energy field, your emotions, and your words. You can reclaim your sovereign nature by aligning with your ability to "state change." When you clean up your energy field, you free yourself from the impulse to be defensive and you begin to retrain your patterns in the way of "inquired response." This is a powerful practice not only for setting personal boundaries but also for not taking on other's emotional states. The process of "state change" takes time and practice, so forgive yourself when your emotions get the best of you. Listen to the call to be an energy-flow worker, an inner mystic, an awake and aware human being who takes nothing personally, who lets go in a flash. Remember your ability to purify with the healing element of water. Liberate yourself from the fear of making the wrong choice. Let go of the societal pressures to conform and please, and nurture yourself the way the mother does a newborn child.

INFINITE CYCLES: BIRTH–DEATH–REBIRTH

Change is the one constant in life. Our entire ecosystem changes, shape-shifts, and morphs with every season and cycle. This is essential not only for our planet's survival but also to contribute to feed the great cosmic web of life. Understanding and acknowledging the different plant, animal, elemental, and human life cycles grants us perspective, renewal, and release. Nature's transformations remind us how we align with this alchemical energy. When we acknowledge the infinite cycle of birth–death–rebirth in all living things, we understand it as an energetic process and a natural rhythm that permits evolution and existence itself. This can give us a deeper understanding of our own lives.

Take for example the metamorphosis of a butterfly. The female lays her eggs on the plant. The egg becomes a caterpillar, which morphs into a chrysalis, from which the adult butterfly emerges. Each stage takes time, precise intention, and braving the elements and predators. There is a flow, a rhythm, and an energetic cadence to this cycle that the butterfly follows instinctually. So simple, yet so complex. When we can stop ruling the show of our lives with our minds and drop into the fluidity and natural rhythm of our own process, we meet less resistance. We meet each phase of our journey with intentionality and with more ease, grace, and resilience.

We can seek counsel in the plant world and receive these insights on a daily basis. To illustrate, let us reverse the order. Take for example a giant yellow sunflower in full bloom. Behind each sunflower petal is a seed, and this seed will fall to the earth as summer turns to autumn. Some seeds will be collected and buried in the earth by a squirrel or dropped by a bird. Each seed will spend the winter dormant—patient and still, maintaining its vital life force inside its shell. When spring arrives, the seed begins to receive energy from the warmth of the sun and water from the spring rains. The perfect alchemy of fire/sun to earth/soil, of water/rain to air/oxygen nudges the seed to root down and shoot up out of the earth. The cycle of birth to life to death to rebirth is renewed. The sunflower becomes a home once again for pollinators—the bees, and the butterflies. The cycle is never ending, never beginning; the cycle is infinite and eternal.

When you attune to your own "flow state" evolutionary journey—both literally and symbolically—your capacity to intuit the moments of divine timing and right action increases. This becomes the work of the inner mystic; to discern when you are in a flow state and when you aren't. This balances your body–mind–spirit integration and heightens your conscious practices. Embodying this flow state energy awakens you not only to the present moment, but it brings you to the precipice of awe and wonder as you truly integrate the life–death–rebirth process. You naturally resonate with fluidity in nature and in your own life. You might feel inspired to make positive contributions towards the collective and global awakening.

You can view the element of water as your teacher within each stage of the cycle; water nourishes, nurtures, hydrates, and shape-shifts. You can ask yourself, "How does this experience nourish me? How am I nurturing myself at this time?" This is an essential practice within the life-cycle stages, for if there is no water, the riverbed will dry up, and if you are careless rather than deliberate, your river will become toxic and polluted. Yet when you continue to evolve your emotional self as a gateway to your spiritual self, you move towards living a creative, devotional, and mystical existence. There will always be drama, triggers, and intense energies to work with. This is a truth based on reality. You cannot always control what happens to you or control what energies come towards you. Yet you can control how you respond.

THE POWER OF LETTING GO: UNDERSTANDING THE FLOW OF ENERGY

Time and time again, we are reminded that when we let go, we generate space for a new perspective to emerge. Just as water flows, and symbolizes this letting-go awareness, we can receive profound insight by softening our grip and releasing our habitual (unconscious) patterns to force our way through life.

We are stronger in our letting go than in our holding on.
Our letting go becomes our strength; it opens the gateway to intuitive
messages and the positive energy of change, renewal, and release.

Here we can attune to our day-to-day present-moment energy. We can generate opportunities to re-seed good and truthful intentions inside us, around us, below us, and above us.

If, instead of letting go, we grip and grasp at what is known and comfortable, we get stuck between the cycles and stages of growth. Our energy channels get blocked. Our emotions become imbalanced. The mind takes over, and limiting thoughts become embedded deep in our brain. These limiting and lower vibrational thoughts turn into beliefs over time. We begin to organize our life around these created belief systems, and our body begins to take on this vibrational energy.

We become our thoughts, and our thoughts become us. The energy of our thoughts becomes embedded in our cells—we may not even be conscious of this process. In this way we block the flow state. Our inner waters become stagnant in specific areas. This pattern can become habitual over time, leading to inertia or guilt about not doing enough or not being enough. The energy within no longer evolves. We may feel confused, angry, depressed, and unmotivated.

This too is part of a cycle. Every part of the cycle is a step along the journey. When we train our eye to the cycles in nature, we feel the resonance in the marrow of our bones. We can liberate ourselves by discerning what cycle we are in; then we can balance our emotional response inside the cycle in order to transform that energy. When we can acknowledge, receive support, and work with the present-moment feedback in all of our channels—physical, emotional, intellectual, and spiritual—we become both the student and the teacher of our own process.

Life is cyclical; we expand, we contract, we open, we close. It is the space inside each transition that enhances the state of flow. When we acknowledge that we are stuck and allow ourselves to feel this way, we are honoring our true selves. This specific honoring becomes the path towards transformation and healing from a place of compassion and love. When we feel ecstatic states of bliss or joy and honor this vibration, we allow it to become embodied.

When we dance with both the light and dark places within, we release stagnation. The inner critic somehow quiets down and softens; we are able to reflect and work consciously with what arises in the moment. When we get intimate with our inner birth–death–rebirth cycles we know that in good time the cycle will shift. The energy will change and the lessons will be learned. It is our ability to listen with a soft intimacy that allows us to seed, grow, bloom, and fade. Thus we cycle through the evolutionary flow time and time again.

We learn to place our faith, trust, and hope in this process. Consider the ancient teachings of the lotus flower: rooted in dark, muddy, fertile soil, it blossoms into the most exquisite flower. Anchored in mud, fluid like the eternal womb of life-giving waters, we will also rise with the sun and rest in the darkest of nights, embracing the journey of expanding to contracting, of blossoming to shedding, of light to dark. This cycle is infinite, vast, mysterious, and cosmic. Living with this energetic alchemy on a daily basis radically shifts our relationship to ourselves, our friends, families, and communities. It deepens our own spirituality, as we contribute to the evolving shifts of our planet.

ADAPTING TO CHANGE:
ELEVATE YOUR INNER ALCHEMY

Change is the one thing you can count on in life. Change can trigger a range of emotional reactions: resistance, judgment, excitement, fear, promise, hope, transcendence, to name a few. Some of us thrive on change, and some of us find it very challenging. Change inside yourself, in your relationships, and your environment allows you to experience the unique personality you embody—and this provides you with the ability to sense other energies. This felt awareness allows you to get clear, to reflect on your chosen path, and to shape-shift. Without change, you would not experience growth. Your consciousness feeds on change and stimulates experience for you to embody your own authentic voice, feeling or action. Then you can assess the situation. Do you like this change? Do you dislike it? When you begin to understand how you process and react to change, you experience greater flow and freedom in your life. This also makes you more compassionate as you grow to understand that we all perceive change differently. Each person's reaction is personal and unique to them.

Change can be a gift; it can bring you to where you must discern which direction to take, whether to say yes or no. You feel into the question, "Will this change nourish me?" Some changes are out of your control, of course. Some are incredibly devastating. Yet once you understand your habitual resistance to the small changes in life, once you recognize your desire to control, then you can learn to let go and flow with the energy. Through this process you become more resilient for the expected and the unexpected events in life.

Change brings duality, duality brings heightened awareness. Awareness eventually brings clarity and unity. The next time you find yourself at the crossroads of change, ask yourself, "Is there a hidden treasure or a deepening within my own self that will come with this change?" Change contributes to your growth, your capacity to stay fluid, to receive insights and live from your instincts. When there is great resistance, you may find yourself feeling exhausted, uninspired, and living in a lower vibrational field of energy. There is so much power to be sourced when you can connect to the way water moves you, guides you, and allows you to maneuver through life's greatest challenges. Letting go, staying fluid, clear, strong, creative, and resourceful feeds the cycle of water's gifts. Moving away from seeing only through a literal and rational lens, you can shift into the mysterious, the intuitive, and live your life with deep awareness of the energy cycle. Step inside the spiral and see the current of life through the lens of wonder.

Hold yourself within the mystical realms of the goddess of life-affirming waters. Form a relationship with her, the divine feminine that nourishes, nurtures, consoles, holds, soothes, and heals. She is as grand as life itself. She is the ocean, lake, river, stream, rain, and waterfall—her presence dwells in all water. Water is life. You began your nine-month creation journey in the waters of your mother's womb. The water goddess is calling you home. She is the one that nourishes on a deep soul level. She heals through touch; she teaches you how to flow from the macro state to the micro state in a droplet of rain. She teaches you how to receive just as much as you give in life.

Water is the teacher of the "flow state" and guides you to transcend your imprint of being separate and feeling alone in the world. As you are enveloped in her watery womb spaces, you are held in the sacred. Your ego softens and you return to the source of your purest inner alchemy. Your emotions rebalance, your spirit recalibrates, and your unconscious wisdom emerges. You hear the callings, the whispers, the stirrings of the deep blue oceanic life force within.

Your intuition rushes forward like a raging river. Can you stay awake to catch those flashes? Can you soften enough to hear the call? Can you allow your ego to swirl, shape-shift, and change directions just the way the currents shift in a lake? Can you be fluid between the states of form and formlessness? Can you sense and attune to the energy around you just as much as you pay attention to your emotions? This is how you enhance your inner alchemy. Pay attention to every experience, whether it be grand or minuscule. It is part of the journey. One single droplet of rain might allow the deepest message to come through and shift your energy body in ways you never thought possible.

Be like water; stay fluid through all the realms, through all the dimensions.

A Prayer To Honor Water

I open to the element of water as the sacred teacher of change, creativity, and renewal. I greet the setting sun in the west and honor the purification that comes through the darkness of the night's journey. As I rest and renew, I await the messengers, divine timings, coincidences, symbols, and mysteries into my energy field as soul medicine. My salted tears pour out of me and flow back into the spirit waters. I trust this is all part of the great flow of life. Yesterday, today, and tomorrow is another day of change and momentum. I flow with my evolving mind–body temple as I hold strong to my sovereign nature, and live out the best version of me. Like water, I enable my energy body to shape-shift in a flash.

A BALANCING ACT: YOUR EMOTIONS AS GUIDE

Understanding, harnessing, and learning to transform our emotions may be the greatest gift we can give ourselves in this lifetime. The word "emotion" is from the Latin word "movere," which translates as "to move." We can see this as the process of moving energy and consciousness throughout the body—to move it through and out. To "emote" is to transfer information and energy from the unconscious to the body–mind field of awareness. This brings change and movement inside the body. When we can understand and feel into this more clearly, we can welcome movement as a healing balm to clear out repressed emotions, stagnant energy, and chronic stress.

It is part of our deeper soul's calling to experience emotional highs and lows, from absolute bliss to sorrow, from unconditional love to anger or hatred, from joy to depression or anxiety. Witnessing children in their emotions is a great teacher of how emotional energy can move and be expressed. They feel and play out their emotions in the present moment and move on to another state very quickly. It is healthy to feel a range of emotions in our life. It is not healthy to repress our emotions. We are robbed of our flow state when we shove our emotions down or project our fears and difficulties onto others. When we repress our feelings and emotions, we become susceptible to both physical and emotional illness.

It is empowering and life-changing to learn how to work with emotional energy, transmuting it into a vibrational field of emotional understanding and acceptance. This requires present-moment awareness, letting go of guilt, and releasing the desire to win or to be right. It requires speaking our truth, as well as a deep-seated trust that we can endure challenging times. We can become the medium for a range of emotions to be worked with, sculpted, released, and integrated. This we do for the greater good inside our own soul and for the greater good of humanity. We can wake up and become a vessel of energetic sifting, coding, understanding, processing, and managing—in essence we become our own therapist. We can discern what emotional energy is ours and what is being projected on us and then we learn how to manage it. We become both a student and a teacher of our own emotional patterning. We become a tracker of imbalanced states and an alchemist of energetic states.

As an example, let us work with the emotion of guilt, which is associated with the lower abdominal energy center. When guilt and other highly charged energies such as fear, shame, anxiety, or grief take over, your intuition shuts down. Your intuitive light switch goes off. Your ability to sense and communicate with your gut instincts gets overpowered by your emotions. To clear and enhance your intuitive capacity, it is necessary to do our personal emotional and shadow work. Imagine you stay in an unhealthy or mismatched relationship because you feel guilty. Your guilt over hurting the person in your relationship, your guilt that somehow you have disappointed your family, your partner, and yourself for not being able to fix the relationship. This guilt then takes a hold of your inner systems. You begin to shut down and hide from your own emotions. You are no longer flourishing in other areas of your life, and you begin to self-medicate— drugs, alcohol, zoning out with media—losing yourself in the energy of avoidance, addiction, and habitual patterns. This becomes a mind–body takeover. This is the moment where you can become aware of how you may be feeding the situation. You now have a chance to reroute, shapeshift, and practice your way towards a balanced emotional system. When you get connected with your emotions, and practice working with them as opposed to having them rule you, you land at home inside your signature essence. This signature essence is the gift of who you are. It's authentic only to you, it fuels what you love and stand for and generates your ability to live a joyous, balanced and soul-infused passionate life. When you can hold your emotional intelligence as a moment-to-moment balancing act, you can recognize and transform difficult emotional content. You can track it like a hawk, transform it with compassionate inquiry, and eventually move forward feeling lighter, more clear, and perhaps more free.

"Embodied Tracking"— A Practice to Transform Energetic and Emotional States

What follows is a step-by-step system to support your emotional wellness when you are in a triggered state.

Begin by finding a visual or an image that represents your emotions, for example a swirl or a ball of energy or a basket that holds your energetic capacity in all of its dimensions: the highs, the lows, the good, the ugly.

When a wave of energy comes through you or towards you that is heavy—feelings of lack, scarcity, fear, anger, jealousy, or comparison—and you want to clear it by transmuting it into usable, valuable material, here is what to do:

1　*Acknowledge the energy inside the emotion*. See the energy for what it is, acknowledge its presence, attune to how it feels in your body and its location. Acknowledge that you have a right to feel this way. Remind yourself that you can move your emotional energy field. Pause in this space and take three deep breaths.

2　*Anchor into your personal affirmation.* Call forth your essential nature and recall a positive and truthful affirmation about yourself, for example, "I am a good person. I can endure challenging times. I hold the capacity to love myself unconditionally." (It's very important for you to find your own personal affirmation. It may change and evolve, but have it on the ready.)

3　*Cut energetic ties or attachments and let go.* Visualize yourself getting behind the energy of the emotion. See yourself holding your basket or your ball of energy. Without allowing it to fully penetrate your inner self, imagine untangling your own attachments from the situation. See yourself with a pair of scissors cutting the energetic cords that come with a triggered state. See the emotions for what they are, and without needing to fix or solve or remedy immediately, let the emotions bounce or deflect off of you. This is a letting-go process.

4 **Gratitudes and permission.** Express your gratitude. Create an inner dialogue that gives you permission to see this emotional state as an opportunity to do your inner work while fully acknowledging how you feel. For example, "I have a right to feel this way. Thank you for this opportunity to practice letting go. I am a vessel of connection, love, and truth."

5 **Transmute the energy.** Clear it out of your energy field by visualizing the heavy emotional energy detaching from you. Simply let it move out of your body; witness its ability to transform, and return to your personal anchor of love, truth, and connectivity.

6 **Move your body as a channel.** Find a way to physically move your body to clear the energy. Remember, the root meaning of emotion is to "move out." Stay open to the perspective you receive while moving your body. Your body is a channel.

7 **Find solace in nature or in a meditative space.** Find inspiration, solace, and connection in nature. Seek counsel from the trees, plants, flowers, the sky, the waters, the warmth of the sun, the animal kingdom, the plant beings, the elemental allies. When you train your inner eye to see the beauty in the natural world, you receive that beauty inwardly and it allows your emotional energy to shift.

8 **Forgiveness.** Forgive yourself so that you can forgive others. Letting go of emotional hooks can free us of toxic energy that can grip us with such force that we begin to walk away from our own soul's calling. When the time feels right, ask for forgiveness of yourself so that you can ask forgiveness of others and forgive others as well.

9 **Speak your truth.** If possible, wait until the time is right. In some cases you need to speak your truth right away, but in others cases you can hold back, allow the energies to settle, and speak from a place that is not harmful. Working with your ego, your pride, fear, and vulnerability will support your process of discerning what needs to be said and when.

10 **Creative lens.** Replenish your vitality through a creative or expressive lens: write in your journal, pick an oracle card, call a friend, get exercise, cook a meal, garden, take a bath, read poetry, craft, collage, make love. Trust in your process as you turn to practices and energies that soothe and connect you back to your own energy field.

DEVELOPING YOUR SIGNATURE ESSENCE

Developing your signature essence is what lands you inside your own authenticity. This may come in the form of daily creative and fluid mind–body practices such as meditation, breathing technique, exercise, intentional rest, or artistic and nature-based activities. Observe how your mind–body states shift when you immerse yourself in what you know to be positive and transformative for you. Committing to polishing and refining your core gifts is a lifelong practice. Over time, you can learn to stay grounded and steady by consciously committing to a mind–body–spirit existence. Listen for the call of your genuine nature to wash through you. Become intimate with this feeling and embody the vibrational field you want to live out in your life. Find the quiet and spacious moments when you can feel the calm waters flow through you. Allow this fluid consciousness to become a part of your daily rhythm. Your daily rituals can generate a rhythm for you to become fluid, vast, and steady all at once. If this flowing consciousness is not cultivated and crafted, it simply will not grow.

Listen for what is genuine inside your signature essence with no attachments, projections, or past or future expectations. Breathe deeply into those moments when you feel so lit up that your body surges with inspiration. Feel the vibration of this surge, align fully with these channels by attuning your senses: listen, see, smell, and feel. When you get close to your own internal workings and eliminate distractions, this becomes the bridge from your unconscious towards your conscious self. This will allow you to build, create, and express your most authentic soul purpose. Your inner workings are fluid, creative, intuitive, and feminine.

Inside the quiet power of your inner temple, hear the song of your genuine self coming alive. Accept the invitation to dance when it arrives. Become intimate with the internal sensory field. Get to know the energetic qualities, let them be felt and acknowledged, and feel the resonance inside this energy. No longer question it. This is the divine feminine coming through you, reminding you of your capacity to live out your soul's calling and your wildest dreams.

This is your intuitive realm; that of the internal. Sometimes soft, sometimes swift—welcome your fluid nature to merge with the divine feminine. You will come alive and awake in a way that is deeply nourishing, evocatively mysterious, cosmically otherworldly. This becomes the conversation between you and the unseen realms. Allow it to open and be held in this knowledge, wisdom, and quiet power.

It's time to redirect our trauma story and enter into a renewed alignment of our human capacity—to lead on the path to collective healing, to renew our spiritual existence, to answer the call to support Mother Earth's needs, to dismantle the patriarchal mindset of aggression and domination. Let us accept the invitation to participate in the shift in consciousness that we can sense in the world today. This is the shift from the power-over mentality to the inner force of the feminine mystique. Her divine source holds the strength of the great Mother Earth herself. Her matriarchal code is calling us to find our own personal evolution so that we can be the light keepers, the shape-shifters, the healers that inspire wellness, truth, beauty, goodness, compassion, hard work, and diligence. A force that can no longer be ignored; a force to be reckoned with.

Find this matrix within yourself. Meet the call of the guide, the mystic, the spiritual awakening in you.

INTO THE DREAMTIME: CONNECTING TO MESSAGES, GUIDES, AND INTUITION

When we begin to pay attention to the dreamtime and open ourselves to trust the messages we receive—the inner whispers or deeper callings—we become a receptive conduit for our intuitive nature. Water is a healing channel that supports us in letting go, softening our impulse to control or dominate. It holds us in a container of inner listening and knowing. It puts us in a flow state, where we trust in the non-ordinary realms that come to us in our dreams, our visions, and the messages channeled through our intuitive realms.

If we resist or push away the inner calls, we lose an opportunity to fulfill our relationship with a greater force. Call it the divine, the great spirit, intuitive callings, the angelic realms, the ancestral realms. Find a way within yourself to connect to the energy that brings you into inquiry and relationship with the unseen realms. We all have supporting guides and messengers, and when we begin to open ourselves to them, we can see our guides both in human form as teachers or mentors and in the otherworldly realms.

Look to them for support, wisdom, and energy—from the stranger you met at the grocery store to the hawk flying overhead in that exact moment where you pondered a deeper life event, to the way the water ripples just as you feel yourself gripping and tightening, to feeling the warmth in the marrow of your bones under the sun, to an elder visiting you in your dreamtime. Take these signs to heart. Accept the invitation to activate mindful and soul-fueled practices that make you feel not only empowered but fluid, open, and receptive to seeing energy. You will begin living through a creative, resourceful and widening lens. Just as you train your inner eye to be touched by the exquisite beauty in the natural world, you can also use your devotional practices to be in a fluid relationship with the existential, universal, and spiritual realms that have existed since the beginning of time.

This must be a unique journey in order for it be authentic. Pay attention to the events you have had in life that touched upon a spiritual experience. The times the veils thinned and extraordinary moments occurred where you felt another presence or received a sign to take another path. You saw light, patterns, codes, formulas; you saw yourself as an elder. These are the moments to remember. When you can open up to these mysterious happenings, not defining them by an exact outcome, but embodying them into your spirit as an energy source, you begin to uncover, decode, and reveal the "why" behind your soul's whispers. You accept the invitation to go forward, inwards, outwards, and onwards.

Begin to track your dreams, and journal about them. The dreamtime is a way for the subconscious mind to unravel, express, and bridge into your consciousness, like an internal compass merging with your soul to generate depth, perspective, and insight into your external world. Begin to awaken to the dreams that have powerful and lasting messages, not the recurring ones, but the very specific dreams that wake you up at night or leave a lasting impression when you wake in the morning. Write them down. Keep a dream journal beside your bed, and as you wake, begin to write down anything you can remember. Do not take them in a literal sense, but begin to get behind the energy of the dream. What message may it be bringing to you, and how does that relate to your current life? Before you go to bed, you can ask for support from your guides or from your higher self to shed negative, toxic, or depleting energies. Not so much from your intellect, but rather allow it to come from your creative, fluid, watery self.

Ask for support from your guides or higher self to receive signs, symbols, and messages that support your soul in order to rest. Hold the intention that through the resting state, you will receive rejuvenation and guidance that will allow you to thrive and flourish in your day-to-day life. There may be a deep desire that you may want to inquire about or a prayer you want to make. You can call this forward before you go to sleep in a fluid, creative, vast open space. It is crucial to truly release yourself from the attachment to the desired outcome as you do this. Keep it fluid and body-centered; release the mind completely, and open to receive supporting insights from the unseen, spiritual realms.

COMMUNING WITH SPIRIT: CHANNELING YOUR PRAYERS

If you want to seek counsel from the spiritual realms, find a quiet and sacred place where you can speak your prayers, call on your supporting guides, and ask for support and guidance. Build your altars to be compelling and magnetic so they draw you into a sacred space—light your candle every day and sit inside the medicine of your own inner healer. Speak your visions out loud, or let them come through you as a felt sense. Drop out of the mind chatter and open to the images, symbols, sounds, and words that want to emerge. Simply allow them to appear.

This is a profound and wildly intimate practice.

At first it can feel awkward, like you are simply speaking to yourself. When you allow your body to be the channel, what begins to come through is the letting go of emotional cords and attachments on the surface level. Then you go deeper and begin to touch the awakenings of soul expression. Here, your intuition opens and a conversation begins between you and the supporting energies all around you.

When we shed the toxic layers— products of the monkey mind and societal and familial conditioning—we begin to truly listen and hear the sound of our own genuine energetic alchemy and signature essence. This allows us to discern what is good and right for us, when to let go or move on, or which direction to take on our personal journey. This grants us perspective and a cosmic awareness that our personal process is unique. This radical, cosmic awareness brings us closer to our own personal mission in life and keeps us connected to the whole—to our communities, the plant and animals realms, to the life-giving waters around us and within us. When we allow our bodies to be a channel, we become acutely aware of when to let go, how to recalibrate, and where to direct our attention. Our habits of over-working, over-consuming, or feeling unworthy begin to slide off like a snake shedding its skin. We return to the watery state where our fluid, creative, and wildly intuitive gifts become channeled and expressed out into the world.

FEWER DISTRACTIONS, MORE SPIRITUAL CONNECTIONS

Limiting external distractions and reducing the drama in your life will increase your ability to connect with your intuition or your "gut instincts." Distraction, avoidance, and an excess of unresolved emotional energy cloud intuitive processing. Living the extreme highs and the extreme lows will cause burnout, confusion, depression, and anxiety. A disconnected system lives in constant fight-or-flight mode.

When our emotions become the rulers, we simply cannot feel, sense, or hear our intuition, even when it is knocking at our door. When we over-research, over-think, and over-process, this creates excess information that can lead to confusion and overwhelm. Ultimately this disconnects us from our gut instincts. This is why a mindful practice is so essential in our modern technological world. We have access to any information we want, therefore we begin to make decisions based only on what we think, other people's opinions, and societal influences or pressures. But as humans we are innately intuitive. Our primal instincts for survival are coded into the cells of our body. Through technology and mass consumerism, however, we have disrupted our ability to listen from within and hear the whispers of our intuition calling.

Because of the conveniences of our world and our disconnection from the land and waters, we no longer feel the sensation in our gut guiding us, allowing us to discern what is good or not good, what we want or don't want, or what we need vs. what we desire. When we get still and practice present-moment awareness, we begin to discern what we truly want and need, and how to get there. Think of intuition as an insight that arises spontaneously without conscious reasoning. It is a form of unconscious intelligence. It may come as a flash of energy through the body, sending either a message, a pattern of shapes, lines of energy, or it may be a direct call to action. When we get quiet and have fewer distractions and less white noise around us, we can begin to sense a whole other level of energy. Yes, our mind is tricky, and our ego is extremely complex. This process of inner listening takes patience, commitment, and trust.

When we do the personal work to harness our emotions so they are contributing to our life and not stealing energy from us, then we get to access other energies. We become effective, efficient, and intentional in living our life in alignment with the goals, values, and dreams that contribute to our higher self. We use our life experience and our knowledge to tap into the resources and gifts that we were born with. Living an intuitive life comes with practice.

Think of your intuition as a muscle that needs to be exercised and your emotional wheelhouse as a sacred temple. It needs to be cleaned, cleared, sorted, organized and adorned on a regular basis. Come home to yourself, get quiet and name what is truly going on for you, as painful as it may be at times. Only then can you begin to free yourself from a weight that will continue to push you down and keep you from living your dreams.

DREAM YOUR LIFE INTO BEING

To dream your life into being requires deep personal work, an understanding of the "why" behind the dream, and an unshakeable commitment to removing doubts and fears. Where there is untruth, doubt, and muddled motives, the path will not present itself. When you hold true to the core of your vision, you can see it clearly and connect to merging with its energetic field.

Let go of your doubts, the fear of failure, and embrace that you are already here. Be inside the process. Trust in every step on your journey. See yourself living your dreams in the here and now. Get crystal clear on who, what, where, why, and how. Imagine the whole picture of you living your fullest life. Merge with this energy in your visualizations and let go of your attachment to the perceived outcome. Then you dance with spirit. Spirit has a way of answering the call when you are in truthful alignment. At the core of your highest self, ask yourself, beyond the material manifestation, what is the core essence of what I am calling into my life? Find the source and connect so deeply with this vibration that it becomes part of your inner matrix.

The universe works in mysterious ways. Most often when we embody the vibrational field of our dreams, it will deliver. It may not look exactly as you thought it would, but it may lead you to the next cycle. In hindsight you will look back and understand that divine timing was on your side and you were being supported to get where you are now. The journey and the process of manifestation are interchangeable. There are no mistakes; each piece of our history brings us to another cycle in our journey. Every time we fall, get misled, and revert towards negative and toxic patterns, we have an opportunity to accept the invitation to get back on the path. The process is never-ending and always beginning.

As much as we want things to be linear and straightforward, life proves itself to be cyclical, mysterious, cosmic. When we dance with this attitude we instantly open our channels to receive the call of our own genuine song. Our creative genius comes alive, we find ourselves in a state of flow, and we trust our inner knowing so deeply that we free ourselves from any past, present, or future limitations. We heal not only ourselves through this process, but we inspire others to do the same.

Follow the desire, release your attachment to the outcome.

Connect with your life dreams by understanding the "why" inside the dream. See yourself living the dream as your current reality. Let go of your attachment to how you get there and what it looks like and connect to the source of the dream's vibrational field.

This is how you get there.

Visualize your desire in its manifestation; speak, feel, sense and see it in real time. It's already happened, can you connect to this realm? Where are you … who is there … what is happening … what does it feel like … what colors, shapes, patterns do you see? This process holds an energetic key and vibrational capacity that supports you in actualizing your deepest soul desires.

You are already there.

Rituals to Awaken Flow, Creativity, and Intuition

Connect with the element of water to generate new pathways of flow within your internal and external life. Learn breath practices, movement techniques and guided meditations to ignite the power of creativity. Receive tools on how to work with change and let go in order to access your dreams and prayers.

1. Breathing Techniques to Increase Flow and Creativity

Ocean Flow Breath

1 Find a comfortable, tall seat or sit cross-legged on the floor.

2 Place both hands on your navel center, relax your whole body, and take three deep breaths in through your nose and out your mouth.

3 On your inhale, visualize your breath entering directly into your navel center like a flowing river. Slow the breath down and spread it out throughout the whole pelvis and lower back area.

4 On the exhale, visualize the sacred water moving up your spine towards your heart and your mind. The purification of the water in your breath is now merging with your central energy channel in your spine, informing your heart and mind to flow and merge with this universal life force.

5 Repeat this for two to three minutes; inhale water swirling through your pelvis and navel area, exhale water flowing out of you and around you.

6 Pay attention to the color of the water. Place your intention on this being a deeply nourishing breath that reminds you of your creative, fluid, and intuitive self.

The Trio Wave Breath

1 Find a comfortable, tall seat, place your hands on your lower abdominal area, and relax completely. Set an intention to welcome in a fluid, transformative, and calm experience with your breath. Connect with the element of water—how it nourishes, hydrates, and purifies the inner body.

2 On the first third of your inhale, your hands are on your lower abdominal area. On the second third, move your hands to your rib cage, and for the last third, place your hands on your upper chest.

3 On the first third of your exhale, your hands stay on your chest. On the second third, they move down to your rib cage, and on the last third move your hands back to the lower abdomen.

4 Repeat for two to three minutes or until you feel you connect to a fluid three-part inhale to a fluid three-part exhale. The more you practice, the easier this will get. Once you find the rhythm, think about the thirds expanding and contracting in your back body as much as your front body.

Liquid Nectar Breath

1 Find a tall and relaxed tall seat position.

2 Begin to attune to your breath and set the intention to let go of excess mind activity and get connected to your intuitive and creative energy.

3 Place your hands over your ears, take a full breath in, close your mouth, and exhale out your nose and hum loudly. Generate the humming sound from your navel center and allow it to move up your spine towards the center of your forehead.

4 Repeat six to twelve times, relaxing all muscles in the face. Open to what you may see, any traces of light, patterns, or snapshot images. This is a powerful tool to awakening your intuition. Think of it as the nectar inside the center of your essence that is the messenger of your intuition.

Seated Sensual Rocks

1 Find a tall seat, either in a chair or sit on the floor cross-legged.

2 Set your intention to state change: welcome in flow, let go of imbalanced, stagnant, or excess mental activity energy states.

3 Interlace your fingers behind the nape of your neck. On your exhale, round your spine and bring your chin towards your chest. On your inhale, lengthen your spine as you lift your chest and gaze upwards.

4   Repeat for two to three minutes. Once you find the flow, bring
    awareness to your pelvis and let it initiate the spinal movement. Relax
    your shoulders and your spine, and visualize your pelvis as a bowl of
    water that initiates the flow in your spine.

The Ripple Effect

1   Find a tall seat in a chair or sit cross-legged on the floor. Soften your
    shoulders and relax your lower abdominal area completely.
2   Place your hands on your knees.
3   Visualize warm fluid water in the bowl of your pelvis.
4   Begin to create circular movements from the very base of your spine,
    almost as if you are doing hip circles or belly dancing in a seated
    position.
5   Imagine the bowl of water jostling freely and let this fluid energy
    ripple up your spine, almost like your spine is now completely fluid
    and free. It may travel all the way up to the back of your neck and into
    your brain.
6   Now move in the opposite direction for the same amount of time.
7   Let this movement be sensual, free, creative, fluid, and soul stirring.
8   When complete, come back to the still point within and observe the
    alchemical vibrational field inside you. Embrace the sensations and listen
    for the intuitive whispers coming through.

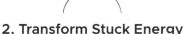

2. Transform Stuck Energy

Part 1
Illumination Meditation

1   Close your eyes and come into a place of stillness. Begin to attune to
    your breath and slow it down to a count of six on the inhale and six on
    the exhale.
2   Either visualize a body of water before you, or do this outside beside a
    body of water, or place your hands in a bowl of water on your altar.
3   As you slow down your breath, begin to gently sway your spine forward
    and back, then side to side, and continue this easeful release pattern for
    two to three minutes. Release the back of your neck and jaw and allow
    your lower abdominal area to completely soften.

4   Visualize the sun setting in the western skies and receive the colors of the sunset into your inner body. Now, welcome the darkness of night and visualize yourself safely meeting and embracing your shadows, your fears, and the unknown. Let go; you are safe, held and supported by your guides. Welcome them into your healing circle. Receive any gifts or insights they may have for you. Words, mantras, positive affirmations, symbols, animal, or ancestral guides.

5   Visualize a healing body of water before you and bless yourself in the water. Free yourself of the deep core beliefs that limit you. Liberate yourself from fatigue, burnout, and imbalance. Shed all of the existing roles you play, all of your responsibilities—just for now.

6   What does it feel like to be free? Welcome that energy into the waters of your pelvis. This is your birthright; this is your soul's calling.

7   Listen for any guidance, a way of being, a direct call to action, an empowering affirmation. Listen to the call of your own signature essence.

8   Bring your awareness back into your body, return to the space you are in. Prepare for Part 2 with a pen and journal.

Part 2
Discover Your Signature Essence

From the visualization you just completed, begin to write down who you are at your core level. What makes you unique? What are your greatest gifts? Write down words of encouragement to help you live with freedom, creativity, emotional intelligence, and inner radiance.

It may be supportive to include what you released and invited in during the visualization.

This will be very personal to you. You can repeat this exercise frequently, and it will support your ability to understand, visualize, and actualize your dreams and goals in life.

An example:

I am a conduit for truth, radiance, and creativity. I actively release the thoughts, words, and actions that come from a place of negativity. I am fluid, calm, wild, and strong all at once. Every day, I commit to my sacred practices that align, awaken, and ground me into my loving presence.

3. Purification Ritual to Activate Your Intuition

1 Light a candle.
2 Create an altar to welcome flow, creativity, and intuition. You may be inspired to create a water altar by filling a bowl with water and placing items inside it. There are no rules here. You can use essential oils, spices, flower petals, driftwood, seaweed, or a candle that floats. It is wildly supportive to call the energy of "flow" forward in this way. You may also feel like having music that plays water sounds.
3 Have a journal and pen ready.
4 Set an intention. Remember, your intention is what creates a potent ritual. For example:

> *I am stepping into the flow of my life. I release the feeling of being stuck. I welcome support from both physical and spiritual planes to move into my purposeful and intuitive flow at this time. I am an ocean of change. I am flow. I listen to the knowing in my gut, the rising of my intuition. I honor my process, trust in divine timing, and pray for guidance on the right action at this time. To my supporting guides, I am here. I am ready to receive messages and signs. I am ready to listen and activate when the time is right.*

5 Close your eyes and come into a place of stillness. Begin to attune to a slower breath and find a rhythm that feels nourishing for a count of four to six on the inhale and four to six on the exhale.
6 Welcome the healing qualities of water: softening, letting go, flowing, nourishing, nurturing. Visualize water before you, behind you, and inside you.
7 Allow the element of water to calm you and take a deep fluid breath. Begin to take on the properties of that body of water. Imagine it running through your veins, swirling around your organs for rejuvenation, filling up your lower abdomen and spine with the pure, clean properties of water. Flow this visual into your heart, your throat, your mind, and see yourself perhaps floating, surrounded and held by this warm, pure, clear body of water. Feel your whole back body receive the softness of the water. Now visualize your whole body completely supported by the body of water.

8 What are you ready to release into the water at this time? What is holding you back? Does anything feel stuck? Do shame, guilt, frustration or fear of change keep you from pursuing your dreams?

9 Sense old energies or stressors coming out of your body now. Give them permission to move out of you into the body of water. They are ready to be released. You may feel lighter, calmer, your mind liberated from old narratives.

10 Open to an invitation of wisdom: a symbol, sign, repeating mantra, colors, objects, a messenger, a guide, or an ancestor. Welcome this wisdom as a gift for you on your journey. Welcome whatever came to you and allow it to be a guiding light for your flow and creativity.

11 Seal your ritual by giving thanks to yourself and gratitude to the supporting energies present. Take one minute in silence. Simply receive nourishment through your own process and have gratitude for any messages received. Journal about your process.

4. Sacred Bath Ceremony

1 Fill a bath with water. Add any Epsom salts and essential oils (four drops of lavender is calming). You may also be inspired to add rose petals or any seasonal items such as cedar, lavender, rosemary, etc. You can also place your crystals right into your bath. Light your candles. Play music if it supports you to get calm and connected to your inner body.

2 Set your intention. Is there a question you are working with right now?

3 Is there something you are ready to release?

4 Is there an invitation from spirit to be supported?

5 As you welcome a state of flow, creativity, deep renewal and relaxation, visualize every cell of your body being replenished. Visualize the center of your brain getting spacious and filled with light.

6 Dunk yourself completely underwater several times with the intention of letting go of your stressors, triggers, negativity, and emotional imbalances. Visualize this energy coming right out of your body, your mind, and your heart. Go for as many dunks as it takes until you feel that you have cleared out the energy that does not serve you.

7 Relax your body completely and connect to a soothing breath. Welcome the divine feminine into your space, the energy that is

unconditionally nurturing and nourishing. Merge your energy field with that of the divine feminine.

8 Now visualize your body as a conduit for illuminated source energy that is purely positive and filled with wisdom. Merge into this field of energy and let it surround you until it is embodied in you. This energy reflects your goodness, your beauty, and your truth. It wants to come alive and be expressed.

9 Call forth what you are inviting into your life at this time. Do you wish for support? Understanding? A vision to become realized? Do you have a question on your path? Begin to speak out loud as if you are speaking to your best friend. Speak to the divine feminine. Share anything you want to release with her; any habitual patterns you are ready to let go of. Pray for the truth and for the right action to unfold. Let spirit know that you are ready to receive support, ready to listen and to hear spirit's call. Let this divine feminine know that you will also support her and advocate for clean and clear waters on the planet. Be in a reciprocal conversation as you call your dreams and visions forward.

10 Then listen for what will support your vision to become realized. Get real with accountability, wash your ego clean, receive the core and the heart of the vision, and understand the "why" of what you are asking for. This will support your internal cleansing and vision activation.

11 To close your water ritual, thank any guides or messages that came to support you, thank your higher self for your commitment to the spiritual path, and bless the sacred life-giving waters all around you for their teachings.

5. Water Blessing Ceremony for Letting Go

*Water purifies my life force and renews my energy body so I may
let go, forgive when needed, and dance with all that life brings.*

1 Find a body of water to commune with. If you do not have access to one, fill a large bowl of water and sit before it.

2 Create a bundle from nature: stones, sticks, plants, flowers, leaves, etc. Arrange and attach them in a way that reflects what you are currently letting go of. Take time to sit by the water's edge. Listen

for the sounds and embrace the qualities of flow and surrender. Find the softness in your strength and the strength in your softness. Give yourself permission to shed a few layers of energy that feel tired, like old narratives, imbalanced emotions, fears, anxieties, stressors, or other people's energy you may have taken on. Ask to be supported by your guides or spirit or whatever the "divine" is to you.

3 Hold your objects as you begin to find a deeper, calmer breath. Allow the objects to be symbolic of your letting go. Release them into the water. Place your hands in the water. Then follow with your feet or your whole body. Allow your body to be a conduit for flow, purification, creativity, and change. Surrender completely, and allow any guiding images, words, mantras, or symbols to come to you. Say a prayer for all of the living beings in the water and for the spirit of water herself to be healthy and in harmony. Speak a mantra, a prayer, or a positive affirmation while you are in the water, allow the water to cleanse you, and be a reflection of your highest self. For example:

I am in the flow. My body is a river of change, my mind is open like a vast ocean, my heart like a channel to the divine. I am in the flow where great mystery abides. I am letting go of my desire to control every aspect of my life. I am softness in my strength and strength in my softness.

6. Finding Flow and Creativity: Moving Meditation

Be in a safe space, know your boundaries, and use a blindfold if you find it supportive. This movement can be done with music or in silence.

1 Begin by kneeling with your hands on the ground, shoulders over your hands, hips over your knees.
2 Sway side to side, nod the head yes and no to release tension, and connect to your breath to free the channels in the body.
3 Cat/Cow poses: On the exhale, round your spine, chin to chest. On the inhale, tilt your pelvis, look up, and soften your abdominals. Repeat twelve times or more if desired.
4 Hip circles: Place your feet wider than hip width apart. Relax your whole body and begin to circle the hips. Do any kind of movement here

that frees up your pelvis, lower back, and lower abdominal area. Allow it to be sensual, soft, fluid, and feminine.

5 Let this be the gateway into five to ten minutes of improvised movement focused on letting go of the desire to control what it looks like. Instead, follow the flow inside the dance. Be sensual, get wild, express sounds with your movement, allow your body to become a channel, and *let go* completely!

6 Find an end to your movement with a silent meditation, or simply lie down to rest and ground yourself.

7 Observe: How do you feel after moving in this way?

7. Prayer for Flow, Creativity, Change, and Activating Intuition

I remember that I am a part of the evolutionary flow that lives in all things, and I release my tight grasp on preconceived notions. I let go, soften, and acknowledge that I am composed of water. The song of the winding rivers calls me home. I roll with the deep dives, the vast open plains, the stormy rides, and the still waters. I know change is the one constant. I give myself permission to trust that everything will be different tomorrow. I accept the invitation to journey as creatively through this portal as the great mother ocean herself— at times, fierce, other times, still, but always and forever moving. I accept and generously host a complex ecosystem of stirred emotions, thoughts, and feelings. This sacred body vessel knows how to navigate through the cycles and rhythms, the ebbs and flows of water, carried by the great mystery and the unknowns of life. The births, the deaths, and the cycles continue to flow. Never ending, I begin anew once again.

Today, I unearth my lurking shadows, my guilty patterns, my self-doubt, and my resistance to change. I surrender my desire to control it all. When my emotions engulf me and toss me in the depths of the sea where I can no longer see, hear, smell, touch or taste the truth, I no longer push them down. I become the witness to my emotions, I acknowledge where they came from and why. I forgive myself and grant myself permission to move forward. I hold my emotions like a feast before me, I invite all of them to my sacred table.

*My fluid process holds my dreams freely—refining, polishing, and
shape-shifting them to become embodied. Inside this fluid body
ecosystem, I stay awake to the intuitive flashes streaming though me.
I am ready to listen, be still, and surrender in order to receive the elixir of
my inner knowing. When the time is right, I activate and share my free,
wild, creative, and wise inner stirrings, with no regrets. I never look back.*

8. Journal Prompts

- What currently nourishes you on a soul level?
- What leads to emotional imbalance in your life? Who is involved? What are the conditions or the triggers? Name the emotions that come forward. What contributes to this imbalance, and what can you do to prevent this from happening in the future?
- How do you adjust to change? Give an example of a current situation in your life that brought you the lesson of change. How did you deal with it? What did you learn from it? Change can be uncomfortable and can make us feel out of control. How can you formulate a new attitude towards the changes in your life?
- Where do you allow for sweetness and pleasure to enter your life?
- What is your relationship with guilt? Do you currently feel guilt in your life? Did you have guilt as a child or young adult and if so, how did it affect you?
- What generates and inspires flow and creativity in your life? Can you make a creative flow date once a week?
- What steps are you currently taking in your life to activate personal courage in order to align with your truth? In your relationships? Career? Personal life? Write out the words "Courageous acts to ignite personal flow and freedom" in the center of your journal page. Now circle it and write down examples of your courage. Include acts you aspire to.
- What phase of the life–death–rebirth cycle are you in right now? Can you apply this to a specific project and seek guidance into a state of flow?
- Where can you be more fluid in your life? Where are you rigid, stubborn, and convinced things should be a certain way? Can you open up to becoming more fluid?

I am a vessel of change. Water runs through me like a great river.

I am the sweet balance of flow and stillness, of activation and calm.

As I release my firm grip, I welcome in mystery, divine timings,
and spiritual experiences.

My creative flow reminds me how to dance with my shadow and my light.

EARTH
MEDICINE

Strong spine, wild heart, rooted presence, rising spirit.
When we anchor inside the cosmic web of our own signature
essence, we support not only our own personal evolution,
but that of everyone else around us.

Chapter 5

Earth Medicine
Ground, Stabilize, and Generate Abundance

RETURN, REMEMBER, AND RENEW:
ALIGN WITH THE EARTH'S ALCHEMY

To return to the earth's intelligence, rhythms, cycles, and exquisite beauty is to remember where we came from, where we are going, and how to get there. It is to seek counsel, pray, honor, feel, learn, and listen as a forever student of her majestic, unshakeable strength and abundance. Mother Earth's heartbeat, the pulse of her blood runs deep inside the core of this planet—she is an ancient living being. She lives inside you and your ancestors. She is the wisdom keeper; she knows how to rebalance and heal, how to overcome fear and threatening energies. She is renewable, soft yet fierce. Her umbilical cord feeds the source of all life—and she is connected to you. Right at your center, you too are a child of the earth.

Your body is a channel of her abundance and her strength, and she calls to us all now to become earth angels, advocates, earth keepers. She asks us to treat our bodies as if we are Mother Earth herself, treading lightly upon her soft belly as if we are walking upon our own wombs impregnated with the next generation.

See no separation between you and the earth. Your body is a channel for the earth's alchemy. She is a source from which you drink the nectar of her wisdom. Plant your roots deep within her belly—this becomes the daily ritual of the inner mystic. We must begin with the earth first. Step into the sphere of her wisdom with respect and intention. Honor her cycles; fall to your knees in awe of her numinous ways. When your heart skips a beat because her beauty takes your breath away, you are taking in her pure life-source nectar.

Observing nature's beauty becomes a daily ritual. It allows space for your present-moment awareness to grow. Observing your environment grants you perspective; a heightened awareness comes alive within your own internal climate and you merge your external and internal systems. You feel more deeply attuned to the magic and wonder of life's great mysteries when you remember the evolutionary process and how life came to be on Planet Earth. As cosmologists and scientists have discovered, humans are made of both stars and mud. Billions of years ago, shooting stars descended upon the earth, transformed into the microbes, and evolved into the human species. When you shift to this evolutionary perspective, you open your awareness to an intimate relationship with the earth and with your own body as a channel of Earth's epic strength and her most tender softness.

Be like Mother Earth. Source your strength inside your softness and your softness inside your strength. Trust in this cycle, and the pauses in between which are profoundly rich, potent, and incredibly fertile.

The root system of a tree is crucial to its existence. The roots absorb and transport a combination of water and minerals from the soil to the tree. If the roots are disrupted by imbalances in the soil or other external conditions, the tree will no longer be anchored enough for the roots to feed the tree. In winter, the roots become the storage system for the nutrient reserves needed to produce the spring leaves. Trees communicate through their root systems; dying trees can even send nutrients to their neighbors—even of differing species. There is a whole unique and complex system that lives in the underbelly of the earth; a labyrinth of hidden messengers between tree roots, soil, insects, and fungi. This remarkable web lives below us; a thriving community that produces essential gases and keeps our planet alive.

When we shift our consciousness from our individual human needs— away from striving, competing, from mass consumerism—to a "planetary consciousness," we not only become earth advocates, but we begin to see life through a different lens. Every tree becomes a messenger and inspiration to live with this planetary consciousness. Each garden, forest, and flower brings a remembrance that our own roots and our own grounding feed our ecological balance. Our inner harmony can become rebalanced time and time again through nature's wisdom.

When we get caught up in our own personal drama and struggles, we forget that there is a greater force all around us that we can lean into and receive energy from. When we align with Mother Earth, we honor the earth's most delicate, vulnerable state. We acknowledge the earth's pure abundance and experience this quality within us. We too are of this tender and dynamic capacity—from the lava inside volcanoes to earthquakes, landslides, avalanches, forest fires; to the way trees communicate and support their dying neighbors. We live in awe of our natural world, carrying the spark of soul care simultaneously for ourselves and for our planet.

May we rekindle our relationship with the earth through our prayers, our offerings, our advocacy, and our willingness to be in a loving and supportive relationship with her. We must speak to her, pray with her and for her, and teach our children to garden her soil in reciprocity. The earth's sap lines are like our own bloodlines, the bloodlines we inherited from our ancestors. Complex, diverse, connected—each tree and each person with their own unique story and song. This perspective opens many doors. No longer are we just this or that. We begin to receive messages from nature; the gateway to the intuitive and the unseen realms opens. We can feel them as our ancestors. We can speak to them, form a relationship, hug them, read them poetry, and continue to be in awe of the whispers, teachings, and feelings that come through.

For any seed to take root in our lives, it must be nourished by nutrients, water, community, and love. We need peaceful moments in order to survive chaos. When we endure the complexities of life, we learn that we too can overcome personal challenges. We find true resilience by weathering the storms. We understand that we can be strong in the face of adversity. We can be soft and vulnerable in the eyes of our loved ones. We can widen our lens to be a student of life's most delicate and intricate weaves. With humility we bow to the earth, we fall to our knees in prayer for goodness, beauty, and strength; for our families and communities to learn through love, to lead for love, and to generate the change that we know is necessary for the healing of all people, cultures, and the planet. We remember how to do this by cultivating a steady, daily self-care practice. We return to the earth as stewards and keepers of her medicine, her well-being, and we renew our own bodies as we channel her grounding alchemy.

We must be rooted in our own authenticity; we must feed our own passionate song through the earth's most precious gifts. We understand the process of grounding our vision seeds deep in the earth before they can rise and become actualized. If we push only for productivity and results, we push against the natural cycles of planetary evolution; we end up burnt out and perhaps living a life that lacks love and true meaning. When we step out of the blindness that comes with the intellectual striving-mind and we drop into the synergy of what happens when we root, ground, feel, sense, and then think, we align with a true force that creates lasting change.

EARTH KEEPERS: INSIDE THE WEB OF LIFE

Mother Earth is calling us to be in a reciprocal relationship with her abundance, to open our senses to the grandness of her beauty. She is calling us to live inside the cosmos of her web, to cooperate with her, to harmonize our heart intelligence with hers and to be her advocate. We then become the stewards of her body. Our needs and wants no longer rob her of her vitality but align with a sustainable future. She is beyond generous; she has given unconditionally since the beginning of time. Now we find ourselves on the precipice of a climate crisis. Humanity has pushed her so far that she has been responding through forest fires, earthquakes, and tsunamis, no longer tolerating the pollution of imbalance.

While the environmental crisis can make the future seem bleak and daunting, we can meet this era with responsibility. Personal accountability is the call of the inner mystic, along with an intentional lifestyle that contributes to the planet's sustainability. May we listen to the youth, who all across the globe are already clamoring for change, and may we do this for our grandchildren, for future generations so they may experience the earth's exquisite beauty.

The element of earth is wildly abundant, full of sustenance, dependable, prosperous, sensitive, strong. It is the place where we root to rise and ground to physically manifest our needs and wants in the world. We can visualize our own root system, originating from our navel, streaming down through the tailbone, through the legs and feet, deep into the underbelly of the earth. This gives us a potent awareness of our natural grounding process. Take for example the state of fight or flight, our body's natural instinct for survival and protection when we experience fear. Our heart beats fast, our palms sweat, our breath shortens, and our mind begins to race—perhaps even spins thought after thought, strategizing in order to get ourselves out of that situation. Our survival mechanisms kick in and we want to run, fight, or hide, to change the dangerous situation as fast as we can.

The tricky part is that our internal systems do not actually know the difference between real danger and perceived danger. For example, we could perceive danger in feedback from a colleague that was intended to be helpful but ends up feeling like an actual attack. We get defensive, our heart rate increases, and we are in a state of armored reaction. This is not an efficient and effective way to be in the world. Our clarity becomes muddled, our mind spins, and we sever our roots—we lose our grounding. The more we get curious about how perceived danger vs. real danger may be affecting our capacity to be clear and calm, the more we learn how to live life with less drama and internal stress. We can learn how to not take things personally and how to widen our lens in the moment, bringing us out of a state of reaction, defense, and armor into a space of inquiry, non-judgment, and overall understanding of the bigger picture.

When we practice daily grounding techniques and a nurturing self-care regime, we can reroute the spinning, ungrounded expressions that result in fear, anger, grief, or shame into stability and resilience. We reclaim in a moment our grounded strength. We send our roots down, we remember we are as resourceful and abundant as the earth, and we connect to the bloodline of the ancient self. This process is wisdom in action. When we open ourselves to feel the gravitational pull of the earth, we become embodied and we attune to our senses and our body's rhythms. We develop a relationship between the earth's energy and our own energies. We release separation, and we open to a conversation not only with our bodies, but also with the earth. If we practice this regularly, we begin to view our lives through the lens of love, forgiveness, and compassion.

In the pagan wheel of the year, the earth element is associated with the direction north and the winter solstice is honored—the longest night and the shortest day of the year. This honoring ushers us toward inner reflection, stillness, darkness, and resting. In that dark quiet space, our dream seeds can be renewed. At every solstice or equinox, a transformation occurs. When we are conscious of the earth's pivotal transitions, we too can align with her forces. We can evolve our own beings, deepen into our own personal work, and understand how stress, fear, anxiety or grief has been gripping our souls and directing our lives.

When we honor the turning points in the wheel of the year, we pause, draw inside, and begin to embody the present moment. We understand that every day we live on this planet is an opportunity to grow, feel, and sense the great mystery that lives in the natural world. We stay awake to the pivotal moments in our life, and we experience the deeper levels of consciousness that come forward. We see ourselves on the precipice of a new journey, an exciting adventure on the horizon. A visceral sensation in the body calls to us, and we receive clarity on which direction to go, what decision to make, and where to focus in order to live our fullest life.

The conversation between you and the earth's rhythms is the process and the journey. It's just like the conversation you have with your own body. Can you begin to greet your body and the earth like this every day?

Good morning my body—my temple! May I treat you with compassion today. Mother Earth, may I walk softly and consciously upon your fertile belly. May I remember to be your ally, your advocate, and your champion as I make intentional choices with what I consume, how I recycle, and the lifestyle I choose. May I tend your gardens in a way that is nourishing and sustaining for both of us. May I be an earth angel today, living with a nourished love for myself, my community, and the greatness of your expansive dimensions. May I hug trees often, and may I teach my children and my communities to do the same. May I walk through the forest, the open plains and the gardens, palms open to receive and to give with a radiant vital force.

If we can open a conversation with the earth, giving her an image or a personality, then we can see and feel her spiritual existence. Remember this. Talk to her. Listen to her. It is the spirit of Mother Earth and her kingdom that shows us how to pray to her and for her. This becomes the church of the modern spirit seeker.

As a young child, I felt a very strong pull to be in a spiritual relationship with the earth. I knew deep down that the earth was my religion. The moon called to me. I became mesmerized by the lunar and earthly rhythms. Under the light of the moon and upon the sanctuaries of the earth—this is where I would play and pray, build sculptures and habitats, devote my energy and attention; where I would seek counsel and solace. The earth was the wisdom keeper, the knowledge holder, the place where I would plant my dream seeds—some of them realized through the cycles and seasons of my own life, some of them returned to the earth to nourish her.

What if we prayed every day, not just for what we wanted in our own lives, but for Mother Earth herself? For the first inhabitants of the land, for the indigenous wisdom keepers, the stones, the insects, the creepy crawlies, the four-leggeds, the two-leggeds; for our ancestors to guide us. Our perspective shifts, the dance of the mundane of everyday life begins to soften, and we open ourselves to dimensions we did not even know existed. Perhaps we encounter earth angels. Messengers from the spirit plane come knocking at the most unassuming times, so pay attention!

You may awaken to the ravishing beauty of the sunrise or the scent of a rose garden. Wherever you find this source of joy and beauty—move into this energy field. This is how you sense the unseen energies. With devotion and a steady mind–heart field, you can trust you will experience a spiritual existence in the physical form. Magic, mystery, and unforgettable soul-stirring experiences are abundant on Planet Earth. It simply requires us to slow down enough to feel this earth spirit energy around us. We can practice this by simply observing nature's majesty.

WORKING WITH FEAR AS A CATALYST FOR TRANSFORMATION

Life brings a series of cycles. There will always be new beginnings, moments of pause, transitions, and endings. There will be fears, heartbreaks, unforgettable love, radical epiphanies, and spiritual experiences. When we begin to track where fear-based thinking rules our life, we instantly widen our lens of perception towards the truth. The winged perceiver comes alive, the veils of illusion lift, the grounding force of earth awakens, rumbles, shakes, and brings our vision to life. We begin this inner journey by naming our fears. This channels them towards living life based on authenticity, present-moment awareness, clarity, and inner strength. We drop deeper into the experience of meeting our true nature as we are no longer guarding, hiding, or running away.

When fear arises, observe it, work with it, breathe deeply into it. Let go of how others perceive you in the moment and redirect the energy of fear towards the opportunity that is knocking on your door. Fear brings deep personal inquiry and wild state changes. The evolution comes through when you allow yourself to name fear in the moment; to look it deep in the eyes. You open yourself up to dismantle, decode, understand, and reroute the fear into compassion. You are the channel, the mystic, the warrior. Stay open to what life brings. Seek the mountain peaks—fly, dive, dance, tumble, roll, fall, swim. Commit to your personal goals and visions in a way that is louder than the fear.

Understanding when fear takes over is a key step towards living with liberation, love, and joy. Ask yourself, "Where do I practice vulnerability in my life? How do I respond to fear?" Seek to understand the back story, the sideshow that feeds imbalanced reactions. In this way you can clear and cut the ties that feed the back stories—the ones that direct your life in ways that do not serve your highest self.

Your body sensations, where your mind goes, how you speak and listen, what you consume—these are all signposts along the fear-tracking journey. To be the huntress of your imbalances is to tend to all of your separate selves in order to bring them back home with safety and compassion. When you dig into the experiences and stories of your wounded inner child, you begin to understand where your personal triggers originated from. When not tended, the hurts, shames, and disappointments that span across life experiences will affect the quality of your life.

You can simply begin by acknowledging when you are not grounded and having the conversation with your inner self: "Here I am again, I see you, I feel you, I know you." You honor your process and you acknowledge that you are in a state of non-clarity, and that this is okay. This begins the process of dismantling fear-based living. When you allow for this present-moment recognition, whether it is towards yourself or in your relationships, you allow the softening required to pause, breathe, and ground. No longer do you feel the need to prove you are right. The warrior doesn't need to fight and win every battle in this way. When you see clearly the actual situation that caused the fear to arise, the wounded warrior of the past reroutes with a clear, grounded vision and a new perspective.

When fear triggers a state of overwhelm and defense, you sometimes put your armor on. You get ready for battle or retreat or disassociate in your own unique way. It's uncomfortable and you want to avoid the pain. You want to numb the sensations or go straight into problem solving. You get so consumed by these habitual patterns that you miss the opportunity for personal growth.

When you find yourself in the murky abyss of emotional overwhelm, simply begin a conversation with your body and say "Here I am again, I feel my heart pulsing, I feel fear churn in my guts, and I know my mind is muddled." Try saying, "I am unclear in this moment." It is this kind of inner dialogue that gives the body permission to soften, and in this moment you gain perspective. You become the witness to your unclear thoughts and sensations. This is the key to opening the next door on your personal evolution. This becomes the most positive, vibrant, and quintessential opening into your healing process.

Here I am, beautiful body. Here I am, abundant-vast-tricky mind. Thank you for this opportunity to grow, evolve, and interrupt the pathways that once served me. For I am widening my perspective and I am open to learning new ways in this moment.

RECLAIMING YOUR RIGHT TO BE HERE

If you are living your life from your wounded inner child, you are less likely to be in connection with the abundant nature of the earth. You may be unconsciously living from a place of lack, fear, and scarcity, not only in the physical realm but also in the emotional and the spiritual realms. It is now time to reclaim your right to be here and become a channel for your dreams. Listen to the earth, let her inspire your inner work so that you can be present, awake, and activated. She will become your guide. This alignment will generate your grounded nature. You will be more invested in the healing, grounding, and rising evolution of your signature essence. Through this you can contribute to the positive shift that lives inside the consciousness of the collective and support the investment in our future generations.

If you were brought up to believe that you didn't have the right to have nice things or you grew up in a house with poverty, abuse, or violence, you were constantly in overdrive—trying to cope and survive daily life. Though this experience, you may have been taught that you do not deserve abundance and success. This belief, either conscious or unconscious, causes you to push away abundance, reject self-care, and feel that you do not have the right to have love or success in your life. If you do not unearth the familial patterns and do the work to heal your inner child, those old wounds will continue to rule your life.

The work of healing your familial, and ancestral wounds is essential for personal liberation. The childhood wounding manifests when you are in intimate relationship, especially as you become a parent yourself, and it affects how you grow and evolve into adulthood.

The work that needs to be done can be broken down into simple steps that will bring clarity into the spaces where you find yourself repeating patterns that keep you from generating abundance. Begin to observe when you are living your life with your cup half empty. Perhaps you use sarcasm or judgment against others who are living out their dreams. Perhaps you are a workaholic, addicted to stress and productivity, or maybe you feel worthless.

Observe the times you can't make a decision or you become overwhelmed. Your nervous system goes into overdrive, and your survival instincts become muddled because they are over-functioning. This could be in a triggered state where you feel threatened, where you have to prove, defend, and exaggerate or lie. When this happens, go through the steps below.

Tracking the Inner Child: Reveal to Heal

1 Remember to breathe. Acknowledge the emotions troubling you and visualize your roots from the base of your spine down into the earth. Hold the intention to meet your inner child with healing and compassion.

2 Soften your exterior, calm your interior, and acknowledge the energy in your body and mind. Remind yourself you have a right to be here and to feel your emotions.

3 Recall the situation that caused your emotions to become imbalanced. Track back to yourself as a child and recognize any patterns, coping mechanisms or learned behaviors. Open to receiving a new perspective.

4 Visualize your adult self holding your child or teen or young adult self, and let her/him know you are safe, there is nothing to prove or fear. Merge the different sensations and feelings together in a way that feels compassionate and healing.

5 Acknowledge the healing process happening inside you. Remind yourself that you are grounded, soft, spacious, and strong, like Mother Earth herself. Call on an affirmation that will support you in your grounding and abundance; the right to be here and the right to dream big and get what you want.

6 Forgive yourself so that you can forgive others when the time is right.
7 Call forth your gratitudes and engage in a nourishing activity to seal the experience, for example a nature walk, a warm bath, comforting food, talking with a friend, journaling, etc.

This kind of healing holds an energetic vibration. We don't always have to know where it comes from. What is essential is that we listen, feel, acknowledge, and attune to the vibration. It may be ancestral or karmic. It may be the very essence that we were born with as a gift towards personal liberation and global evolution. The world we grew up in is no longer the world we live in now. We must evolve consciously with the rhythms, patterns, and events that are happening here and now.

If we do not allow ourselves to shift out of stubbornness, pride, ego, and fear, we are feeding the paradigms that have contributed to violence, oppression, racism, sexism, and patriarchy. If we remain confined in what others expect of us, we continue to feed these constructs and illusions. Our body takes this on as muscle memory and we find ourselves as martyrs, as victims. We'd rather sweep the hard times under the rug, push those stories down, and trudge on like a wounded warrior in battle. With an armored heart, murky mind, and ungrounded body, we forget who we are and live a life that was not meant for us.

At the end of your life, will you be able to look back and know that you lived a life true to your heart and your soul mission? Find your inspiration to keep doing the work, stay true, meet your challenges with a fierce grace, and reclaim your right to be here with the humility and courage of a warrior and the love and compassion of an earth angel.

When we liberate ourselves from trying to fit into preconceived paradigms, we reclaim our own roots and our fundamental right to live out our soul's mission. Perfection can be an addiction that keeps us away from our personal evolution. It takes a revolution within to battle the perfectionist who holds us back from our wild, creative, intelligent, expressive self. If we play small in fear of making mistakes, our roots cannot grow and extend. If our inner critic gets so loud and beats us down with a kind of emotional and mental violence, we stop growing. We close more doors than we open. Our ability to discern what is real and false gets muddled. Fear takes such a firm hold on us that we convince ourselves we are not good enough to make changes in our lives; we are better off staying in the abusive relationship or the incredibly boring career, or we are better off alone. We have programmed ourselves to trust our fear more than our desire for love. The work of the inner mystic is to liberate your human heart and mind.

When we begin to deeply inquire why we choose what we do in life, we get to know our own inner rhythms with great intimacy. We feel into the yes's, the no's, the "I don't know right now." And that's okay; we acknowledge this process, no longer resisting it. We hold fear like a feast before us, eye to eye, energy to energy, and we begin to trust ourselves that we can do this. We are complex beings in an ecosystem of immense complexity. When we align with the force of the earth's systems, cycles, and rhythms, we discover an inner knowing, fueled by our instincts. Our grounded nature feeds this inner knowing, like a wise elder within each one of us. We have arrived in this moment. It may feel as if we are seeing our life through a completely different lens. Our mindset shifts.

We live by the simple universal truths of peace, balance, love, grief, joy, strength, grace, and compassion. They intermingle with our being; our muscle memory calls to us. We ground, anchor, and merge with the life force of all the earth's dimensions. We remember our soul's calling and we receive the inspiration required to plant our vision seeds deep in the earth. Our intuitive nature comes alive. Our psychic channels open. We begin to receive messages, we choose to take action on them. Like the spiral inside the ancient fossil, we return to the source. We step into the center of our human journey, and we find great strength and clarity as we navigate according to our inner compass.

ROOTING DOWN TO RISE UP: THE BODY AS CHANNEL

We are more effective in our letting go than in our grasping.
Our releasing becomes our pure strength, our divine grace, and
our true unified nature. Over time this softens us, widens our lens,
and enlivens our ability to stay connected to the earthly realms
while conversing with the divine.

Our body is our cherished temple. It is home to the workings of our heart's chamber and soul's purpose. It is the vessel that holds the complexities of our mind, our personal genetics, our senses, feelings, stories, and unique life experiences. The entanglement of energies inside the human organism has the capacity to function like a well-tuned instrument, allowing us to embody our personal potential and live towards our full capacity.

When we embody the energetic art of rooting down towards the earth's alchemy, the body consciousness rises up through the spine. This awakens the heart and feeds the mind. We align with the body as the pure enshrined channel it is.

The catalyst for this body reverence begins with acceptance. We must acknowledge, feel, and love our bodies. We must embrace our ancestral goddess- and god-given bodies with an unshakeable strength and compassion. If we do not make peace with our bodies, we cut the energetic love cords of beauty, goodness, strength, and truth that are our birthright. Now is the time to do the work to love your most cherished chamber; the channel in which you house the many diverse experiences of body, mind, and spirit.

Based on our ancient survival instincts, we experience a plethora of body–mind–heart vibrations. We hunt and gather, we organize and align, we fear and disconnect, we forget and remember. All of these energies become a super-highway within our living body. We are born with the bones and blood of our ancestors. We arrive into our family circle with our own karmic energy to sort and sift. We have our own lessons to learn and gifts to share, and a soul calling to live out.

We are born of the alchemy of star and mud.
The stardust within us keeps us rising. The mud nature in us
keeps us humble. The humbled spirit can rise when we consciously
dance with the dark and light forces we face every day.

When our survival instincts begin to rule our lives through the lens of fear, we disrupt our rooted connection with the earth. We live our history; we live in reaction to fear, stress, anxiety, and the historical structures of racism, sexism, violence, and patriarchy. For some of us more than others, this affects our ability to feel connected, calm, and safe. Our instinctual states of rest and calm do not flourish as the fight or flight mechanism takes over.

For centuries, black, indigenous, and people of color (BIPOC) have experienced this kind of fear. Their commitment to keeping their lineage and cultural strength is what has allowed BIPOC communities to continue speaking loud and clear—they want justice and change. They want to feel safe in our communities. As a white woman and a descendant of Scottish, Irish, and English settlers upon stolen indigenous lands, my work is to dismantle my own unconscious racism and to deeply study how I contribute to the systems of patriarchy, sexism, and violence within my own being. It is my responsibility to share the true story with my children, to educate them about systemic racism, and to raise them to be conscious learners of past, present, and future narratives of all inhabitants on this earth.

My role as a mother, a partner, a teacher, a friend, and a daughter is to stay connected to the earth's rhythms; to remain grounded through daily mindful practices so that my instrument is not only finely tuned but ready to receive and to give; ready to advocate and take action where I can. It does no good to indulge in guilt and to hate my ancestors and those who caused war, violence, and the rape of so many cultures. When we can make peace with our own history—not to accept the actions or the behaviors, but to learn the true stories, we can advocate with greater resilience, compassion, and effectiveness. This is the work the earth teaches us: how to acknowledge, forgive, listen, learn, love, and continue to grow. To teach our children how to live consciously with deep reverence for Mother Earth is to hold space for lasting change for this planet and all her people.

When our roots are disconnected—both from the earth and from our ancestral lineage—we may feel lost, confused about our true purpose, depressed, anxious, and fearful. We become susceptible to living our life half asleep. When we are disconnected from the ground that we walk upon, our body's natural response channels are disrupted. This includes how we receive and perceive the signals from our intuition, how we connect to our self-esteem, inner power, and our capacity to love unconditionally, and how we speak our truth. The receiver signals in the body become severed, the lines break, and the energy gets cut off. We can no longer feel our body's true needs.

We abandon ourselves, we check out, we push away. We over-eat, we under-eat, we blame and judge, we hate and fear, we hide our secrets, we numb ourselves with alcohol and drugs. We do all of these things so we don't feel what is really there. And what is really there is *gold*. This is the medicine of the modern mystic and the mindful soul leader. This is the alchemy of the earth angels. This is the spirit of our ancestors. This is our direct line to our intuition and to expanding our capacity to truly love ourselves—unconditionally. Listen for the divine messengers, the omens, the numinous happenings. They come into our life for a reason, may we open up to hearing their call.

WORKING WITH MINERALS AND PLANTS AS TRANSMUTERS OF POWERFUL ENERGY

Working with minerals, stones, and plants as healing sources reminds us that we are connected to the web of life. Tending to Mother Earth and her exquisite prana or life force, brings profound insight. When we widen our viewpoint to see the teachings inside the stones and the plants, we develop reverence towards the earth. We begin to sense the natural lessons that are willing to come into our energy field.

As we begin to observe the life force in the stones, we see how they have been weathered by many storms. Rock formations shape-shift, mountains form, glaciers move, and fossils are created. There is a healing power in stones. They hold stories, they are living history, and they can speak to us in a way that shifts our perspective. When we find a fossil stone with a center that has been carved into a perfect star, how can we not want to solve its mystery? Children naturally gather stones; they collect the very special ones and hold them in their hands until they become warm to touch, and they blow their wishes into them. They see the wonder and the magic of the universe in a single stone. May we too be in this kind of wonder as we journey through adulthood. May we blow our prayers into our stones, and may we speak to the stones enough so they begin to speak back to us.

You may find a unique stone on your adventures, or perhaps a stone calls to you in a crystal shop. It feels warms to the touch; the energy from the stone feels nourishing, symbolic, and supportive. Or you may feel a strong resonance with the properties of a particular plant, as its scent, color, and its healing properties enliven your senses. In a way this may become your soul plant. Observe the stones you are attracted to, for they carry an alchemy that will both ground and energize you. This palpable energy becomes a unique relationship and a window into working with the stones and plants that nourish you on a soul level. The touch of a stone, the scent of a flower—at times it can feel nostalgic, and at other times completely original. Whether you are drawn to gardening, gathering medicinal herbs and flowers, or collecting stones—take your sacred earth objects to your altar in honor and great reverence to the power of the elemental forces all around you.

We remind ourselves that we are surrounded by beauty, and even on the hardest of days, we can feel the support of the mineral and plant world. We open to see the beauty all around us. This mineral and plant medicine work becomes louder than the inner critic, more powerful than the fear of the unknown, and over time, a lesson in reciprocity. There is an inner knowing that through connecting to other life forms, we receive as much as we give and we give as much as we receive.

The flower blooms so that the honeybee can pollinate and share this medicine throughout the entire garden. This is what makes our food grow, and this is what sustains life. The earth angel inside of us comes alive, determined to share the love and compassion known to change lives, transform states, and re-align with the simple universal truths of a strong and peaceful life force. Like the honeybee he listens for the call to return to the earth to source the nectar, and then she goes out to share it with the world. She gathers, collects, sifts, and gives—her medicine runs deep in the underbelly of the earth. She carries a radiance that allows everyone around her to blossom.

How Does Crystal Healing Work?

Historically, ancient cultures have worked with crystals as a source of healing, clearing, and transforming energy. Crystals can enhance the wellness in body, mind, and spirit through both physical and spiritual realms. Everything in our universe is made up of energy, from the fabric of the clothes you wear to the metal in the bicycle you ride, to the hair on your skin—they all contain unique vibrations of energy. Although you cannot actually see or feel these vibrations, the cells inside your body and the energy inside crystals also contain their own unique vibrations. Imagine the workings of a magnet. It can both repel and attract energy, and this is also how healing crystals work.

When you hold a crystal in your hand or move it over an area in your body, your body responds through a pulsing or a shifting that you may or may not feel. This inner pulse can raise the vibration inside your body in alignment with the crystal's energetic healing property. Both crystals and our human bodies contain the mineral silicon dioxide. As a result, we are naturally receptive to the vibrations of the stone's healing quality. The energetic interaction between you and the stone creates a charge, and this alchemy can create a state change or a felt sense within. This could be anything from clearing negative energy to encouraging restful states, to relaxing the nervous system—all depending on the stone.

When you are fatigued or stressed, when your emotions are imbalanced, you can work with crystals, along with raw stones we find in the earth, to balance areas of disharmony and nourish our energy. It's important to purchase ethically mined crystals, and when collecting stones from the earth, check in to receive permission. The stones are like conduits. The unique properties and history they carry can be channeled into you through the induction of their particular frequency. Picture how a light source turns on when it gets plugged in; there is a similar stream of electricity when a healing crystal gets placed on your body. You receive the benefits from aligning with the crystal's energetic properties. Visualize how a magnet draws up pieces of metal. This is how crystals can pull out imbalanced energies in your body.

There are many ways in which crystals can be used to heal, connect, and generate positive state changes in your life. They can be arranged in your home or on your altar, you can wear them, place them on specific body parts, hold them while you are meditating, or put them under your pillow while you are sleeping.

As crystals attract, absorb and repel energy, it's essential that you keep your crystals clean. If you are using crystals specifically to draw out negative energy, be sure to cleanse them before you use them again. Soak your crystals in sea-salted water, or rinse them in ocean water. Under the full moon, you can put your crystal in a bowl of sea-salted water to cleanse them and give them an extra charge of energy. As you cleanse your crystals, place your intention on rebalancing their healing properties so they can return to their full capacity.

In today's fast-paced, technological world, stones and plants can support your mind, body, and spirit in a highly effective and healing way. As you choose your stones and welcome the natural healing of plant medicines into your life, you will also begin to awaken your intuition and tap into your higher self. This journey of crystal and plant healing is for all ages and stages of life: from children, to teens, to mid-life, to elders; we can all benefit from raising our frequency to that of Mother Earth's finest gifts.

OPENING TO BEAUTY AND
JOY EVERY STEP OF THE WAY

The song of the hummingbird awakens the medicine inside the flowers.

The ritual life brings rhythm and steadiness into our days. It brings meaning to our inner life—the spiritual life—in ways that words cannot express. This becomes a "felt" sense where we experience the sacred on a visceral and somatic level. It's devotional and deeply personal. From our center of gravity down into the earth and up to the sky, we simultaneously stay in a grounded connection and a rising consciousness. We dream our biggest dreams into the realms of possibility while embodying a calm and practical mind–body state. We embody all of the elements at once. We become dimensional, we diversify our portfolio, and we open to beauty and joy every step of the journey. We light our candles, we greet the day with reverence, we welcome in the wonder of a child, we visualize how we would like to walk into our day. We practice a spiritual intimacy that becomes vulnerable, mysterious, and reciprocal as we cast our prayers out into the universe.

Weaving the threads of the body–heart–mind creates an open tapestry. We get to choose what, how, where, and when to create. We get to choose who we want to share our deepest, most intimate, and sacred moments with. Sometimes, our most soulful work happens in relationship to nature. Find whatever the divine means to you. What stirs your soul, pulls you up from the ashes, reminds you of your courage to carry on? From the quiet meditative moments to epiphanies—let each moment, calm or wild, guide you into your soul chamber.

Can you find those moments in your day when you are not engaging in life's dramas and demands? This becomes your work. Seek counsel through your own channels. Become the love mystic you are. When you step into your truth and healing in this way, when you practice adoration towards your own spirit, you inspire everyone around you to do the same. This becomes an ongoing conversation. You may be inspired to begin your mornings journaling, or simply engage in conversation with yourself—in the shower, as you are sipping your morning coffee, or even on your commute to work:

Dear mind, I see you, I hear you, I feel you. Let me discern what
is mine, and what is not. Grant me permission to lay down the

limited thought patterns like the precious relics they are—ready to be transformed upon the earth into the next cycle. Let me feed you with the goodness, beauty, and truth that live all around me. Guide me to your spirit house so I may feel nourished, loved, complete, and whole.

When you seek counsel within your own temple in this way, an open-ended conversation takes place between your most sacred parts; they come alive when they are spoken to with love, held with compassion, and honored for their process. Let this devotion towards the inner life come fully alive— be it through prayer, meditation, mindfulness, creativity, movement, or meaningful relationships and conversations. Open the doors to the temple and tend to your spirit in the same way you would care for your best friend, your lover, your animal, your child, or your ancestors and guides. Open the temple doors! Your guests are ready to take a seat around your ceremonial fire and warm their hearts and hands while basking in your divine grace. This is the way to deepen your life experience while aligning with your soul purpose. This is the process and the journey of nourishing the soul unconditionally, and this is ultimately what brings sustained joy and beauty into your life.

When we weave our devotional practices into the fabric of daily life— not just when we are in crisis—we become a vessel for the mystical guide to emerge. Our inner life becomes vast, fertile, and so energetically abundant that our outer body merges with our inner soul. The dark well of restlessness, fatigue, doubt, and fear that we unconsciously sourced from in the past dries up, and we become unified on another level. Our internal conscious feminine and conscious masculine energies intertwine with the forces of both the light and the dark. They catch each other when they fall, they hold each other in a divine embrace, and they encourage one another to keep fighting the good fight. This unity consciousness within feels fluid like water, fertile like the earth, radiant like glowing embers, vast like a clear blue sky, and cosmically aligned like the ethereal energy that surrounds the spirit of life. Just as the song of the hummingbird awakens the medicine inside the flowers, our call to direct our lives with a purposeful, meaningful, and conscious intention allows the song of others to awaken alongside our own. Our daily rituals tether us to the earth. Through the earth we feel how the devotion of a spiritual life awakens beauty and joy in every step. And our own personal evolution inspires and awakens others to do the same.

CONNECTING WITH YOUR
ANCESTORS AND GUIDES

May we be good ancestors.

May we show up and do the work required to heal not only from our ancestral hardships, but may we understand that our choices and actions will directly affect the next generations.

What are we willing to pass down and pay forward?

What are we willing to do to become a good ancestor?

Some believe that on a spiritual or a cosmic level we choose our own parents, and some believe our parents choose us through the natural creation process. Whatever your belief is, there is a sacred contract between you and your family. We may not always understand why we were born into our family, and it may be part of our life's work to discover how to be in a healing relationship with them. Or we may feel deeply connected to our family and have a very strong feeling of why we came to the earth in this lifetime. Others might find their spiritual or karmic family through devotional practices, religion, or nature-based spirituality.

When we learn about our past and make peace with it, we mine the gold of our personal ancestry. Sifting through family history, stories, traditions, beliefs; learning the languages they spoke, the wars they fought, the plagues they endured, the traumas and the milestones—all this is part of understanding who our ancestors were and what we can do to honor them.

Developing this relationship with our ancestors engenders compassion for their journey and their life experience. War, violence, hatred, racism, sexism, and patriarchy are part of our history. When we can forgive and understand that our ancestors' choices were based on survival, perhaps we can understand and forgive. We learn to do better. We can make good choices for the times we are living in. We can uncover our own unconscious bias and unconscious racism and begin the journey of evolving our heritage.

We can heal, mend, forgive the past. The world we live in today is very different from the world of our ancestors, and even the one we were born into. We can heal the pain and the injustice our ancestors endured through weaving this prayer into your morning meditation: "I come from good people. May I embody the heart and spirit of what it takes to be a good ancestor. May I be a good ancestor." Welcome this affirmation into the marrow of your bones. Let it fill your heart with the warmth of the sun. Open up your energy field to communicate with your ancestors and to carry forward their strongest, most loving, wisest attributes.

As the consciousness of our times shifts, and the limiting societal structures become dismantled and questioned once again, we can weep for the events our ancestors had to endure; for their broken hearts, for the trail of their tears, for the hierarchical forces that caused them to steal land and take cultures away. We can communicate with their spirits through our meditations and dream states. They may come to us in a flash, or we can honor and acknowledge them when they whisper to us in the darkest of nights. When we align with our ancestors in this way, we feed the hungry ghosts no more. We untangle ourselves from their trauma or pain and we enter into the goodness, the mystery, and the wisdom in their hearts.

Untangle your mind from the hooks of toxicity.
Feed the hungry ghosts no more.
Rise above the clouds.
Feel into your own evolution.
The star-kissed web is waiting for your return.

When we track our personal ancestry in this way, we understand which ancestral qualities we want to weave into our present life—strength, wisdom, and character. Simultaneously, we clearly see what toxic patterns to shed— addiction, greed, sadness, trauma, and violence. Whether these patterns manifest consciously or unconsciously, doing the work to uncover and reveal historical truths can empower us to have compassion and make different choices. We become liberated by ending certain toxic cycles, making peace with our past, and choosing to live life from a place of sovereignty. We reclaim our roots, we unearth the secrets, we overcome the universal human desire to hide from our ancestral trauma. We name our history for what it is. We call forward the untruths, the written narratives in our history books that came only from the colonial white male lens. Now is the time to evolve through listening, through widening our understanding, through becoming a good ancestor for the collective consciousness.

This work is worth doing—we not only make peace with the secrets, the unknowns, and the pain of the past, but we also become channels to receive support and guidance from our ancestors and our guides. We no longer romanticize the illusions we grew up with or the bubble we were sheltered in. When we step inside the global historical narrative, we begin to see, feel, sense, and become a conduit for change. We speak the truths. We name our freedoms, our right to be here, our right for our voices to be heard. We begin to patiently and steadily dismantle the embedded paradigms based on external systemic narratives.

Living in these wildly shifting times is a privilege. Our ancestors did not have the information or the truth and freedom we have today. In 2020 we saw a necessary uprising that has shaken the world awake—a global pandemic, along with movements such as Black Lives Matter and Indigenous Lives Matter. Global consciousness has evolved, and yes, we still have so much more work to do.

This journey of acknowledging, processing, and liberating our inner bias is the work. We have a choice right now to stay awake. Let us no longer participate in the ancestral and habitual patterns that contribute to a life-denying mentality—power over, push forward, dominate, control, we must make more money and buy more things. If we continue to feed the social constructs that we want to shift, we continue to live inside that box and contribute to these lower level vibrational paradigms.

When we open our body–heart–mind field as a channel to give and receive not only in the ordinary world, but also in the spiritual or unseen worlds, we open our consciousness to our ancestors' gifts and strengths. This journey may come in the form of a creative process or time spent in nature, or through our ability to fall in love with both our light and our shadow. We honor our ancestors and celebrate their wisdom and gifts. We can make peace by rekindling their spirit through our personal self-expression, through our devotional and meditative practices.

THE GIFTS OF DOING THE WORK

A sacred space exists between how much effort we put into our life and how much we allow effortlessness to channel through us. It takes great effort, energy, commitment, and dedication to fulfill our desires. However, we often forget to include ease, grace, spaciousness, and effortlessness. Effort and effortlessness must be in a symbiotic relationship for true abundance and soul nourishment to exist. We must commit to this question: "What nourishes me on a deeper soul level?" and "How can I embed this nourishment into the fabric of my life?" For example, if spending time in nature is soothing for our soul, how can we organize daily life rituals to include nature time? The earth is such a profound teacher to us in her ways of creation, manifestation, cyclic evolution, growth, resilience, and resourcefulness. Think of the tiny sapling that pushes through the crevice on the mountain's edge and grows into a healthy strong tree. Keep that image alive the next time you face fear or challenge. Remember to dance with the forces of effort and effortlessness. When we push too hard in one direction, the universe will remind us there is a simpler way. And even when our own vision seems too far out of reach, when planted with intention and expansiveness, it will take root, even in the toughest, most unlikely conditions.

We can work with fear through grounding and present-state awareness techniques that open us to the vast landscape all around us. There we have the opportunity to walk the path of life with joy and love. We listen and attune to the earth's abundance, sourcing inspiration and positive energy through our own physical, emotional, mental, and spirit channels. We seek counsel through the reflections from our personal work and we hold space to touch upon the primal, ancient, and mystical teachings. Thus we learn to live liberated and whole, to dwell in wonder of the universe, to touch upon the depths of our own ancestral and karmic healing.

The whispers of Mother Earth's call inspire us to meet each cycle and phase of our life with a wild, untamed, loving embrace. When we allow ourselves to feel this, we go out in the world and we express ourselves free of judgment and unafraid of the unknown. Our inner passion becomes more important than our inner critic. We source our internal desires and stream them out into the world; our soul's destiny unfolds before our eyes.

This is how the inner mystic calls to us. Sometimes she comes in the divine feminine form. Her creative, deeply nourishing earthen arms and fertile belly swaddle us, imbue us with the remembrance of our own divinity. She will catch us upon her soft heart, even when it's bleeding and we fall from grace in despair. She will hear our prayers and remind us that things will shift in good time. Return to her pure source of fertility, deep in the rich darkness of her soil. Receive her when she comes. She will always remind us to rest so that our dreams may be realized. Our soul will continue to evolve and support the alchemical transmutation that is necessary for her sustenance. We do this for our mother, our grandmother, our great-grandmother. Like the moon, our divine feminine cycles through darkness to radiance every 29.5 days. She teaches how to embrace our inner wisdom, no longer doubting, fearing, pleasing, or worrying. The moon follows her cycle—steady, strong, mysterious, ever changing and always evolving.

Like the sun, our divine masculine instinctually knows how to give intentionally without asking for anything in return. We call forward the goodness in our father, grandfather, and great-grandfather. We burn brightly and inspire radiant growth inside us and around us. We open our heart–mind–body as a conduit for the divine masculine to come through us. The strength and goodness of our ancestors taught us how to be determined and how to activate our clean inner power. To wear our hearts on our sleeve and express our inner passion to bring positive change to the world. Inspired by the sun, we work with the force of light to manifest our visions and to sustain the earth.

With intention, anything and everything transforms into something. Lean in and commit to the things that light you up, even if they scare you, even if you are afraid to fail. Tend to your dreams as if they are seeds planted on a rocky peak, and listen to the messages coming through you. As you plant your dream seeds, see them already in the manifest; get connected to the feeling inside the dream. Visualizing the conditions inside your future dream—who is there, what the landscape looks like, and how it feels—will greatly support you in manifesting your dreams. Observe when your inner critic wants to come in and sabotage, belittle, or judge the dream. This becomes the healing process towards radical self-love and reclaiming your right to be here and deserving the dreams you are putting out into the world.

Ask yourself: What is the cost of not following your dream?

Let this question inspire you to keep going. Discern what nourishes you on a soul level and get crystal clear on what does not. Take action from this place. We are complex beings, and so is the world. Turn to nature's exquisite complexities for strength; she will guide you home again and again. Sing, pray, write, dance, meet your inner artist, your inner mother and inner father. Engage them in an intimate and open conversation that will guide you towards a deeper relationship with yourself and the earth. Write love letters to the earth, and become a channel for what you wish to see and be in the world.

Today I embrace the dance between my softness and my strength.
Rooting down into your soft belly, sweet mother, I intend to serve you,
to be a potent love channel to nourish your intricate web, your cosmic
roots—to feed you with the goodness, the truth, and the beauty that you
reflect back to me daily. My own abundance alchemizes as I remember
to live through the widening cosmic lens of the physical to
the spiritual realms. I live in reciprocity with all beings,
with you sacred mother, and with myself.

Come to me in the dreamtime, good ancestors and guides, remind me of
how to be an earth angel and advocate. Wash me clean of my lack, my
fears, my worries. Remind me of my truth, my purpose, my gifts.

I traverse the plains through the cycles of birth—death—rebirth when
the time is right, planting the vision seeds necessary for my personal
evolution and revolution. I am listening and I am awake.

Come supporting guides, ancestors, animal, mineral and plant messengers.
Remind me of your legacy teachings. Inspire me to tap the roots of my soul's
calling with joy, ease, grace, and sheer strength. Grounded like you, wildly
expansive, harmonizing relations inside this exquisite ecosystem.

Signs, symbols, sounds, smells, tastes, touch. I merge with your song.
Tapping in. Rooting down. Rising up. The intricate weave of your wild
alchemy. I am with you, sweet mother, I am with you.

Rituals for Grounding and Abundance

Deepen your relationship with Mother Earth through grounding techniques, daily gratitude practices, and guided visualization practices. Learn how to transform fear into abundance, connect with your ancestors to receive guidance, and acknowledge the spirit of the earth as the ultimate healing balm.

1. Daily Gratitude Practice

Practice
Best done first thing in the morning.

1 Light a candle and sit in silence. Attune to your breath, honor your body as your temple, and call forth three gratitudes.
2 Rehearse how you will move through your day.
3 Call forth a personal symbol, a word, an element, or an inspiration to carry you through the day. For example:

> *"I am grounded, like an old growth tree. I am deeply rooted
> and wildly expansive. Today I choose to reconnect with
> the love, joy, and freedom that are my birthright."*

2. Circular Breath: Awaken the Body for Grounding

1 Find a comfortable seat on the floor or in a chair.
2 Set your intention: To spark joy, to ground, and to let go.
3 Take six to twelve deep breaths in through the nose, and sigh out through the mouth. Simply attune to your body as a channel of grace and ease. Let go completely.
4 For two minutes, inhale the essence of joy into your navel center. Exhale to ground your roots down into the earth.
5 Visualize the energy of joy, beauty, grace, and compassion filling up your soul on the inhale, and on the exhale visualize being nourished and rejuvenated at the core of your being.
6 Move your awareness to the four corners of the room, or if outside, to the landscape around you. Visualize the corners as pillars of grounded radiance and vitality. Put a color to this energy.
7 Welcome this colorful energy into your awareness and visualize pulling each pillar into your spinal column as a radiant life force. Let it weave and integrate between your vertebrae. Allow this clean energy to ground towards the earth for her healing. Then allow it

to rise into your heart, your mind, and the stars to connect with the spirit realms.

8　Now visualize the shape of a sphere all around you. Feel the safety of this protective layer, and from the base of your spine, visualize your inhale moving up your spine to the crown of your head. On the exhale, visualize your breath moving from your head down the midline of your body towards your pubic bone.

9　Breathe up your back body to awaken your relations to your ancestry— blood or karmic; your family lineage is supporting you. On the exhale, attune to your unique signature essence and let it become aglow and charged with your good energy.

3. Sacred Sit Spot

Find a space in nature where you can go on a regular basis to meditate. If you don't have access to the outdoors, create a space inside your home. Commit to sitting in this sacred spot once a week for at least 10 to 20 minutes.

1　Put your phone away.

2　Set your intention to revitalize your energy body.

3　Gaze into nature's beauty. Become one with the elements and the seasons. Notice the colors, the shapes, the beauty all around you. Give thanks for this gift of life. Give thanks for your able body that allows you to breathe, to love, and to express. Receive this time. Let all concerning thoughts go, and welcome the beauty of the present moment. This is a deep reset.

Each time you return to this space, choose three things you are letting go of and three things you are inviting in. This will ensure that you stay current to your process, your own grounding, and your ability to align with your spirit.

4. Quartz Crystal Visualization: Connecting from Earth to Spirit Realms

I Find a quiet place where you can relax in a sitting position or lying down.

2 Begin to soften the outer shell of your body and consciously start to activate your breath. Exhale out your mouth to release any excess tension or stress.

3 Set an intention: Call forth a desired outcome. For example:

> *"I am a channel for abundance. I give permission to any residual fear to leave my body now. I am nourished on a soul level. I am grounding into my true nature; my divine essence is rooting to the earth and rising toward the sky."*

4 Imagine a calm and relaxing landscape with a very large clear, quartz crystal before you.

5 Visualize yourself now sitting inside the quartz crystal. This is your healing chamber. Welcome in the energy of this spirit stone. Allow your body to receive its healing quality to expand your consciousness and receive insights from the spirit realms. Welcome the healing of the crystal into the very core of your being.

6 Now bring awareness to the base of your spine and feel a connection between the base of your spine into the crystal, perhaps even further: send your roots through the crystal down into the earth. Welcome the strength of your grounded earth essence. What do the roots look like? What is their texture?

7 Attune to your breath. Begin to slow it down for a count of six on the inhale and six on the exhale. Become aware of your front body, back body, and side body, the space below you and above you.

8 Look around inside the healing crystal. Can you sense, feel, or see any colors emanating from it? Can you sense the colors of the rainbow inside the crystal and welcome them to clear and clean your energy body?

Red: At the base of your spine for grounding and releasing fear.

Orange: In the bowl of your pelvis, lower abdomen, and lower back for creativity, emotional intelligence, and generating abundance.

Yellow: In your solar plexus for inner power.

Green: In your heart and lungs for unconditional love, compassion, and forgiveness.

Blue: In your throat for speaking your truth, listening, and discerning untruths.

Indigo: In your third eye for awakening intuition.

Violet or white: At your crown, for connecting to your compassionate and helping spirit guides, for channeling spiritual energies, and for trusting in divine timing.

9 Now call forth your intention for abundance, for grounding, for the release of fear. Ask for guidance and support from any guides, elements, plants, animal, or mineral allies.
10 Is there a repeating symbol, a flash of a pattern, an outline of a supporting energy? Welcome this.
11 Return to your breath. Release the lower half of your body towards the earth, and lift your upper body towards the sky. Focus your awareness on your navel center, and welcome any symbols, patterns, images, or positive affirmations that come to you.

5. Transform Fear into Abundance: Meditation for Transformation

This can be done indoors or outdoors if you have access to nature. Set your intention as clearly as you can and write it in your journal. For example:

"I am calling in abundance on all levels.
I release fear of lack and scarcity.
I am wildly abundant and deeply rooted to the source of my divine essence."

Altar Creation

1 Collect items from nature to connect with the season. As much as you can, gather fallen items: leaves, flower petals, branches, stones, etc. If you want to pick something living, check with its energetic feel. It may be supportive to you or you may feel it's not necessary. Follow your instincts. This is a creative, conscious, and healing experience.

2 Begin to create your landscape altar; allow yourself to be completely free. There are no rules. Place items in a way that feels good. You can choose any shapes, colors, textures, and structures. You are creating a piece of earth art. Hold reverence in your being for Mother Earth and honor her rugged, wild beauty as you create.

3 If it feels healing, you can represent your relationship to any fears, doubts, stressors, or anxiety currently in your life. The more you can process and not repress these energies the better.

4 How can you represent your relationships: to yourself, to others (partners, children, family, pets, etc.), and to your career?

5 Where can you plant the seeds for abundance? For the release of patterns that are holding you back?

6 Can you portray your relationship with your supporting guides, your relationship to spirit? Offer your whole self to this creative process. Place your hands in your earth altar and begin to slow down your breath. Begin to sense your body as a conduit of abundant energy. Listen for any guiding words, remaining open to repetitive symbols or flashes of light, images that may be like a photograph. This is intuition coming through.

Meditation

1 Connect to your spine and take some deep breaths to establish a connection with the earth. Now, from your navel to your tailbone, imagine a "grounding cord" or "roots" that reach down deep into the earth. Welcome a weighted feeling, like you are unshakeable in your seat.

2 Sense the space you are in, and invite the directions into you as a way to ground and call forth sacred space. Welcome the east—give thanks for another day to rise with the sun and the pure air you are breathing in. Welcome the south—the element of fire and your ability to transform energies that come into your field. Welcome the west— give thanks to the element of water for flow, purification, and hydration; honor the setting sun, the starry night skies, and the mystery and

unknown of the dreamtime. Welcome the north—the earth before you and all around you; the great generator of abundance, the exquisite beauty of the forests, gardens, mountain peaks, fields, and valleys. Welcome the element of ether —a light source plugging into your navel center, connecting you to the expansive, clear, and pure source energy that interweaves all of the elements.

3 Merge all of the directions and the elements into your spinal column now. Visualize all four corners of the compass enlivening your spine. Notice any colors you see. Allow this powerful source energy in and let it integrate by calming your breath.

4 Now visualize the rising of your spinal column from your navel through the crown of your head, like a fountain of clear energy right from your crown towards the sun, moon, and stars.

5 Allow your whole being to receive this abundant elemental energy.

6 Visualize a blue cocoon of energy around your whole body. The chrysalis has edges and form, yet is malleable—it has movement. This will set strong boundaries without cutting yourself off from connecting to both the physical and spiritual realms. Negative energies will bounce off of you with this energetic chrysalis. Open yourself to feel this energetic transmission and recalibration.

Spirit Letter

Write a letter to spirit and read it out loud. Let go of any inhibitions. There is a deep healing and a wild recalibration that comes with this practice. If you prefer, you can improvise and speak your prayer as it comes.

Dear Creator/Earth Mother,

Today as I walk upon your sacred womb, I am struck by your rugged yet refined beauty. I am here, bringing healing to you. I am here, committing to the practices of supporting you as an earth advocate.

Today, I submerge my whole being into you.

I open to your ability to move through the birth, death, and rebirth cycles with strength. I feel your expansive field of abundance. And I align myself with this field of abundance. I call in abundance on all levels now.

Earth Mother, I enter your dark rich nutrient field of energy.

Like you, I am a vessel of wild abundance. I let old narratives of lack and scarcity fall away and regenerate themselves into new seeds of growth inside and out.

I am abundance in all forms.

6. Connect to Your Ancestors

1 Find photos of your ancestors and arrange them on your altar.

2 Represent the four elements on your altar: earth, air, fire, and water.

3 Place a small portion of food on your altar, along with a glass of water.

4 Light your candles.

5 Look into your ancestors' eyes, gaze into the photos, or recall in your memory their characteristics and their mannerisms.

6 Close your eyes and begin to connect with an easeful breath.

7 Welcome your compassionate and loving ancestors into the room. Begin to align your inner radiance with their inner radiance. Visualize being held in a blanket of warmth and love, and extend this energy towards your ancestors. Welcome them to eat and drink from your altar.

8 Pray out loud. Let your ancestors know of all the positive attributes and qualities that you inherited from them that you are carrying into the world. For example, you might say: "I remember the time when…" or, "I remember hearing stories of the time…" or, "I miss you…" This will support you in becoming a channel for their energy to come forward.

9 You may feel inspired to ask for guidance, starting, for example, with these words: "I am willing, ready, and open to receive support and counsel in this area of my life…"

10 Place your hands on your heart, and open your body as a channel to receive any insights, words, colors, patterns, and memories that may come up.

11 Seal your ritual with a prayer for the healing and spiritual evolution that comes through your family line. Trust that you are supported to do good work for your ancestral bloodline to affect positive change in the world.

12 Close the sacred space by thanking your ancestors for being on this journey with you. Blow out your candles and journal about your experience.

7. Journal Prompts

- What nourishes you on a soul level? Take five minutes to write free-flow about all the things that feed your soul. When you finish this, read it over and choose three things that you can activate in the coming week.
- What inspires you to learn more about your personal ancestry? How can you gather that information?
- What family patterns are you ready to heal from?
- How can you improve your practice of recycling and your earth advocacy? Can you commit to this for the next year?
- What activities, experiences, relationships, and habitual patterns are you ready to let go of in your life?
- What grounds your energy and makes you feel like you are living towards your true capacity and potential?
- What brings you lasting joy? How can you commit to sourcing this on a daily basis?

Go forth now, release what binds you—for it is not you anymore.

Draw from the well of life that takes your breath away, brings you to tears, and drops you to the earth in prayer.

What do you have to lose?

THE SACRED MOVES
THROUGH YOU

Mystery occurs quietly,
in small hidden worlds.
From ancient to ephemeral,
in the space between realms
lives magic—
No longer fear something is missing.
Chop wood and carry water,
let this simple task continue.
Go so deep into the mundane
that it becomes sacred.
The micro moments become
the macro cosmic eternal web—
casting out into the abyss
from you, out into the ether.
Striking, isn't it?

Chapter 6

The Sacred Moves through You
Spirit Is Calling

THE UNSEEN REALMS: ANSWERING THE CALL

When aspects of our physical, emotional, intellectual, and spiritual self become out of balance or disconnected, they will call to us in a way that demands our energy and attention. With compassion, mindfulness and a steady mind–body practice, we begin to wholeheartedly answer the call by recognizing where the healing is needed. Once we arrive here, we begin to understand how to align with the unseen realms—the etheric or spiritual forces—for support and guidance. Through observation and the willingness to stay present, the cosmic forces and divine timings come alive all around us.

If we seek to experience life only in the mechanics of day-to-day living, placed inside the black-and-white box of the mundane, our experience will play out through this frame. As we go about following only the routine happenings, we may not be equipped to stay steady when the deeper twists and turns of life take us for a ride—leading to feelings of emptiness, lack, and loneliness. We may turn towards the distractions of media, social life, or constant busyness in order to fill us up. Yet, over time, we may still feel there is something missing.

Perception and perspective are everything. If we become too preoccupied with our personal life, we get caught up in an unconscious bubble where we cannot see through the dense clutter inside our minds. The armor around the heart tightens, we lose our ground. We abandon the flame that lights us up and inspires our soul's mission, and we numb ourselves from feeling and sensing the beauty, truth, and goodness that lives all around us.

If we simply live in the space of the literal, we leave no room for magic to exist. Essentially we cut ourselves off from hearing the whispers of the extraordinary, from the wild, untamed joy, love, and mystery that comes when we open to the numinous happenings that exist all around us. When we shut down, dismiss, or ignore the spiritual forces at work all around us, we miss out on the deeper, richer, symbolic teachings that come through the non-ordinary spaces and places—what can be referred to as the unseen realms.

When we develop a closer relationship to our own centers, a mind–body conversation opens and establishes a living, breathing anchor. We dig deeper and tap into the roots of pure source consciousness—the energy that is independent of wants, needs, or others' influence. It is the energy that grounds us into living an intuitive and spiritual life. If we journey on the surface of the earth only, we may never access the garden of the spiritual life waiting for us. Opening to the magic a child sees in cloud formations, the wonder of the starry night sky, or standing in awe of a breathtaking mountain—this is how we move from the literal to the non-literal. Life begins to take on a deep symbolism when we get out of our heads and allow our felt sense to be touched by the mystery and beauty all around us.

When we open ourselves to trusting in the experiences that do feel sacred or spirited, we begin to receive guidance and support from the non-literal occurrences, and we walk hand in hand into this life with a force greater than we can understand. We climb mountains with spirit at our back, we sit at our meditation cushion surrounded by unspeakable love and devotion. We go to the ocean and offer her rose petals from our beloved gardens, we make ceremonial fires and let go of the ways that no longer serve us.

We call on the divine, our ancestors, and our guides and we honor their support and compassionate work. We take these signs to heart and we open our body as a conduit for energy to sense the magic of source consciousness—pure untapped energy in motion. When we live our life through this lens, our perception shifts and our perspective becomes vast.

Pure source consciousness is the energy of the non-judgmental, non-literal realms. It is like the power of the sun on a seedling, the nourishing soil feeding the roots. Combined with positive intentions and prayers, and aligned with support from the cosmic web of life's body of knowledge, its growth can be immense.

It comes in simple moments, for instance, a flash of a long-lost friend comes across you, and she reaches out the same day. The pull you felt to go on a particular hike, and you were met by an owl. The moment you turn your awareness to the skies, the most stunning alchemy of clouds and light forms. It is as if spirit is speaking to you and reassuring you to trust and love deeply on this life journey.

As we begin to train our inner being to observe the unseen realms at work, we open our life experience to a richer, more fulfilling, and more joyful existence. Everyone's interpretation of this is personal. Some love to dig deeper, while others love to dance with the lighter energies in life. When we release our judgments of others, when we no longer feed the inner critic, the doubt and the fear, we open our mystical channels to a different experience. We begin to dismantle and reroute the limiting thought patterns that doubt our own psychic and intuitive channels. And we listen. Sweetly, softly, with reverence, wonder, awe, and trust, we experience the mystical in the form of the human body.

Daily rituals—be it prayer, meditation, visualization, solitude, quiet, creative practices, or kindness—not only bring you balance and fulfillment, but you receive energy and insight from the unseen realms. You will feel supported on your chosen path when you become a channel for clear and clean energy to move through you. You will make the world a better place as you step in the shoes of your own inner mystic. These shoes have been waiting for you.

It's time. The mystic is knocking at your door. Open the door every morning. Pray at night to let go of the human desire to stay small, stuck in the inner critic. Feed these lower vibrations no more! Heart open, mind clear, body as your temple; spirit calls in the most unsuspecting of places. Listen, love, give and receive in a balanced, respectful, embodied way. The modern mystic is ready to come alive. Can you hear the call? Can you feel the nudge?

Lean into what lights you up and commit to daily acts of compassion and goodness. The healing path, personally and collectively, will be revealed and ignited through your steadiness.

ETHER: UNDERSTANDING THE FIFTH ELEMENT

The fifth element is ether. It is known as the element of spirit. It is every-where, all around us. It cannot be seen and therefore it is not talked about as much as the other four, more tangible elements: air, fire, water, and earth. Einstein spoke of ether as the element that occupies the space between all objects. The Greeks describe ether as higher than the earth plane. In the metaphysical tradition, it is known as the element at the center of sacred space or the life force that lives inside the center of the mandala—which the ancients considered the center of the universe. The colors black and white are associated with ether, and the spiral symbol is used to represent its energy as circles moving inwards, representing never-ending movement. There is an indescribable energy that exists in this fifth element, which can be thought of as the energy that connects all living beings together. All living beings have the alchemy of ether inside them.

Ether acts as a bridge between the earth and the body, between the spirit and the universe. It is a conduit between the body and the soul. Just as the element of air brings perspective, fire offers transformation, water inspires fluidity, and earth evokes grounding, the fifth element of ether brings us to the gateway into the spiritual and soul dimensions.

Think about any experiences in life you have had that you would describe as "spiritual." Did you feel energy in motion? Was there a sense of divine intervention? Or was there an outer-body experience or a shift in your alchemical process or body awareness? This is the energy of ether moving through you. It is wildly mysterious and deeply personal.

For the inner mystic and the inner healer to come alive, we must begin to open our awareness to this element. Begin to observe the body sensa-tions and signals you receive when your breath is full, your heart is beating fast—after exercise for example—or what happens when you are con-sciously relaxed, what sensations arise during sex, or when you are deeply engaged in a creative process. Become the tracker of these subtle energies. Observe them without naming them. Experience them fully with present-moment awareness. The ancients explored various techniques and devo-tional practices to access the ethereal realms and reach states of nirvana.

In thirteenth-century Turkey, the Sufi order of Islam started a medita-tion practice that involved "whirling," a form of turning dance. Wearing long white robes and conical hats, the Sufi "dervishes" would fast for hours before they began their dancing ritual. The intention was to have a transcendental experience of releasing the ego and entering the unseen realms. Thus they experience complete liberation. The whirling dervishes spin and spin until they contact what they perceive as the center of a mandala. Their intention is to connect to the divine mind of the mandala, described as the sacred universal life-force energy. Once this contact is made through the constant spinning, they set their intention to understand the divine will inside the divine mind.

We can recreate these experiences through free movement, trance dance, the use of psychedelics or plant medicine, meditation, breath work, prayer. They can be facilitated by body–mind counselors, Reiki practitioners, and gifted healers. Any of these practices can bring us into an out-of-body experience. During a somatic healing experience—meaning "of the body," ethereal energy allows a powerful healing to take place. It allows stuck traumatized energy to be released out of the body.

The wisdom, mystery, and magic of ether is like a lighthouse in our soul. It lights the way into this energetic realm. These spiritual experiences become available to us when we release our attachment to the outcome. This becomes the journey and the process. Psychics, mediums, channelers, and healers work with the element of ether in order to receive information—to access and communicate with the deceased, to channel light healing energy, and to support others in accessing their own spiritual nature.

These experiences can come through shamanic journeying or visioning sessions, meditations, visualizations, and dreams...the list goes on. We gain insight into our supporting guides, awaken our intuitive nature, reveal a childhood memory; this becomes a step towards our healing journey. A flash of an unborn child comes through long before the child is born. A project or a career opportunity comes in the form of a vision; it strikes us energetically, and images or symbols arise to support our vision. This is the energy of the ethereal realms at work. Begin to observe where this kind of magic exists on a daily basis. This is the training of the inner mystic. How we speak and listen, how we attune to sound, and how we receive and awaken to the resonance and rhythm of life's vibrational waves is a large part of how we embody energy.

The throat and back of the neck is the gateway for the channels of energy that stream from the lower body up into the heart chambers and further up into the mind. This is a two-way channel; the energy patterns in our mind also stream down into the heart center. Personal power, creativity, intuition, and your grounding nature arise from the lower body, and if the channels are clear, they will enliven the heart and pass through the neck/throat and awaken the mind. If solid and connected, the upper realms of the heart, neck, and mind enable you to speak your truth, to listen and call out untruths or exaggerations.

As discussed in previous chapters, the core beliefs that cycle through our body–mind–heart field become our reality. This is why it is so very important to understand the ways in which we speak, hear, listen, and express ourselves in the world—for it has great weight and meaning. Not only are the throat, ears, and mouth the gateway to transmuting our limiting or negative ways of speaking and listening, it is also how we attune to sound resonance and rhythmic vibration—and this becomes the journey into our own personal experience of mind–body–spirit integration.

The art of communication allows us to feel connected in the world. It's a way for us to express our thought process, helping us to make greater sense of our own consciousness as we walk the tightrope between the literal or physical and the non-literal or abstract. The literal and physical planes support the manifestation of the non-literal and the cosmic. When our consciousness dwells in both realms, we are like the artist who receives a vision in the abstract realm and then goes to paint it on the canvas in the physical realm. This is how the mystic observes, dreams, visions, and manifests. Through the vibration of communication, we become attuned to activating and sharing the unveiled visions that come through, without judgment. In order to truly hear and receive these visions, we must have inner solitude and quiet.

In quiet, mindful, nature-infused moments, our internal energy becomes settled in a way that opens our ears to our own intuitive voice. We let down our guard; we allow nature to be the healing balm for our busy minds. Details, stressors, doubts, and triggers begin to fall out of our energy body. The oscillating vibrations that surround us will eventually come together, and over time these energies will entrain with each other. This entrained rhythm occurs naturally when we get intentional and align our own internal rhythms with that of the seasons and the elements. We no longer feel alone, our material searching decreases, and we seek counsel at the seat of our own unique resonance. We open to the macro lens where a greater universal faith exists, one that is endless, ancient, ephemeral, and wildly mysterious, allowing our micro self to merge with this energetic realm. We take a seat in our own hearts, we drink from the endless well of truth, and we become whole through trusting that we are a greater part of the cosmic web that ebbs and flows, ever evolving.

DIVINE TIMING:
YOU ARE THE CONDUIT AND THE CHANNEL

The concept of divine timing awakens a collaborative process within the dance of life. It teaches you how to be patient, to listen, and to activate the universal life-force energy. There are two approaches to being the active creator of your life. One is to have an exact plan of what you want and to execute the plan by taking the steps to get there. The other way is to get connected to your heart and your higher self. Get genuinely clear on the vision, and work to weave these energies together. In collaboration with spirit and your commitment, you cast your visions and prayers out into the world.

When you take the first approach—the exact plan—you may fall victim to pushing, over-pleasing, and dissociating from your true nature in order to achieve the result. You may lose your heart and soul along the way, and find yourself confused, imbalanced and living a life you do not find satisfying; you are not happy or fulfilled. You close yourself off from the signposts that come with living a life based on divine timing. When you live with the attitude that all things will come in good time, or in divine timing, you open yourself to staying devoted to your soul mission while simultaneously listening and sensing the possible rerouting pathways that may actually make your life more joyous and fulfilled.

An example may be choosing a career based on making your family happy, or based on financial security. Yet you find yourself disconnected and not at your full potential while in the job. The external pressures do not meet the internal desires. Then, along comes divine timing with another opportunity to shift your career focus. It comes at you from many angles, you connect with people in that career, you receive an opportunity to begin training or learning more, and you receive an intuitive flash where you see yourself already living out your new career. This is a divine timing intervention, a wake-up call from the universe to follow your dreams and allow them to manifest. This requires inner listening and the development of mindful, intentional, and awakened states. It requires a sensitivity to trust and have courage to live in this realm of possibility.

Divine timing comes to us when we have removed old emotional weight and baggage. And this gives us a beautiful push to keep doing our personal work. As we engage in the healing of our inner child, in the deep work of learning how to love ourselves fully—which actually may be the biggest work of our lifetime—we hear the whispers, see the signals and omens, and experience the shifts in consciousness. The power of observing and inner listening can come through our awakened body–mind channels and our dream states with great potency. Traveling our life's journey through feeling, seeing, and sensing this alchemical process—this is the element of ether at work. It holds a vibration that, when listened to and felt, can change our life. The divine will calls to us in many ways, and it's up to us to attune, align, and hear the call.

You are deeply connected to your environment. Attune your senses to the quiet power of observing the beautiful, the sacred, and the divine in every step and breath you take.

Move from seeing only the ordinary into walking hand in hand with the universal life-force energy that exists all around you.

Grant yourself permission to live a spiritual existence on a daily basis.

Pay attention to the divine timings and the messengers coming to you.

CO-CREATING WITH UNIVERSAL LIFE-FORCE ENERGY: OPENING TO RECIPROCITY

Universal life force is in every breath you take. It is the subtle energy that exists inside the physical, mental, emotional, and spiritual realms in all life forms. At a base level, life-force energy regulates and supports your life, first to experience good health, and then to experience the joy and the peace of mind that comes with a connected, unified, and embodied life force. How we increase our vital life force, through conscious and mindful work, is how we receive feelings of deep love, intuitive mind–body integration, and blessings from the divine. When we show up and do the conscious work on a daily basis, we generate the space to explore inside the stream of unity consciousness within our own unique life-force energy. This space is like the sacred pause in the breath cycle—if not consciously noted, it will be not activated or developed. It is unique to every individual.

The roots of life force exploration date back to the ancients. Mystics, healers, shamans, spiritual leaders, and medical practitioners have always worked with the alchemy of the physical-emotional-mental-spiritual planes in order to restore well-being and vitality to their patients. Historically, every inhabited continent had a cultural context and a system of beliefs in relation to universal life force. There was a commonality in connection to subtle energy, which can be described as the force that generates and sustains all of life. Ancient practices such as breath, movement, prayer towards sacred artifacts, deities, or landscapes, in collective ceremony or individual ritual, were experienced in order to increase and engage with the subtle energy fields.

Indigenous cultures practice oneness with the spirit of the land and towards their people, animals, plants, ancestors, and majestic places in nature; all of these things are believed to house spiritual power. This oneness increases personal life-force capacity and whole-body vitality. These channels become integrated and flow in a way that generates abundance, higher vibrational fields of fullness, wholeness, and mental wellness. It's the difference between living your life from a place of opportunity, faith, and possibility vs. negativity, lower vibrational fields of anxiety, fear, shame, guilt, and toxic mental build-up.

Life-force energy is visible to the human eye on certain levels. We can see when something is vital and healthy, and we can see when something is lacking vitality or well-being. Individuals who are gifted with psychic or clairvoyant abilities may be able to see where the life force is blocked or stagnant and may be able to receive insight on how to remedy this energy.

On a fundamental level, life-force energy is responsible for the health and well-being of the body. Being blocked or disconnected from this energy can result in illness. Finding resonance within our own energy channels is essential for our own healing process. When we anchor into our mindful and soulful practices, our intuition has an opportunity to awaken, our systems have an opportunity to flow together, and we may receive insight into our own healing process.

What if our meditation each morning was to invite our body to unify in such a way that it heals itself? What if we spoke to our body, mind, heart, and our own spirit in a way that was so deeply compassionate and so wildly loving that our systems aligned and we set our healing in motion? When we walk through our daily lives in this space—personal inquiry and reverence towards our whole systems, not just the ache in the back or the anxiety in our minds—we see the potential to heal through the lens of universal life-force energy. Your sacred body will speak to you, grant you colors, resonance, vibration, images. It will guide you in the way you need to be healed if you listen, trust, cultivate, and take responsibility for this relationship between body–mind–heart and personal life force. It's an ongoing conversation. Speak to your own sacred being as if you are speaking to your best friend or the soul mate of your dreams.

You can practice tuning into your own life force by placing your hands on your heart and navel center while in meditation. Over time you will begin to get a sense of what is going on for you. This is how to develop intimacy with your intuition. This is how to practice radical self-love and cultivate a deep reverence for your own vitality. It will speak to you; it will tell you what it needs—rest, better nutrition, prayer, nature time, speaking truth, simplicity, a breakup, a breakthrough, a thirst for learning, loving more. You may have this feeling when you place your hands on someone who is ill. Or naturally place your hands on your body when you get hurt. This is how you attune to universal life-force energy.

Our energy flows into the spaces to which our attention is drawn. Think about energy flowing in only one direction. For example, if we only allow ourselves to believe limiting thoughts or negative viewpoints, this becomes our reality. If we only see from our own viewpoint and base our entire life experience on this attitude, we cannot see where others may be coming from. We get lost in our own forest. There is not a reciprocal relationship with energy.

Visualize your life inside any box you imagine right now. Inside the box is your entire life history, including your dreams, prayers, relationship to your career, higher self, in addition to your secret and shadow self, your connection to past experiences, family, lovers, and your community. And it's all wrapped and tied with a perfect bow (so as not to get too messy). As you are reading this, visualize every side of the box falling open—no more box, even the bottom of the box falls open. Then what? What if? What now? Infinite possibilities zoom into this open space. Your universal life force meets its own receptive channels. We have to truly give ourselves time and space to think and live outside the box.

You now have space and time to give and love freely, space to dream. You can pour compassion, patience, and forgiveness into the complex pieces that are healing. You drink in the richness of the energetic exchange; when it is done without conditions and with pure intention, you can give and receive energy in all forms. Streaming from the core of your goodness, beauty, and truth, you do this freely. You give without asking anything in return. You give out of love and truth.

However, when you give out of social expectations or duty, your shadow side grows, resentment builds, and you begin to project your own shadows and experiences onto others. This clouds your own perception and keeps you living inside the box. It holds you back from living your dreams. When you stay steady on a daily basis, your reciprocal life-force thrives and blossoms. No longer do you have to gather your separate selves, or think one way and behave another, or speak untruths in order to prove yourself or stroke your own ego. Cleaning up your inner dialogue and practicing devotional self-love will radically shift the way you naturally express yourself in the world. Your visions and intentions will come alive in a way that is crystal clear. You will be less fatigued and confused and more powerful as you take action and become the director of your life.

When you stop the pleasing, hiding, numbing, and unworthy game,
your life force instantly grows with a fearless, radiant power, and like
the sun, charges everything around you.

As we attune to the resonant rhythm of the universal life force that surrounds us, we instantly remember that in each moment, we have an opportunity to inhale, exhale, and get truly present. But we forget—damn, we forget again and again! We get busy, stress takes over, our defensive mechanisms rise up, we fall to pieces. Our shadow self begins to feast at our own table. Yet we can shift this perspective very quickly. Can we open to falling into this feast as the *gift?* Because it is at this very moment of falling that we remember how to get back up and return to the source of our inner knowing and flowing. We fall off the path in order to remember how to get back on the path. Failure is no longer a part of this process. Shame, fear, and guilt no longer feast on you. A simple forgiveness card allows you entrance into the world that is ready and waiting for you.

The quiet universal truth of finding beauty in nature becomes our anchor—in the spring seeds rooting and shooting, the summer's wild abundance, the autumn harvest, the warmth of the winter's candles aglow. Our human ability to revel in nature's exquisite evolution, from bulb to blossom, from thunderstorm to rainbow, breeds hope and faith. Every time we forget, may we remember that we too are part of this evolutionary growth. When we shift our viewpoint of lack, scarcity, and negativity towards the wonders of life-force energy, we begin to feel no separation between ourselves and our environment. We know that we are able to weave the hard times, the quiet moments, the chaos, along with the times of breathtaking beauty inside the fabric of our cosmic journey.

We set our boundaries strong and free all at once; we choose which energy to invite into our personal field. Building this connection with our life-force energy not only awakens us to the present moment, it also grounds us and uplifts us. While we cannot control what happens to us in life—nor what happens in other people's lives—we can control how we manage our own. This is the freedom piece in the puzzle. May this bring our inner radiance, vitality, decision-making and visions alive. The ripple effect is strong as Mother Earth, powerful as the oceanic tides, and celestial as the starry night sky. Our life force can and will contribute to the healing of the collective consciousness that surrounds us all. This is an evolved planetary consciousness steeped in great mystery. May we channel this expansion through our own evolved, balanced, and harmonious life force.

BRIDGING WORLDS: PHYSICAL, MENTAL, EMOTIONAL, AND SPIRITUAL CONNECTIVITY

Inside the deepest well of our personal essence lives the capacity to bridge the separate selves of the physical, mental, emotional, and spiritual energies into one cohesive, connected, and unique unit. An intimacy grows inside of us as we begin the process of awakening to our full potential. When we unpack who we are on all of these levels, we see more clearly the personal work that is essential in order to weave ourselves into a space of union within. This becomes the catalyst for traveling to another plane of consciousness. Through the awakened heart, we begin to access routes and pathways toward other levels of consciousness.

This can be an uncomfortable process. Like a snake that sheds its skin only when it's ready, we too will naturally give our attention to the parts of us ready for transformation. This is a process that we can trust—whatever is knocking on your door, pulling on your heart strings, or occupying the monkey dancing inside your mind, that is where you direct your attention. When we work with this body–mind connectivity, we can liberate ourselves from the struggle to fix and heal everything at once. This will only lead to burnout, and generate more anxiety. We may be feeding the greater problem of a divided self. We must remember that patience is our greatest virtue when we are working within the spiritual realms. When we get quiet enough, we can hear which seeds need to be tended to first. There is a sense of spiritual sequencing that lives inside the web of your soul work. Utmost attention must be placed on trusting the inner knowing, the intuition, along with an attuned heart, a clear mind, and a fluid, connected body. These become the rivers that feed the ocean of your body; an ethereal inner to outer, embodied wisdom.

When we are ready and willing to bridge our separate selves into one unit, an invitation will present itself in the form of a shifting viewpoint. This may feel quite different from what you have experienced before in your life. It becomes an inner "felt" sense, and it is authentic and different for each person. When we work with the element of ether and actively place our awareness towards accessing different planes of consciousness, we begin the journey into the mysterious realms of the curious inner mystic. Nothing is to be forced here. All is to be sensed or felt internally. When in a state of mind–body intention, you may feel that your inner body vision begins to align with the force of gravity, as if you are rotating downwards, perhaps down to the center of the earth. Think roots, darkness, and the crystal planes. It may feel uncomfortable at first, but this becomes the invitation to enter into another plane or field of energy in order to access the ethereal energy field.

As you feel your energy pull you down into the center of the earth through this portal, there is a felt sense that you are entering another plane. The physical body does not change or move; this is an internal sensation. This shift in consciousness may feel as if the gravitational energy pull takes you down into the belly of the earth, and you then arrived into the starry night-sky plane. You sense the glimmer of the stars inside your own being—inside your heart, your navel center, your mind, and in your bones. Receive the invitation to swirl this otherworldly formation inside your physical body. You may sense helping and compassionate beings present and ready to support you. They welcome you into this field of consciousness. These beings of ancient wisdom and love are ready to support you.

It is through the practice of unshakeable and wild self-love that you can journey with an open heart and access other levels of consciousness—the fifth dimension or the Akashic fields of consciousness. This becomes the daily journey and the process of integrating the workings of divine timing, present-moment awareness, energy in motion, and the ability to travel through different realms and state changes—all symbolic and characteristic of working with the element of ether. The element that weaves earth, air, fire, and water together—the space between space, the pause of the sacred, the awareness and willingness to engage in the great mystery of the unknown. The cosmic truth teller, the ancient call of healing, the journey backwards and forwards to receive messages. The messenger of truth, faith, goodness, and beauty.

Spirit calls to you in so many ways. How can you listen, soften, and open yourself to answer the call? This daily question, "How is spirit currently knocking on my door?" brings present-moment awareness. It helps us move from the ordinary realms where resentment, fatigue, fear, and inertia can build up. It can replace lower vibrational energies with those of a higher frequency.

This process can take its own shape and form. Like a revolving door, it can come suddenly and knock us over when that door opens, or we may sense hints of light streaming through the crack below the door. Observe when you sense other levels of consciousness around you. This is how you begin to understand how to receive and access the unseen realms. The daily devotional practices, the processing of your emotions, the moments of pause and solitude in the swirl of everyday life; it is here that you begin to cultivate a relationship with the sacred.

Daily soul-care rituals enable us to move through these planes where we can access more expansive states. What we discover over time, with faith, trust, and practice, is that these higher vibrational states are here for us whenever we need them. When we simply ask with pure intention, we receive access and the doors open for us. As life's dramas take over and we get busy, we forget that we have access to these other dimensions. This becomes the work—to remember every single day to take our personal work to our altar, to our meditation cushion, to our journal pages, and straight inside the well of our hearts.

Steps to "State Change" and Access a Divine Portal

The simple formula below helps you to bridge the heart–mind field so that you can organize the whole self together and access the divine energies available to you.

1 **Process + Practice:** Work with your emotions before they get the best of you. Practice present-moment awareness.

2 **Soften + Let Go:** Observe your inner critic, soften your body, visualize yourself free from criticism, and remember that letting go is your super power.

3 **Trust + Support:** Remember your capacity to receive support from compassionate and helping energies all around you. You are supported when you step into this work with consciousness and pure intention to heal and to speak from honesty and truth.

4 **Move Energy + Journey:** When you are ready, shift your perspective by time traveling down to the core of the earth and into the starry night sky: lay down your fears and imbalances, and be open to receive insights that support your core values and soul purpose.

5 **Integrate:** Move back into your life with this knowledge and wisdom, give it the time it needs to integrate and become embodied. Observe how this process shifts your energy. Journal about your experience, and share your learnings with a friend you trust.

The integration of the energetic streams of all parts of your unique self shape-shift and evolve over time. Wisdom comes with life experience, as does the art of embodying the disparate planes in which we feel, sense, and integrate information channeling through us. The organization of the body–mind–heart field bridging into the spirit field is a true mystery, a place where the unknown dwells. When we can continue to return to the center of our own physical bodies, our center of gravity, we inhabit our own life force with rigor, connectivity, and an integration that goes far beyond the intellect.

Each morning, awaken to your own abundant center. Imagine you are literally stepping into the center of a circle or a web that is symbolic and reflective of your own life's journey. Have curiosity and believe you are deeply rooted in your own alchemy, yet you have access to other dimensions for support. The center of the web activates your inner knowing, where you give and receive unconditionally. It reminds you that you are a spiritual being in the form of a human body. It encourages you to take the risks of a spiritual warrior and to soften your own inner critic so that you can become a conduit for intuitive messages to channel through you. This cosmic web reminds you that you are not alone on your spiritual quest.

It holds you in the most tender embrace, whispering the love songs of the ancients into your heart. It guides you to places and spaces where you are surrounded by kindness, grace, and numinous glimmers. The web has unlimited access to the nectar of life's simple joys and greatest mysteries. Step into the circle. Spirit is calling you home.

DEVELOPING YOUR INTUITION: OPENING, BUILDING, AND TRUSTING

Devotion to the divine can be an intuitive practice. When you cultivate a commitment with the divine, an intimate relationship with the sacred runs through you like a river. The quiet pause you feel in the dead of summer's heat, the universal life force that ripples and swirls inside you, sometimes fierce, sometimes quiet—this is what keeps our spirit alive. We rekindle our connection to the pulse that lives inside the roots of the earth, our bones sing, and the steady drumbeat inside our hearts comes alive. We engage and merge with the numinous. We remember faith, receive support from spirit, and above all, we trust the inner knowing that allows us to endure hard times.

The spirit of ether calls to us through all of our ranges, cycles, and dimensions. It sees us inside our present life experiences, understands our past, and knows our future.

When the energy of spirit calls in this way, do no longer ignore the call. This is the inner reckoning, the inner rumble that can be uncomfortable, at times bittersweet or reflective, at others like ecstasy or bliss. It is our sixth sense. Ride the flow of intuitive flashes as they arise—this is how to ignite and engage with rhythm and ritual inside the dance of everyday life.

The gifts from spirit are wildly abundant, each one carefully crafted, designed by intuitive forces, collected for unforgettable reasons—from literal, to karmic, to cosmic, to facts—spirit ignites a unique and unforgettable relationship.

And when fostered, our historical collection of narratives willingly cycle through space and time in order to reclaim the healing necessary to turn the page. A new chapter begins. We do the work so we can continue to evolve, relish, fall, rise, return, and catch a glimpse, and then more, of the new ready to emerge.

THE DANCE OF THE MYSTIC: PRACTICES FOR BUILDING INTUITION

To stay inside the current of our own intuitive experience we must learn to discern what our tricky, ego-fueled mind wants, compared to what our inner knowing wants. This becomes the dance of the mystic. Allow this intuitive dance to be experimental and open to the wonder of a beginner's mind. These varying degrees of intuition can range from literal or direct to non-literal or symbolic. In order to develop, trust, and utilize your intuition, there are some key steps and guidelines to follow. Remember this is a process—a way to work with your own universal life-force energy in order to attain harmony and an alignment of purpose in your life.

Listen to your gut instinct; it really is in your gut, in the area of your intestines. Eat nourishing food and take good care of your body so you can feel more in your belly. Your gut instinct is your superpower. The more you can follow it, the more your intuitive nature will grow.

When you commit to a daily meditation practice, you begin to greet your own energy in a calm, rested, non-productive state. This clears away the tendency to live your life from the reactiveness of stress and anxiety, while training your system to feel intuition. This supports you in discerning between your intuitive voice and your anxiety and fears that want to rule you and cloud your vision. There is a fine line between taking action based on your willpower and acting from your anxiety. Cultivate a daily quiet practice where the intuitive whispers call out to you.

The power of observation is key to understanding your own personal life force and how energy affects everything. Begin to observe your energy levels when you are in the company of others, or when you are engaging in specific activities. Notice when, where, why, and how your energy gets depleted. Observe when you feel grounded, powerful, and connected.

Trust the images that come through you. Catch the flashes—whether they are outlines, light tracers, or flashes of the future. Observe where and when this happens so that you can begin to see from this perspective more often. This is your intuition speaking to you.

There are many practices through which you can experiment with and experience life through your sixth sense in relationship to the element of ether. Intentional and simple rituals will support you in moving from the symbolic, non-literal realms to the more direct or literal messages and calls to action. The following two practices can easily be woven into the rhythm of your day, and that will allow you to get connected, calm, and spacious.

Meditating and creating time for intentional, quiet space can radically shift your energy body and awaken your intuition. When you are in these quiet moments, you may choose to ask for clarity on an event or situation that you are currently experiencing in your life. Go further and ask for a clear intuitive experience about this particular topic in the near future. Let go of the outcome completely. Observe symbols, shapes, colors, patterns, outlines, etc. in your meditation; trust that they are coming into your field for a reason.

Committing to a daily *journaling practice* is a potent way to tap into your creativity and your intuition. One way to connect to the ethereal realms in a journal practice is to write freely and uncensored every morning for at least five minutes. Allow the focus to shift from the events or hardships of life, towards a free-flowing style, as if you are channeling the energy around you, within you, and continue to work with the other elements—earth, air, fire, and water—to connect you to the ethereal and spiritual realms. Immerse yourself in nature's beauty. If it feels right, allow the writing to flow into this question: "What will serve my highest self at this time?" Along with your writing, open yourself to write out symbols, sketches, poetry, etc. Ask yourself: "What would I celebrate, subtract, or add to my current situation?" Listen for the words and symbols that flash before you, and stay open to discerning their meaning.

LEARN TO TRAIN YOUR INTUITION

Consciously place your awareness on your ability to sense, feel, capture, hear, and smell information. Experience this as if it's coming from your sixth sense—the source of your inner knowing. Placing your awareness and attitude in this way will open many doors for you. Trust that your intuitive nature will channel through your body at the most unsuspecting moments—forest walks, witnessing the sunset, on your commute to work, during your solo kitchen dance parties. The work is to stay open and awake enough to feel the surges inside your body.

Your intuitive eye awakens in your meditations to radiate visualizations of health and vitality through your whole body. Your intuitive ear opens into the dreamtime to catch the whispers of guidance, and your intuitive heart becomes the sacred nest in which you channel love over fear. Receive and embody the symbols, signs, omens, shapes, and energies that come through your daily activities. They are coming into your energy field for your healing and for your personal growth and transformation. Allow your senses to guide you on a daily basis. Give them space to grow. Release the desire to be guided by others only, and generate expansion for the quiet power of your own intuitive guide to emerge.

The way we perceive, receive, and interpret energy is wildly unique and fascinating. We build our compassion and letting-go muscles when we understand that every person we know and love experiences life differently than we do. This becomes the baseline towards living with non-judgment, empathy, compassion, and from a space of true, expansive reflection. Our intuition supports our ability to maneuver through life in all of its unpredictable, complex, and mysterious ways. Through visualization, meditation, non-attachment, and the commitment to living and loving from a place of devotion and faith, we start seeing through an expansive looking glass.

However, there are times when the power to visualize gets interrupted or muddled, places where our vision gets muddled, murky. We may even self-sabotage the vision. When we can take a good hard look at this, we find the path towards clearing the debris that culminates inside our psyche—be it unconscious or conscious.

Fear, anxiety, doubt, and guilt come into play here. Lack of clarity or confusion about what we actually want will also deeply affect our ability to manifest through our visualizations. These energies rule and feed our tricky mind, attaching to our ego like glue. The work to clear the glue is well worth the effort—it's what can liberate us from playing small and leading unfulfilling lives. It can free us from over-working or running in circles and repeating past patterns. If we continue to set goals and put our visions out into the world, but we still don't believe we deserve this or are capable of it, we block our dreams.

Interferences could also come from others. This is potent to recognize—not to put the power in others but to understand the energetic environment in which you live in the present and lived in the past. Attuning to your personal vibration will allow you to feel others' vibration. This is a win-win situation. Your own energy levels will tell you whether this energy is supporting you or taking away from you. We cannot change how others see us and approach us, but we can change how we show up for ourselves and make our decisions based on this information. We can choose to breathe peace, happiness, and joy into our homes and hearts.

This is where we come back to looking at our limiting core beliefs and how they affect our life. Inside this wellspring of material, we have an opportunity to gather our courage and generate lasting transformation so that we can live out our birthright. This life is an invitation and an initiation to touch upon both what liberates us and what binds us. It's the space between the wild expansions and the complex contractions; it's about navigating our higher self through the realms of the still point and the wild.

We come into this life to feel deeply, to heal, and to express our soul fully in this incarnation. When we tap into the roots of our instincts, tracking like an animal, fiery and fierce, soft and sensual, from the literal and mundane to the symbolic and cosmic—we spark the flame that lights our way to see with clarity. This becomes the gift that we receive when we listen and attune to this journey. We begin to trust our instincts, and through this, we live out the life we want, not the life we were falsely striving for or the life that was expected of us by others. Track the interruptions, the tests, the hard times and the complexities of life like a dedicated mother wolf sourcing food for her babies. This becomes the material in which you follow your inner compass and find your way towards the next portal. When we meet our resilience with openness as opposed to a hardening, and trust that this is the essential fuel necessary for our personal evolution, we can move out of that state more quickly and effectively.

Accessing the still point with ease and enjoyment becomes the path and the process. The place where the sacred pause meets the universal life-force energy; the pulse that lives inside the roots of the earth, our ancestral bones, and the beat inside our heart. It is here that we engage with the sacred. We remember faith, we feel held in this liminal space, and above all, we trust in our own inner knowing that allows us to endure hard times. We are reminded that each cycle, so unique and unforgettable, is a part of our collection of stories—a new chapter ready to begin again.

Seeing and living through our intuition is fiercely subtle. Through training our minds to empty of clutter, we can learn how to focus our minds beyond the literal and the high-drama demands—we can see what is happening before us, just the way a best friend could give counsel. This is the work of the intuitive. We must practice in order to see. Take the seat inside your soul, begin to visualize your dream life from a place of honest clarity, grounding, curiosity, creativity, and inner strength. This is where you find the space of illumination and inner beauty that ultimately leads to living a joyful, meaningful, and fulfilling existence.

CULTIVATING FAITH:
THE SPIRALED JOURNEY OF SPIRIT

As you mature naturally through life experience, so does your relationship to personal faith. Be it secular or religious, whether it's found in nature or at the church, be it under the light of the full moon's call or gathering for a sacred meal. Your faith may be found inside the quiet of daily meditation practice or in your evening prayers. Be it fire ceremony, sweat lodge, tea ceremony, yoga practice, playing music, ecstatic dance, or kitchen dance parties. Be it your journal practice, turning pottery, or summiting a mountain.

What is your conscious practice where you build your house of faith? Where do you fill yourself up on a soul level? What consciously and wholeheartedly lights you up and brings you lasting joy? It is a truly personal and unique experience to call forth your core values, find the faith in which they exist, and devote to this practice. If you do not have faith, you risk losing connection with your elder wisdom and the deepening of an embodied joy. You open yourself up to a path of resentment and negative bias, which leads to limiting, habitual patterns.

Through faith, all of your life experiences begin to weave together and make sense. You grow to be at peace with of all the choices you have made. Honor your life journey as a spiritual quest, flowing in and out of the literal to the symbolic realms, working with the daily tension between effort and ease, productivity and grace, levity and gravitas. This becomes the process, the daily work, and the journey.

You are not alone on this journey. When you can follow the path of faith that truly lights you up, holds you in your sacred power, gives you freedom to be who you are, and connects you to a higher power—this is the path of the modern mystic.

This is how we can enhance our personal faith, which ultimately contributes to raising the collective vibration. We become messengers of peace over war, love over hate, and wisdom over ignorance. We do the work so all sentient beings benefit.

This would make our ancestors proud. This would warm the hearts of our guides, the mystics, and the ancient ones gathering around the fire as they discuss the secrets of the world and send us signs to guide us to the next portal of humanity.

Part of the connection that tethers us to our faith is the support we feel on our spiritual journey. This becomes a very personal experience, and each of us finds our own way to the temple on spirit mountain. When we get settled into our faith, when we engage in our soul-fueled practices and allow them to become embodied, we arrive home, again and again. For some this could be a forest walk, for others attending church, or greeting the morning with a candle, tea, and meditation. Whatever this may be for you, with consistency and dedication, the body of faith grows strong and we find the resiliency to weather the strongest storms. We find delight in nature's beauty, and we surround ourselves with the teachers, leaders, and mentors whose message holds resonance and enlightenment. For some, the spiritual quest takes many paths, follows diverse lineages, and threads together a personal devotion that gleans the gold of many traditions. For other folks, one particular faith becomes the strong line that holds the spirit body.

Once faith is restored, grown, sculpted, and practiced in a way that is no longer questioned or abandoned, a deeper level of embodiment takes place. This practice brings not only hope on a daily basis, but an infusion of living grace and integrated resilience that allows us to travel up and down the spirit mountain. We no longer forget; we continue to remember where, when, how, and why we seek counsel through the energy available to us.

You may find support along the journey in opening the cosmic spirit web to communicate with ancestors, spirit guides, angels, gods, goddesses, creator—one who has a thousand names, yet is nameless. This is the spiraled journey of spirit. It is not one path, nor is it a straight line. If you begin every morning with one minute of prayer/intention, you may find yourself more open to receive the insights or messages that will support and restore your faith.

Dear Spirit,

Here I am, ready to receive support today. I am open to hear, see, and feel the teachings coming to me. Guide me to the spirit mountain for I am open to the journey.

This kind of devotion grants you the attitude and alignment necessary for you to work with all of the energies in your life—the good, the hard, the visible, and the unseen. This is the bridge towards calling in other supporting energies in the spiritual realm. You may feel strongly about honoring your ancestors, and maybe one ancestor in particular guides you. You can visualize their face and let them know you are there, ready to give and receive support. You may be connected to the elements—earth, air, fire, and water—and you find yourself going into nature to tap into the wisdom energies present.

The divine timings, the animal spirits speak to us; they visit us up on spirit mountain every time we go to be immersed in nature. We can speak our prayers and our questions to the altar of each element, bringing offerings. It may be that our faith is inspired by the pastor, rabbi, monk, nun, or the yoga teacher, the counselor, the poet, or the artist. These teachings become the catalyst to taste spirit, to feel it swirl concentric circles inside our vessels. When we can find the deeper callings to faith, not to blindly follow, but to learn and be fully engaged, our systems align, energies merge, and we land inside spirit mountain with a basket full of curiosities supported by a circle of our supporting guides. There we no longer hunger or thirst.

We are no longer lost—we remember we must continue on the spirit journey every day as if it's our first one. The beginner's heart–mind takes you on the journey every day, surrounded by supporting guides that give you standing ovations for your commitment, guiding you to the support systems within your own body of knowledge and the support of your faith community.

When you close your eyes and visualize your most loving guides cheering you on, who is there? Begin your conversation with them. What exactly do they look like? How do they hear you calling? How do they support you? What is so unique about their essence? How do you communicate with them?

When you open your vision field to work in this way, you will see and feel more spiritual support surrounding you. From the owl, the eagle, the wild rose, fossilized stones, and snake energy, to an ancestor or karmic guides, each of them has a specific feeling and symbolism. Symbolism matters. It allows the intuitive voice to guide you towards your own spirit mountain. You can attune to this practice by closing your eyes and connecting to what animals or landscapes would most support you in your life at this time. What essence do they bring to you? Reflect on their symbolism and invite them all into your spirit web as you bow with humility and pure joy every time you catch a glimmer of their presence and every time you receive a message.

Rituals for Calling In Spirit

Grow your daily intuitive capacity, connect to the etheric realms and become a bridge for physical, mental, emotional, and spiritual energies to align and become embodied. Discover rituals of sound resonance, song, breath, dance journeys, and dream states to ignite transformative mind–body states and generate powerful healing techniques.

1. Unity Breath Activation: Ignite Your Life-Force Energy

1 Find a comfortable seat, light a candle, welcome the present moment, let go of your daily roles and responsibilities, attune to your breath, and connect to the bounty of universal life-force energy.
2 For inspiration, think about your favorite space in nature, the place that feeds your soul. Set your intention to raise your personal frequency through breath and vision.
3 When you feel settled, bring your palms together and vigorously rub them to generate heat. Cup your hands over your eyes, breathe in universal life-force energy, and breathe out universal life-force energy. Repeat this three times.
4 Bring your palms to touch in front of your heart. Circle arms out to your sides and above your head, bring palms to touch, and pull them down the midline of your body. Repeat circles 6–12 times inviting life-force energy in.
5 Continue to breathe deeply and visualize your whole body merging with a field of light-force activation—pure clean and clear

high-vibrational energy waves, like sunlight streaming from your navel center.

6 Place your left hand on your heart and your right hand on the earth. Breathe fully and let go of anything you are holding on to. Let go of grief, fear, and the need to control.

7 Reach both hands to the sky and open yourself as a channel of receptivity. Expand your inhales and exhales—make them big and full.

8 Open to become the conduit between the ethereal realms, and the universal life-force energy all around you.

9 Give yourself time to connect to this energy. Take pauses when you need to. Can you see, hear, or sense any shifts in your energy body?

10 Are there any colors, symbols, or messages that want to come through you?

11 Ask for support from your guides and your intuition for this cycle in your life.

12 If there are words or prayers ready to be expressed, speak them aloud or write them in your journal. These moments are sacred, they matter, and they contribute to your personal evolution.

2. Vibrational Sound Resonance: Clearing the Throat Center

Intention
To connect with your voice, to raise your life-force energy,
and to connect to the intuitive and unseen realms. In this exercise,
you will use a series of sounds to connect with the elements
and specific energy centers, starting at the base of the
spine and working up to the crown.

This is quite a personal practice—find a way to express yourself that feels liberating and satisfying.

This ritual can be done seated, lying down, or standing with movement.

Generate the sound of the energy center as shown below, connect to its elemental property, and sense into its property. Let the sounds come out freely, three to six times per location.

Sound	Instruction	Energy Center	Element	Quality
O	As in 'om'	Base of the spine	Earth	Grounding
U	As in 'you'	Lower abdomen	Water	Creativity
A	As in 'may'	Solar plexus	Fire	Inner power
Ah	As in 'awe'	Heart and lungs	Air	Compassion, self-love, forgiveness
E	As in 'tree' (with high pitch)	Throat, neck, shoulders	Ether	Speaking and listening for your own truth
Mm	Humming 'mm'	Center of forehead	Light	Intuition
Ing	As in 'wing'	Hands over head, lifting from the crown	Stars, moon, sun	Transcendent consciousness

Mantra Medicine
Intention
To transform lower vibrational energies to higher ones and
inspire present-moment connection, faith, and grounding.

Mantras can be used to open or close a ritual or a ceremony; they are a powerful way to embody the resonance of the element of ether. Mantras can be spoken, chanted, or sung. It is the repetition that allows the mind–body state to shift into another vibration.

Self-Affirming Mantra

I am the light of my soul
I am radiant
I am rested
I am spacious
I am, I am.

Repeat at least six times. This practice is for all levels, ages, and stages in one's life. It is powerful for children and youth to discover a self-affirming mantra that supports their highest essence. And for anyone going through hardships, trauma, grief, and times of transition, this becomes a powerful way to transform energy.

Write your own personal affirmation and put it into a mantra or a short series of sentences that you can repeat.

Make up your own or use this as a guideline:

> *I am the _____ of my soul,*
> *I am _____,*
> *I am _____,*
> *I am _____,*
> *I am, I am.*

Short Mantras and Chants from Around the World

Repeat each mantra or chant for two to four minutes until it becomes so deeply embodied and integrated that you feel a shift in your energy body. Let it take you over completely, and welcome the freedom that comes when the mind becomes still and the body–heart field grows.

Celtic Pagan Chant

This body, this temple, this is the goddess/god in me.
This breath, this spirit, this is the goddess/god in me.

First Nations Chant

Earth my body,
Water my blood,
Air my breath,
Fire my spirit.

Hopi Prayer

I walk in beauty,
Beauty before me,
Beauty behind me,
Beauty all around me.

Om Mani Padme Hum

Tibetan Buddhist in origin, this mantra translates as "the jewel that resides within the lotus flower." Visualize a lotus flower with a glimmering jewel in the center of your heart. This symbolizes unconditional love and universal wisdom.

Om Shanti Shanti
A Hindu chant meaning "I am peace."

Ahim Prema
A Hindu chant that translates as "I am divine love."

If it feels better for you to sing and dance to recorded music, find soulful music that opens your heart, and sing along and move your body. There is so much healing in singing, dancing, and finding expression through voice.

3. Spirit Is Calling: Honoring the Ancient Ones

Intention
A visualization and prayer to open you to the ethereal realms
and to honor the ancient ones who came before us.

1 Find yourself in a comfortable seat. Begin to slow down your breathing and relax your whole body.
2 Visualize an umbilical cord from your navel center, both in the front and the back of the body.
3 This cord expands like a cosmic web from earth to sky, from the ordinary to the spiritual realms, from east to west, north to south, sunrise to sunset.
4 Each part of the web was spun as your lifeline to your most ancient self. Honor the blood and bones of your ancestors, your karmic guides—the stardust and stone of the ancient ones living inside you. This widens your lens, grounds you into real time, allows you to remember, feel, sense, and see where you came from and where you are going.
5 Call forth a prayer from within this cosmic web, and step into the field of gratitude and grace.
6 Listen for a call to action; you may receive insights or images to support your service to the world at this time.
7 Allow yourself to soften and become fluid.
8 Ask for guidance and support from both the physical and spiritual realms.
9 Return to a state of gratitude; practice non-attachment by letting go of any outcomes.
10 Seal your prayer, giving thanks to all of the energies supporting you.

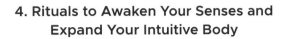

4. Rituals to Awaken Your Senses and Expand Your Intuitive Body

Intention and practice

Make a date with your intuition. Consciously engage in these activities without wanting a final outcome. Follow the desire, release the outcome. As you experience these open-ended practices, place your attention on attuning to your senses to enliven your intuitive nature. Put your devices away and enjoy the freedom of being free inside the creative process.

Dance Journey

Intention

To release tension, be fluid, and open the channels to your intuitive body.

1 Prepare a playlist or put on a track of music that is long enough so you don't have to get on your device.
2 For at least 15 minutes, let yourself dance to the music.
3 Place your intention on freeing up the channels in your body and inviting in flow. If you are in a large enough space, you may want to move with your eyes closed.
4 Let your mind be free, integrate the radiant and free channels inside your body, let your heart speak to you through your movement, and dance as if your soul is coming home.
5 Instead of making beautiful dance moves, follow the natural impulses that arise and allow them to be expressed.
6 Letting go of any final outcome and moving with a sense of freedom will naturally allow your intuitive field to expand.
7 When complete, come to the still point and journal.

Journal Questions

- What would my intuitive self tell me now?
- What specific area in my life—intimate relationships, career, personal health, etc.—can I direct my attention towards at this time?
- Is there a specific resonance, symbol, practice, or direct call to action that would support me?

Heart Meditation Journey
Intention
To enliven your intuitive nature and expand your capacity to love.

Purpose
To call forth an intuitive prayer to magnetize your heart field.

1 Prepare a cozy space for you to sit in for a 15-minute meditation.
2 Set your timer. Light a candle.
3 Call in your compassionate and loving guides to assist you in your journey.
4 Begin by placing your hands on your heart, and slow down your breath to a count of six on the in-breath, six on the out-breath.
5 Breathe in the essence of love and compassion, and breathe out the essence of love and compassion.
6 Call to your higher self to accept this invitation of deep unconditional love and allow its vibration to integrate into every cell in your body.
7 Place your hands in a comfortable position on your lap.
8 Visualize your heart now like a nest and attune to something that you love deeply. This could be something from nature, for example a rose.
9 Visualize the rose being held inside the nest, expanding its radiance, vitality, and beauty as you tend to your breath.
10 Naturally, this energy becomes magnetic inside your heart field. Let it grow and grow.
11 Call forth a heart prayer from your intuition. Speak the prayer inside or even out loud.
12 How was the prayer received? Can you let it in fully?
13 Observe what thoughts, symbols, and energies present themselves.
14 Seal in the sacred space, visualize your room filled with radiance. Thank your guides for their support and honor your intuitive power.

Journal Questions
- What would my intuitive heart speak to me now?
- What will serve my heart capacity to grow and expand at this time in my life?
- Is there a direct call to action or a guiding affirmation that will restore my heart's capacity to love fully at this time?

Walking Journey
Intention
To explore, be open to how your senses direct you,
to feel spacious, to let go of all your agendas, and
to awaken your intuitive nature to guide you.
This can be done in nature or in the city.

1 Set out on your journey like an explorer. Allow yourself to simply be guided by the trail, the next street corner. Find delight in following the pull of your own center of gravity. (If you're on a hike, make sure you have a map just in case.)

2 Allow your navel center to be your guide. Let your mind simply relax.

3 Attune to your senses and feast on this freedom—no hidden agendas or motivations. Pause when you want to, find a pace that feels right, untangle yourself from the stressors of everyday life, engage in the beauty before you.

4 Each step, remind yourself to walk in the field of the universal life-force energy all around you.

5 You are held in beauty and grace. You are a moving vessel of strength and unconditional love. Your heart–mind field is a source of spiritual embodiment. Vast, free, and curious. See through the wonder of a child's eyes. Be free—there is no final destination.

6 Look up often at the sky, see how the cloud formations shift. Sense the *prana* in the earth. Observe what is growing at this time; ingest the colors. What does the air feel like on your skin? Do you feel the force of the sun's radiance? Or is the moon visible in the sky? Is there a place where you can take a rest?

7 Notice the mind's pathways. Is there a thought that feels persistent? Is there a message coming through you? A letting go, an understanding, a direct call to action, a prayer? A moment of profound insight? Are there any messengers from the plant or animal world? Do any earth angels or human messengers spark something inside you?

Journal Questions
- What did you notice through your experience?
- Was there a feeling of being directed by your center rather than your mind? How did that feel?
- Was there a moment of insight, awakening, or letting go?

Dream Journey
Intention
To invite your intuition to be the messenger inside
your dreams, to support you in clearing out everyday fears
and stressors in order to rest well and open the bridge
towards intuitive dream reflections.

1   Have a journal beside your bed.
2   Do a five-minute conscious relaxation in bed with the intention of
    letting go of daily concerns, resting deeply, and opening a portal
    towards your higher self in order to receive intuitive guidance.
3   After the relaxation, write in your journal what you wish to let go of,
    how you intend to rest deeply and restore your vitality. Ask a specific
    yet open-ended question around something you are looking to gain
    insight into. For example, "I ask for guidance on the direction of my
    spiritual evolution at this time. I call upon my loving and helping guides
    to attune my body–mind–spirit into the vibration of healing, resting, and
    receiving. Sweetly now I rest.
4   There may be an affirmation that will support you into the letting-go
    and resting state. Repeat it three times.

Peacefully now I rest,
Peacefully now I rest,
Peacefully now I rest.

5   When you wake in the morning, welcome a state of unconditional
    gratitude, even if you didn't get a great night's sleep. As you awaken, you
    may remember your dreams. Journal about them.
6   Consciously begin to welcome in this new day. Call forth this prayer:

I step into my day with gratitude for being alive, opening myself
fully to receive all of the messages, teachers, and insights ready to emerge.
I will give and receive equally. I will rest and activate equally.
I will listen to all the messengers, in all the forms they come.

7   You may remember some of your dreams throughout the day. Write
    them down as soon as you remember them. There may be insights for
    you. This practice will highly charge your intuitive channels.

5. Guided Journey:
Embodying the Elemental Spirits as Teachers

Intention

To receive guidance, to let go of the old, and to welcome a
cosmic reset in one's current life journey. This can be done
seated, lying down, or expressed through movement.

1   Create an altar that represents earth, air, fire, water, and ether. You may
    wish to have some drumming music playing to foster a steady heartbeat.
    Clear the energy in the space by opening the windows or by burning
    incense, herbs, or essential oils. Light your candle and call forth sacred
    space. Welcome the four directions and the elements as your teachers.

2   State your intentions out loud. If you are doing this in a group, each
    person takes a turn to share by passing a sacred item around the circle.
    You may want to share one energy you are releasing and one energy
    you are inviting in.

3   Bring your awareness to the base of your spine. Send your grounding
    cords into the earth. See them transform into a supporting root
    system deep inside the belly of Mother Earth. Send your awareness
    into the womb of the earth as you soften your whole body and
    breathe deeply.

4   Visualize the spirit of the earth. Is there a shape or a form in the earth
    that can now become your guide? Open to a compassionate and
    supportive earth spirit. Is there a face, an outline, a landscape? This
    earth guide is ready to support you now.

5   Bring your awareness to your pelvis. Imagine it's filled with high-
    vibrational water. Feel its movement; you may even sway with its flow.
    Visualize bodies of water—oceans, lakes, rivers, streams, waterfalls.
    Allow yourself to feel internally nourished and hydrated by them. Now
    see the spirit inside the water. What shape, outline, form, energy does
    it take on? This is a compassionate and wise water spirit, and it's ready
    to support you now. There may be the image of a gift or a message that
    comes through the water to support your highest self.

6   Bring your awareness to the center of your body and visualize a
    flame just above your navel center. Upon each inhale the flame grows

brighter, and with each exhale the flame becomes refined. Visualize a fire in front of you, and welcome the supportive spirit inside the fire. Connect your flame with that of the large fire before you. What shape, energy, outline, form does the compassionate fire spirit have? It will support you in your ability to transform energies rapidly. What energy would you like to transform in this moment? Give it to the fire. Watch it burn. See inside the flame. What message are you ready to receive?

7 Take intentional, slow breaths, filling out the capacity inside your heart, lungs, and upper chest. Welcome the element of clean, pure, air into your whole upper body. Allow the vastness of the blue sky to swirl inside you. Connect to the spirit of air as a compassionate guide. What shape, form, outline, or energy does it take on? Let this supporting teacher cleanse and awaken your heart center. What wants to be released? What wants to be expressed? What wants to grow? What does your spiritual heart want to share with you? Take all of this to heart, for the sky is a great teacher and guide.

8 Bring your awareness back to your navel center. Imagine a web streaming from the center of your body, all around you. The web is supporting your current journey. Feel it below, above, in front of you, and behind you. Welcome the element of ether—the sacred, the unseen, the mysterious. Let it swirl through your mind, washing it clean of negativity. Let it become a light source at your third eye. Welcome ether to clean your throat, so you may speak your truth and be impeccable.

9 What shape, color, form, outline, or energy does the compassionate spirit of ether become for you?

10 Weave this spirit down through your spinal column into the roots of the earth—go there with the force of ether. From the darkness of the earth's womb, look up and discover the portal into the starry night sky. Now allow your whole being to be bathed in the light of the stars. Welcome their alchemical medicine into your soul. The formation of stars embedded in your cellular memory comes alive.

11 Receive this transmission and let it swirl into every crevice of your body. Weave the stars into your spine, your heart, and the pathways inside your brain.

12 What is the teaching in this moment? Are there symbols, words, shapes, flashes, outlines, animals, ancestors, guides, landscapes coming to you?

13 Soften your whole body as a channel of elemental wisdom, receive fully, allow your experience to be integrated. Merge with the earth, air, fire, water, and ether energy once again.

14 Take six expansive breaths and return to the earth energy below you.

15 Come back to a seated position and gaze at your altar. How do you feel?

16 Seal your sacred space by giving thanks to the teachers and guides present. Merge with the earth, air, fire, water, and ether energy once again.

17 Journal about your experience.

6. Journal Prompts

- What were the most memorable spiritual moments in your life, when you felt there was another presence or energy guiding and supporting you?
- How did these moments affect your life?
- What did you learn?
- What kinds of self-care practices nourish you on a soul level?
- What kinds of activities do not serve your highest self at this time?
- When and where have you felt your intuition call to you? Name the particular time and the conditions.
- What is your intuition saying to you at this time in your life? Are there any ways you can support the activation, clarity, and expansion of your intuitive nature?
- What are the soul gifts that you were born with? How can they support and influence your life and the world at this time?
- Journal about the qualities of each part of you: physical, emotional, intellectual, and spiritual. Reflect on each of their superpowers or their most connected qualities—what you love about them. What are the pieces that do not align with your core values? How can you work towards aligning each part of you with your core values and your embodied beliefs?
- Are there any daily rituals you can do to begin bridging towards wholeness and embodiment of all parts of you? Let this inspire you to weave your whole self with your balanced, aligned, and compassionate essence. Write your calls to action and put them up in a place where you can see them often or take them to your altar.

Her anointed heart temple speaks omnipotent truths.
The mystical planes in which she travels leave hints of ambrosial dreams,
a realm in which all worthy visions swirl into life.

Incantations chanted by the ancients push her forward,
dimensions open like a compass inside her mind.

A shrine of numinous reckoning, transcending time and space,
the galactic door swings open.

A holy remembrance of otherworldly wisdom,
traces of mother of pearl nectar seep into her soul
(like universal truths).

Her gifts too sublime to speak, an inner knowing so regal,
her etheric body, a force of celestial light.

Her devotional touch leaves a trail of stardust,
golden threads merge and weave in all directions—
inside, above, below, behind and ahead.

Tethered to the source of life itself,
a transcendental creature awakens,
the inner mystic birthed into her own oceanic,
cosmic incarnation.

THE MOON'S CYCLE

To believe we are composed only of love and light is an illusion.
There will always be darkness and shadow.
Even on the darkest of nights, the moon remains,
invisible, yet a force to be reckoned with.
Her unleashed wild swells pull and tug us alive.
Ever evolving, an intricate orb of majestic luminosity.
Want to be like the moon?
Build your letting-go muscles, face your fears head on,
trust in divine timing, and observe life's synchronicities
with a keen inner eye.
The signs and signals are everywhere,
they will come to you when you accept them.
Become a conduit of resilience, resourcefulness, and compassion—
this is how you get to the love and light.
This is how to find a joyful existence amongst the most reckless of storms.

Chapter 7

The Moon's Cycle

Ancient Wisdom for
Transformation and Renewal

THE LUNAR EFFECT:
SOURCING PURE CREATIVE ENERGY

Everything in our world is constantly shifting. While it all may seem wildly complex, the moon, the sun, and the stars provide a steady rhythm for our lives. The moon is our compass in the night sky to evoke wonder, awe, and a deeper understanding of life's great mysteries. A way to make meaning of our own cosmic rhythms, a vibrational force so strong it pulls our own tides into awakening. We find comfort and counsel in the moon's celestial reflection, contraction, expansion, and mystical beauty.

Since the beginning of time, humans have gathered under the light of the moon to share stories and songs, to attune to the rhythms of Mother Nature, and to bring forth the power of the divine feminine.

There is something wildly sacred that happens when we gather during the full or new moon cycles. The moon is the ruler of the waters and water governs our emotions. So we can physically get attuned to the waters inside our bodies and consciously create a container for our emotions to be held in a healing way. During the full moon, we are naturally more intuitive, receptive, and creative. The new moon phase brings new beginnings when vision seeds can be planted—a time to fill our internal well with conscious rest and reflection. When we create intentional soul care rituals under the light and dark forces of the lunar mystic, we unearth a deep inner listening and answer a call to our most fulfilled life.

There is a beautiful vulnerability that comes through our whole being when we can directly and radically state what is moving through our emotional, spiritual, physical, and mental state. When we can reveal to our own self, or share with a circle of like-minded beings, how we really feel and what is honestly going on in our lives. We free ourselves from negativity or imbalance and begin to direct our feminine power towards light, love, and transformation.

Every 29.5 days the earth receives the full cycle of the moon's magnetic gravitational force in all of its phases. Through this cosmic journey, the moon shines as its surface reflects light from the sun. The sun creates the moon's darkest shadow to its greatest light—from new moon to full moon and back to new moon. We too receive the celestial wonders as we attune with the moon's cycle from the darkest of night skies to the most illuminated. Bearing witness and aligning with this monthly calendar lets us touch those dark, mysterious places inside of us where raw creative energy is unleashed.

The moon becomes our timekeeper, our tracker, gatekeeper, twin flame, soul teacher, and numinous guide. The moon is always there, ready to pull us back towards our own medicine. The teachings from the moon evoke present-moment awareness and inspire us to be wildly creative, mysterious, deeply reflective, and revealing all at once. Lunar wisdom reflects back to us the teachings of liberation as we consciously acknowledge what binds our personal freedom. We can evolve as we revolve around her majestic strength and wisdom.

The new moon is a cycle of beginnings. A new chapter ready to be written. A reclaiming of truth, compassion, inner alchemy, and unleashed self-love. She holds the divine feminine in ways that can disrupt and shape-shift the very core of who we thought we were. What if every new moon you set an intention to pause, soften, and embrace the energy of your authentic divinity?

The full moon is a cycle of expansive manifestation and illuminated source energy. A time when we receive intuitive reflections and awakenings on how to align with our highest essence. We remember our vitality, our ability to thread our outer expressions back towards our internal prayers in order to live our fullest life. What if every full moon you created space to reflect on what no longer serves you and intentionally stated what you want to invite?

The lunar effect is pure creative alchemy. Her feminine energy matches that of our feminine archetype; her reflected cycles can become our guide in the night sky. Lunar wisdom reflects back to us how to stay steady and connected with our deepest soul stirrings. When we refine our moon work practices, our purest intentions will directly feed the foundations of both our strength and our softness in order to achieve our dreams.

The moon's cycle becomes a spiritual compass. A bond of source energy that is both simple and complex all at once, just as human nature is both simple and complex all at once. The quiet beauty of communing on both the new and full moon every month is to sit inside the well of our personal medicine. This intentional and simple moon work builds into a steady rhythm throughout our life. When we can devote our attention to rhythms sourced from the contraction of the new moon to the expansion of the full moon, we align with the universal life-force energy. Our lunar musings become our soul work.

The moon is a teacher of time, a mirror that reflects our questions, desires, healings, and intuitions back to us—an oracle of sorts. Here we can lay down our entanglements, our complexities, and marvel at the source of life's great mysteries. We train ourselves to observe the simple rhythms of inhale to exhale, expansion to contraction, and light to dark—the journey of life towards death. We begin to see the beauty inside all of the realms.

Answer the call to sit by the fire of your own heart as you cycle through the moon's journey. Be like the warrior, the mother, the maiden, the crone, and the elder in the sky. Tend to your life's calling to nourish, create, and slay the darker forces that may come knocking at the door. Face your fears head on. Muster the courage it takes to toss the lower vibrations into the fire. Visualize them burning up in the flames.

Gather the intuitive messages that are nudging you right now. Lean into this space with the intrigue of reclaimed ancient treasures. These relics are the keys towards unlocking your inner power and your deepest source of love. Curiosity and fear cannot exist inside the same energy channel. As a guiding rule, lean more into curiosity and less into fear. Be as active in the power of observation as in the power of activation. Adorn your inner temple as much as your outer altar.

The moon calls in the darkest of nights. Come home, sweet one, for it is time to work your magic far beyond the earthen realms. Cast your prayers deep into the ether. Get intimate with the core of your own essence. Here inside the very center, the divine feminine spins her web, reminding you of all things cosmic and mysterious. Enter this realm. You will never go back.

ANCIENT CULTURES AND LUNAR SYMBOLISM

The moon's cyclical rhythms have always intrigued humanity. Its enigmatic presence in the starry night sky was a symbol of faith and steadiness. The sun was worshiped as the giver of life and was believed to have a masculine quality, whereas the moon was embraced as feminine and was honored for its ever evolving yet steady and rhythmic monthly evolution.

In some ancient cultures, the sun and the moon represented a relationship of struggle—a tension that created and sustained all of life. As solstices and the equinoxes are determined by the sun's position relative to the equator, the moon provided the monthly cycle, the lunar calendar inside the four seasons.

The accumulated power of the sun and the moon's gravitational force is what sparks life into being. The yang of the masculine sun reflects both the shadow and the light of the feminine or yin lunar energy. Indeed, the symbolism here is rich—highlighting all the phases of light to dark, and dark back to light. As humans we can study the cycles of the moon and generate feelings of acceptance, empathy, and compassion as we endure our own life cycles of darkness to light, and light to darkness.

Since time immemorial, the agricultural cycle was linked to the lunar cycle. The moon's rhythm was followed to predict the tides alongside the sun's rhythm in order to determine when to plant and when to harvest. Seeds were planted either during the full or the new moon, as the moisture was known to rise to the top of the soil through the moon's gravitational force, causing the seeds to swell and resulting in better germination and thriving plant life.

THE LUNAR CYCLE AS YOUR GUIDE

Even in our modern world we can utilize the lunar rhythms to ebb and flow between the conscious and the unconscious, the literal and the symbolic, the feeling realms and the intuitive realms, the forces of the feminine and the masculine, and the light and dark polarities inside us. We can open our awareness to ourselves and our environment in our daily lives, remaining grounded while we tend to the inner workings of our spiritual existence.

Allow the lunar cycle to be your guide and teacher. Welcome afresh this ceremonial journey as you land home and touch down into your present state every month. Feel into this soul work as a way to check in, get still, and pause. A way to understand your feelings and heartfelt desires regardless of other people's judgments, societal pressures, or personal limiting core beliefs. A way to honor your authentic process and find supportive ways to feed your energy body.

Attuning to the moon's rhythms is a spiritual reset, a way to step out of the mundane of everyday life and move into insightful living. You can do this through the lens of mystery, diversity, dimensionality, and otherworldly happenings. Once you plug into her energy, she becomes your loving guide—unconditionally. Once you make a commitment to honor her journey and to be in ritual with yourself, others, and the moon, your inner realms remember and begin to weave their dreams into your outer solar capacities. The moon is the grand elder in the sky ready to hear your prayers, ready to nudge you into a place of opposition within yourself so you can discern where to place your attention, what to let go of, and how to activate.

She is an alchemist at work, an ancient grandmother weaving her web; she is the mystic in the night skies ready to guide you towards a better version of yourself. Her steadiness will carry you. Her darkness will remind you that you can be resourceful and resilient inside life's complexities. Her evolutions weave the stories of your own revolutions. And when you forget who you are and what you are made of, she will be there to hold you, soothe you, and rock you into remembering that you already have everything inside of you to make your love come alive once again. The moon is the weaver, the mystic, the alchemist, the midwife, the healer, the grandmother, the warrior, the artist, the farmer, and the child all at once. Follow her journey every month and you will feel these archetypes come alive in yourself.

Every two weeks—during the new moon and the full moon—set aside time to awaken your inner mystic. Her gravitational pull is wildly magnetic. She will sweep you off your feet, shake you upside down, and return you whole, inspired, and renewed once again. Her lessons are a call from the ancients. Soft at times—like grace inside your heart—other times fierce, like your heart being pulled out of your body and placed on a platter for her to feast upon, only to be put back more whole than before. She will take you to the water's edge, toss you into the cold ocean swells. She will bring you to your knees at the river's bank to pray for the collective heart to heal.

The moon's illumination will awaken you from your slumber and speak universal incantations of magic, power, and love. The moon's pull will bring you so far inside yourself that there will be times of quiet. Trust the quiet. The wood has been gathered, the fires have been lit, the water collected, the winds of grace and strength hearten the journey. Follow her illuminated path through the wildflowers, up the mountain trails, and throw your arms up to her in honor. Allow the lunar wisdom to channel through you. Give her permission to transmit to you from the ancient ones. For she has been with them, and now she is with you.

THE MOON AND THE SUN: HONORING THE FEMININE AND THE MASCULINE ENERGY WITHIN

The moon and the sun generate vibrational frequencies that influence the ocean tides as well as the water inside our bodies. In astrology, the sun signifies our outer world and all things external, including our personality, ego, and identity. This is also how others perceive us in the world. It is known to be a masculine archetype and holds the essence of gathering our personal power and strength of will to follow through with a project, task, or vision. It brings the idea or vision into manifestation. The sun archetype is illumination, strength, and courage. It is the teacher of unconditional giving, the healer. The sun's wild fire power is connected to transformation and growth. We can align with this archetype and burn away the old in order to make way for growth and illumination all around us.

Astrologically, the moon symbolizes our inner world: our emotions, desires, shadows, secrets, fears, and worries. The lunar energy is reflective and connected to our dreams, intuition, feelings, beliefs, and the unconscious realms. The moon can be both teacher and guide; her archetype is feminine and has been referred to as the goddess in the sky. The moon is reflective of our waxing and waning personal cycles, along with our subconscious, which shows us what we need in order to feel safe and fulfilled on an emotional level. Through the moon's reflections, we may source the ability to feel deeply, to heal from the past, and to creatively unlock limiting beliefs in order to express our true essence.

The divine feminine archetype represents the internal process—the creative, nourishing, mysterious, quiet, inner spiritual experience. It is the bridge from the unconscious realms, where we access gifts from the spiritual and intuitive realms and offer them to the world in an embodied form. The divine feminine sparks alive when you honor her, and she becomes your guide to all things internal. Her alchemy is what sustains you and ignites your radiance and brilliance to be expressed into the world. Listen to her when she calls to you. Develop this relationship, speak to her, love her as she comes to you in the form of a guide, an ancestor, and in the daily steps you take in life. Fill these steps with unconditional beauty, honoring all those who have come before you and all those who will come after you. This is how her inner beauty becomes so unshakeable that the well of the divine feminine awakens in others and the world no longer rides on surface happenings where the collective ego is inflated and the collective heart is broken. The divine feminine not only mends the ego and the heart; her power ripples far and wide, touching the minds and hearts of those most in need of her strength and softening.

The divine masculine inside each one of us is steeped in the conscious self. It arrives in you at birth to give you the right to be an individual, to express yourself through light, reason, and right action. He is the teacher of integration through clear inner power, strength, and vitality. The divine masculine is the teacher of right action—when the inner vision is grounded, clear, and organized, it can manifest through action to completion. The idea, like a planted seed, roots down, shoots up, and is nourished enough for right action to follow in the world.

At its highest, the divine masculine is humble and gives unconditionally and directly. Through the clear channels of the mind and heart, the divine masculine sees the work at hand and is able to follow through with precision. Developing this relationship of supple will, creativity, and passion will radically free you from hiding your own gifts. Think about what is currently cooking in your life, and tend to those fires. Be the tracker of what dims your light and brings you to states of inertia and lack. Ask yourself, what is the root cause? What are the circumstances? What are the contributing factors? What if? These questions can become the catalysts for lasting change. Think about transporting yourself to the sun's energy channels—the one that gives unconditionally, the one that knows it can overcome hard things, and the one that gives life to the tree sapling inside the mountain crevice. The divine masculine gives us the strength necessary to fight the good fight, to know when it's time to let go, and how to follow through with our most cherished visions and dreams.

The divine masculine and feminine archetypes live inside each one of us. They can help us understand more fully how to become the best version of who we are. When we embrace the balance of the divine feminine and the divine masculine in our personal alchemy, we access fullness, wholeness, and balance; we become deeply connected to our highest self. Like the sun, we cast our sphere of light—through ideas, visions, actions, and projects—out into the world. Like the moon, we cycle through both waxing and waning, getting expansive and then contracting for rest and renewal. Dance your life through this simple mantra found in all living energies; like a vow to your highest self, speak this mantra with love on a daily basis:

May I find my softness in my strength, and strength in my softness.

LUNAR PHASES

Each month we have an opportunity to align with the symbolism of the moon through an astrological lens. The moon takes the journey of eight phases within a month, which are similar to the four seasons and the midway points in the wheel of the year. Imagine the moon as a compass in the night sky, pointing to both our inner self, or our divine feminine, and our external self, or our divine masculine.

It takes 365 days for the earth to orbit the sun. The cycle of the moon orbiting the earth takes approximately 28 days, resulting in 13 moon cycles in a year. Hence 13 moons in 12 months. So each year, there will be two full moons that auspiciously land inside one month.

The eight phases of the lunar cycle are new moon, waxing crescent, first quarter, waxing gibbous, full moon, waning gibbous, last quarter, and finally waning crescent.

As the new moon ushers in new beginnings, its position sits approximately between the earth and the sun. The sun casts light that reflects on the dark side of the moon, the side never visible to the human eye. Hence the new moon is also known as the dark moon.

The time from new moon to full moon is known as the waxing phase, and is symbolic of momentum, nurturance, and growth.

The full moon marks the halfway point in the lunar cycle, and arrives when the moon is positioned directly opposite the sun. We see the full light of the moon because the sun is perfectly positioned to illuminate its whole shape. This oppositional force can make for an intensely charged time, and it also brings potential for cosmic alignment.

Following the full moon, the waning phase begins toward the renewal of the cycle once again. This period is a time to honor your strengths, release external stressors and internal imbalances, and honor your personal expansion as a contribution towards something far greater than you and your own life.

The Moon's Monthly Navigation Chart

New Moon
Rebirth and
cleansing

Waxing Crescent
Nurture and
support

Full Moon
Intuition and
charging

Waning Crescent
Releasing,
completion

Welcome the new moon as a rebirth.
Cast your intentions and prayers into the night sky
with clarity and non-attachment.
Honor the waxing moon as mind—body nurturance and support.
Nourish your seed intentions.
Embrace the full moon as you release outmoded ways of being and
feeling, trust your intuition as you cast out your wildest
dreams into the alchemical moon's glow.
As the moon wanes, she asks of you to let go of what is no longer needed.
Allow flow, grace, and steadiness to bring this cycle to completion.
Welcome the new moon and begin the cycle again.

New Moon Essence

As the new moon initiates the birth of the 29.5-day lunar cycle, it sym-bolizes a cosmic reset—you can leave the past behind you, nourish your internal system, and allow new beginnings to emerge. Aligning with the new moon's energy grants permission to open up to the realm of possibility through the signs and signals that the universe is sending you. It is a time for embracing new projects, ideas, plans, thoughts, relationships and the changes you desire. It is a time for seeding intentions and opening to the new possibilities that are brought by another lunar cycle. The new moon offers a time of hope, faith, and renewal of our commitments. It brings you inwards to start afresh, reminding you that no matter what, there is always rebirth. It also reminds you to let go of what is no longer in alignment with your purpose and your dreams. The new moon reminds you that for you to bring all that you want into being, you need to clear away what is no longer serving you and generate space for what is to flow into your life.

The new moon holds the essence of darkness, internal alchemy, and mystery. Unseen realms deeply embedded within your own being can be revealed, bringing to light the workings of the unconscious self. Herein lies the opportunity for embodiment of your personal mission. When your vision seeds get planted in this rich dark fertile soil of the new moon, shadows will become illuminated, along with the awakening of your intuitive stirrings. When these inner workings merge with what is happening in your outer life, you find the momentum required for the vision seeds to take root and new energies to emerge. If inner contradictions or misaligned motivations take over, when you desire one thing yet do another, the lines of energy get broken and the continuity between the desire and the action gets muddled.

As darkness washes over the sky, the moon's presence becomes invisible, giving us permission to rest. Her divinely feminine way pulls our con-sciousness inwards for a cosmic reset. The sun and the moon are in the same Zodiac sign during a new moon, and this gives a surge of concen-trated energy to the particular sign's characteristics. New moon energy is a catalyst to pause, get still, move slowly, and connect to your feelings inside the container of your most heartfelt desires.

The moon then begins to grow into the waxing moon phase, including the crescent, first quarter, and gibbous lunar cycles. This building phase is reflective of nurturing and support of the intentions set during new moon. It's a time to feed the seeds so they may take root.

Waxing Moon Phase

The luminous crescent between new and full moon brings a promise of hope and wonder. There is an inner knowing that the cycle is beginning to grow. It takes approximately 14 days for the new moon to build into the stages of crescent, first quarter, and the gibbous phases towards fullness. During this two-week period it's essential to steadily build upon your new moon visions. Ideas and prayers are like seeds; they must be attended to in order to flourish. Allow your dreams, curiosity, and wonderment to be your guides as you stay focused on bringing your new moon intentions alive. This is the building phase.

Keep visualizing and embodying the "felt sense" inside your visions; this is very different from focusing on the end result. If you just focus on the end result and your inner body has not yet accepted the invitation, the energy will be dispersed and you will end up confused. This results in fatigue, inertia, over-compensation, and anxiety. What is important to remember here is that sometimes the universe wants to bring you something or someone in a different capacity than you once thought. This concept reinforces the attitude of trusting in divine timing and believing in the power of synchronicity in order to receive the signs the universe is bringing to you. To walk hand in hand with your true essence, you must be a devoted student, practicing compassion, observation, and activation steeped in goodness, truth, and love.

Observe the moon's symbolism and gravitational pull in relationship to earth, air, fire, water, and the ethereal realms around you. Stay curious to how this energy affects your emotions. The stardust runs through you, as do the microbes of the earth from billions of years ago. When in doubt, remember you are a cosmic being in a steady human form. Be a lighthouse not only for your own soul's evolution, but for that of the collective heart consciousness. You can be deeply grounded, realistic, and a practitioner of magic all at the same time.

Full Moon Symbolism

Midway through the 29.5-day lunar cycle, the full moon arrives at approximately day 14. When consciously and intentionally following the moon's cycle as a compass in the night sky, you begin to feel how the full moon is the outward expression of the new moon manifestations. It reflects a more external, action oriented, fertile, and wild energy.

The sun and full moon being in perfect opposition creates a unique and powerful energy. When the moon's feminine and the sun's masculine energies are complementary, they create the perfect yin to yang alchemy of harmony. There is no shortage of deep feelings and gravitational pulls during the full moon. Your intuitive nature is highly charged, and when you are conscious of it, you can discern what you want and what you don't want. The full moon is a time when your intuitive nature gets an opportunity to express and charge itself simultaneously.

As the surge of the full moon's light ripples through your own energy body, your feelings, emotions, and mental processes can go wild. When this is not understood, your life can turn upside down and inside out. Due to the oppositional position of the sun to moon, you may feel resistance and contradiction or questioning in your life. This energy can highlight the opposing forces of work versus home, light versus dark, inner tension versus external tension, needs versus wants, etc. Emotions and instincts can reach an all-time high during the full moon, delivering a sharper focus into the workings of your home and family life, along with your career and your intimate relationships.

This is the gift, however. The full moon brings to light anything that is out of balance in order to help you discern what is working and what is not. Instead of seeing the moon as a wild, destructive and debilitating force, you can use the energy she unleashes to grow. Through compassion, practice, observation, and lunar awareness, you can shed outmoded ways of being and living. The full moon asks you to let go of what no longer works for you and invite in core values that contribute to personal and collective well-being.

When personal triggers become amplified during the full moon, you can use the following practice in order to address the issues at hand. Imagine a dynamic altar in front of you, holding everything that is complex, challenging, and painful or unfulfilling in your life. Then visualize all the aspects of your life that are working; see what you are grateful for, and what brings you joy. How can you work with the altar items, almost like a game of chess, to make this altar glow, get stronger, be more satisfying and filled with radiance? Like the lotus flower blossoming through the murky dark waters, the alchemical lunar energy nudges you towards working with and for, not against, the lessons coming to you during this particular cycle.

Every day we wake with new potential, a new way to see and feel, a new understanding of how energy works. Through the light of the full moon's exquisite glow, we can reflect on what we don't want, and this brings insight and clarity to the next steps we need to take in order to clean up our own energy and take personal responsibility for our life.

It is in the tension-filled, uncomfortable aspects of life that we receive the insight for renewal and growth. When you consciously bring these aspects forward and name them, you create a catalyst for activation. In essence, tension creates clarity. Complexity generates resourceful solutions. Chaos is the catalyst towards peaceful living. No longer fear the oppositional energies in your life. You will find deep insight in all the realms of opposition. It can become the lift-off point to align with your truest calling. To know what you want, how to get it, when to let go, and where to activate is the greatest gift in life. This is the passion that breathes you alive each day. Bring your salt of the earth heart forward, and trust your own capacity to practice kindness and compassion inside the realm of life's oppositions.

During the full moon, reflect on your new moon intentions or spirit messages. Visualize where you were two weeks earlier and observe what has shifted. Stay open to the course of your new moon intentions, and observe if there are different perspectives and insights coming through now. As change is the one thing we can count on in life, it is essential to feel into how the releasing or the activation impulses may have shifted. And most importantly, be open to receive your full moon spirit message. Call it forth, loud and clear, write it down, share it with a friend, or bring it to your altar in the form of a vision seed ready to blossom.

Having a moon calendar will support you in preparing for your full moon ritual. If it can't happen on the exact full moon time, two to three days before will bring your body–mind into a conscious preparation and body–mind attunement. From simple to complex, from solo to group rituals, landing into conscious space and time for lunar musings will create lasting change in your life. Activating a full moon ritual is a powerful way to be in sacred connection with yourself and others. It becomes the sacred space in which insight, healing, reflection and connections can be created for your highest self and for the collective.

Each full moon cycle is an opportunity to step inside a circle of gratitude. Catch your blessings and remember the fullness of your intuition rising inside of you. Imagine your own capacity like that of the full moon's brilliant light. Her illumination is a reminder of your own radiance—your sensual, sexy, wild, howling, and creative self. Allow it to be an imprint in present time to shake off the lurking shadows of limiting beliefs, a time to call out the inner critic and feed it no more! The inner judge will get hungry during the full moon. It will want to steal your energy to keep you playing small if you are not conscious. Honor those restrictive beliefs for what they are and understand where they are coming from. Every time they come around, you have an opportunity to work with this tension and direct it towards your inner strength. Dig deep down, find the roots, cut the ones that are feeding hatred, greed, or violence within, for they are no longer right for you.

The path of self-sovereignty comes through dancing with your shadows, for they will always be there. Ask the moon's fullness to guide you to your temple of liberation. Attuning to her symbolism and reflections on a monthly basis is like stepping into the center of your life and saying "Yes!"

Here I am, ready, open, and willing to ebb and flow with the tides of life!

Waning Moon Phase

The transition from full moon back to new moon is called the waning moon phase. As the moon begins to gradually decrease in size, it passes through the gibbous, last quarter, and crescent phase until it arrives at the beginning of the cycle once again. In this final phase, the lunar energy moves slowly inward. It is a time of inner reflection, review, and completion. The power of observation is the medicine for this final cycle. When you learn how to live in a space of observation, you dwell in present-moment awareness more often and less in judgment, negativity, or criticism.

This final glimmer in the waning moon's phase symbolizes reflection and observation—a window of perspective before the new moon comes once again. Areas of observation and reflection can include personal well-being, health, creativity, work, and relationships. Journal about these areas and ask what feels stagnant and what feels fluid and balanced. This will support you in casting out your new moon intentions once again with clarity, grounding, and consciousness.

As the moon begins its journey into darkness, there is a pause, a reflective still point, grounded in real time. Acknowledge your inner strengths, accomplishments, realizations, personal growth, and the shadows you experienced during the past moon cycle.

As the waning crescent moon transitions through its final cycle before complete darkness, honor the shadows that reveal themselves to you. Observe your current fears, anxieties, toxic thoughts, and reactive behaviors with compassion and kindness. Bring them forward with curiosity. Name them for what they are, recognize their root of origin, and simply welcome them as messengers to your sacred altar. Embrace your shadow self, your attachments, your ulterior motives, the way you play victim, the way you exaggerate and play the power-over game.

By making your shadow self your soul teacher, you untangle yourself from being ruled by it. As you invite your shadows in, you no longer suppress them, but more importantly, you understand the deeper meaning of why they are there. You always have a soul lesson to receive through our shadow. The work is to pay attention when it gets hungry and feels reckless inside you.

Trust that the conscious work you do through pausing, observing, and reflecting both the light and dark experiences in your life translates into your personal expansion. Know that this contributes towards something far greater than you and your own life. When you evolve by working through complex aspects within your body–mind process, you inspire others to evolve. Evolve you. Evolve the planet. And begin the cycle once again. Every 29.5 days you are blessed to do this good work.

This is the call of the moon worker, the intuitive mystic—to selflessly activate the evolution of who you are for the betterment of humanity. This personal work ripples out far and wide—in ways you may never comprehend.

Moon Bathing and Moon Gazing: A Practice

The moon may be one of the most recognizable celestial beings in the night sky. Her enigmatic glow is forever familiar, unforgettable, and wildly alluring as it ebbs and flows throughout the monthly cycle.

Moon bathing is a practice many of us do already. It simply involves intentionally basking in the moon's benevolent glow as a way to enter into mindfulness and reduce stress. We invite the magnetic energy of the moon to heal, calm, and wash away our attachment to imbalances, judgments, and fear.

Charting the moon's journey and basking in its glow is an ancient practice that is said to reduce anxiety and enhance relaxation through the body's natural ability to release melatonin, as the moon is traditionally associated with fertility, growth, and intuition. Directing our energy towards the moonlight is believed to both heal and soothe the body. As opposed to the sun's dynamic brightness, the moon brings subtle energy that is both lasting and nourishing. Moon bathing is believed to increase fertility, regulate the menstrual cycle, and improve sleep, which supports concentration and increases intuition.

Whenever you can, sit under the light of the moon and meditate with her glowing presence. Breathe into her auspicious and expansive alchemy. Breathe into her teachings and let her medicine swell inside the nest of your heart. Breathe out that which you want to transmute or let go of. Welcome in as well the starry night sky, the planets, and the star formations as a cosmic reset.

Moon gazing, closely related to moon bathing, is the practice of directing your gaze towards the moon for periods of time without blinking. Similar to the technique of candle gazing, this practice promotes mental focus while encouraging the mind to empty of excess thoughts. The body responds with the rest and digest phase; the parasympathetic nervous system calms and enters a resting state. Moon gazing can pull on our feelings with the same magnetism that gathers the force of the ocean. Her power intrigues our imagination—a harvest moon sitting powerfully in the starry night sky as a celestial storyteller, weaver of the dreamtime, and a bridge into the mystical whisperings of ancient times. Such ephemeral cosmic awakenings are unforgettable, and allow us to step out of mundane time and space to bask in the light of the moon's holy radiance.

Whereas the sun is the source of external radiance, unconditional giving and growth—the way we activate our visions in the world—the moon is the keeper of our dreams, the enigma of wonder. She is the ever evolving mystic that holds the key to our feminine faith. We can activate our dreams when our feminine mystic is embodied and integrated. Every time you cast your gaze toward the moon, from new to full, from crescent to quarter, become the conduit of faith, and worship the subtle power of the moon. Fill up your own cup. She is the soul caretaker in the sky. Be in conversation with her, speak to her. She will listen and she will respond. Pray out loud and often, for your communing with the moon will invoke the wildest of openings for you. Unexpected doors will open, paths to otherworldly dimensions will appear, and universal truths will speak louder than the lower vibrational energies of fear and doubt. When she wakes you in the night, answer her call, moon bathe, moon gaze, journal, pray, and allow yourself to receive her medicine.

THE MOON AS MUSE

To connect with the mysterious, celestial, ancient, and ethereal energies is to draw in and cast out your highest intentions towards planetary evolution and healing. Anchor into personal responsibility to heal and evolve for the greater good on the planet. Hold the intention of your spirit work to honor the ancient ones, your spirit ancestors, your blood ancestors, those who walked this life before you, your own ancient healer, and the field of infinite wisdom that lives and loves inside of you.

Being in an energetic conversation with the moon boosts your awareness of the natural world. It allows you to practice present-moment awareness while reducing stress and feelings of overwhelm and anxiety. Pausing to commune with the moon is a cosmic reset so that excess tension can leave body and mind. Your internal body receives illumination and wonder like a medicinal and spiritual transmission. When you observe, pause, breathe, and listen, the moon will become your steady celestial guide, a numinous storyteller, an enigmatic mystical teacher, and a deeply nourishing feminine force to support your way of balance and beauty.

Steep your soul in the alchemy and cosmic ephemerality of the lunar rhythms. You will never see this exact energy again. Let the moon speak love talk to you. Wholeheartedly receive this transmission. She will guide you to the temple of your own majesty, time and time again. Pay attention to your impulses and your desires. They may show up in unexpected ways. They may fall right out of your mouth, or come like a flash…"I am an artist…I am a healer…I am an author…I am at peace…I am wildly loving." This is how spirit works. When you get quiet and still, these signs and symbols will come more readily. Observe, feel, listen, and see these spirit messages and take them to heart. When you do, the messengers will come more often to support you.

Equally important is your ability to be guided into the space of surrender. Let go of your new moon intentions and spirit messages; awaken to a stronger force calling you into action. This is your intuitive moon guide at work. This is spirit gifting you insight.

Write down your own crafted moon spirit message each month. Cast your intentions like a universal prayer or like a code of ethics to follow. This will support your manifestations. During the new moon to full moon phase, read, recall, and reclaim this spirit message. Work with divine timing, synchronicity, and the felt sense of the visions to feed your life experience. Believe in the power of change, and open your awareness to receive the gifts the universe is bringing to you. Observe any shifts in your own self since you wrote this. Update the message as needed.

This is a way to converse with the divine. Sometimes you need to pray out loud. Or take your quiet prayer to the meditation cushion. However it comes, allow it to be free flowing. Hold nothing back. Through your depth, knowledge, and compassion, reclaim your true essence. The only rule is to commit to doing this every new moon. This is the path of the mystic.

Rituals to Align and Source Pure Energy from the Moon

Learn how to create a personalized full and new moon ritual. Discover how to generate a personal altar, including the elements and their symbolism. Connect to the wheel of the year, track the moon's rhythms and learn the art of moon gazing, monthly lunar spirit messages, movement medicine, and journal entries as the remedy inside the ritualist's journey.

1. Full Moon Ritual

This ritual can be done in a group or by yourself. Let these steps be your rough guide; use your intuition, have fun planning it out, gather your people, and celebrate the divine feminine that dwells inside of you and the moon.

Intention
To call upon, support and align your authenticity and personal vision.

Preparation
Gather seasonal items from nature or objects in your home that symbolize your evolving personal vision and authentic nature. Have a candle and your journal beside you. Create an altar that is inspired by nature's five elements:

Air
In the east for living from your heart.

Fire
In the south for shedding ego and old stories.

Water
In the west for flow, creativity to meet your shadow and work with it.

Earth
In the north for grounding and earthly strength to activate your personal vision.

Ether
In the center for connection to all five elements, yourself, and the supportive spiritual energies that surround you.

1 Light your candle, cleanse your space with fresh air or essential oils/incense/herbs to clear away negative energies, and invite a meditative, sacred, and silent space.
2 Connect to your breath, get soft, and surrender completely.
3 Begin to call forth your gratitudes. Allow your body to become a channel of compassion and love. Allow anything you are wishing to release at this time to be expressed through the exhale. Allow yourself to inhale fully what you are inviting in during this lunation. You may be inspired to call forth what you envision for the cycle of life you are currently in: alignments, visions, goals, intentions.
4 If comfortable, speak your intentions out loud. Pray out loud. Speak to the moon. Allow the words to flow like a conversation to your best friend. This is a powerful way to activate energy fields from both the physical and the spiritual planes.

5 Place your hands on your heart. Open your mind, body, and heart to receive any guidance in the form of words, visions, and feelings.

6 Come to a guiding affirmation in the "I am ... I will" format. (For example, "I am powerful in my authenticity. I will trust my unique offerings and share them with the world.")

7 If you are sitting in a circle with others, each person takes a turn to share what they are releasing, what they are inviting in, and their guiding affirmation. Have a talking stick or something from nature to pass around the circle as each person shares.

8 Create: paint, write poetry, collage, make bath salts, massage oils, herbal teas, etc. Being creative brings a grounding nature, a feeling of connection, nourishment and inspiration to your ritual.

9 Seal sacred space: Return to a quiet place within, intentionally sealing the ritual by expressing gratitudes, sharing songs and insights, breathing. Thank the moon for her wisdom teachings this month.

2. Breath Work: Moon Breath Activation

Intention

To awaken and integrate the divine feminine in you, and to balance your emotions while elevating you into a cosmic reset where intuitive messages are received. To be done during any of the lunar cycles.

1 Find a place to sit comfortably and uninterrupted for 10 minutes. Place three drops of lavender oil in your hands, rub them together vigorously, cup your hands over your face and breathe in three to six deep breaths.

2 Slow down your breath to a count of four on the inhale, hold your breath and draw your navel in towards your spine for four. Then exhale out your mouth slowly and completely. Repeat this breath for six to 10 rounds. As you pause, find a connection from your pelvic floor or perineum and lift it up towards your navel as you hold your breath, anchoring towards the earth yet lifting up towards the sky.

3 Place your hands on your lower abdominal area and begin to visualize the shape of the moon in your navel area. Imagine it filling the whole shape of your pelvis. Sense its light illuminating the whole midsection of your body. With each inhale, the moon grows into its majestic and

ancient wisdom fullness. With each exhale, it returns you to your compassionate and embodied awareness. Steep yourself in the moon's glow and listen for any messages that come.

4 Now inhale five short inhales through your nose, hold your breath, pull the divine feminine energy of the earth into your spine, and exhale to the sound of "ahhhh." Repeat five short inhales in through the nose. Hold your breath to integrate your divine feminine essence around your body, and exhale to tone, chant, hum or sing. If your soul had a song— what would it be? Sing it freely, explore your range. Repeat as many times as feels good.

5 Return to a quiet space and seal the sacred space all around you.

6 Close with three circles of your arms overhead; inhale to circle your arms, exhale to bring palms together down the midline of your body.

7 Place yours hands on your heart to close and visualize the moon's feminine nature deeply instilled, integrated, and ready to be expressed through you.

3. Visualization Journey: Moon Glow Illumination and Intuition Activation

Intention

To raise your personal vibration through aligning with the moon's glow while opening channels for intuition.

I Light a candle and sit or lie down comfortably. Have your journal ready to record any observations after the journey.

2 As you close your eyes, soften your entire body from the crown of your head all the way down to the soles of your feet.

3 Set your intention to open and enter into the energy of the moon's glow to receive a positive charge and awaken your intuition.

4 Slow down your breath and allow any exhales or sounds to freely come in and out of you.

5 You can pray out loud—as your words are deeply meaningful, you may feel drawn to list all of the things you are letting go of and the ways of being that you are inviting in.

6 Visualize the shape of the moon before you. It could be full, crescent, etc.

7 Observe its color, shape, and the glow that it emanates.

8 Begin to merge your own energy body with that of the moon's glow. You may feel like you can now enter into the shape of the moon and merge your energy body with the moon's.

9 Invite the moon's glow into your lower abdominal area/womb space. With each inhale the glow expands, and with each exhale any emotions or feelings of blocked or fragmented energy are released. Observe what shapes, patterns, or sensations come forth.

10 Now allow this lunar healing glow to swirl into your heart. With each inhale, see the shape of the moon expanding and illuminating your heart. With each exhale, the moon encourages grief to pour out of you like tears and the armor around your heart to break down.

11 Observe the sensations and images coming to you.

12 Move the lunar glow and presence into the center of your mind. With each inhale, the luminous and spacious energy expands, and with each exhale it pulls out excess thinking and limited mind loops. The mind gets rerouted with the moon's radiance.

13 Observe the sensations, patterns, and images coming to you.

14 Bathe your whole body in the moon's glow. Visualize yourself inside the moon. Relax your whole being into this lunar house and receive counsel from this grand elder's energy.

15 The moon speaks truth. What does she have to say to you? Are there any words of wisdom, advice, or symbolism for you now?

16 Merge this counsel into the weave of your own intuitive nature. What does your intuition want to share with you at this time?

17 Return to your breath, become aware of your environment, feel your whole body return to the earth's solid ground. Thank yourself for activating your intuition and receiving counsel in this way.

18 Journal about your experience.

4. Meditation: Letting In to Let Go

Intention
To connect with your breath, soften your edges,
let go of external stressors, and let in
clarity, peace, and relaxation.

1. Find a comfortable place to sit for at least five minutes.
2. Begin by acknowledging the earth below you, the sky above you, and the horizon line before you. Welcome the vastness of the universe at your back supporting you.
3. Set a personal intention to let go completely and call in positive energy.
4. Bring attention to your breath, soften your lower abdominal area and all the muscles in your face, and slow down your breath to a count of six.
5. Gently begin to do neck rolls, moving your head in half circles to free up tension.
6. Then move your shoulders in circles; six times forward, six times backwards.
7. Bring your shoulders all the way up to your ears, make fists, and tighten all your muscles. Hold your breath, and let everything go on the exhale. Get intentional about specific things you are letting go of each time you release. Do this six more times.
8. Return to stillness, track your breath, inhale to let in pure, clean energy, and exhale to let go of fragmented pieces or murky, confused energy.
9. This mantra can be supportive: "With each inhale I welcome in clean energy, with each exhale I release completely."
10. Let in to let go. There may be a symbol that supports the focal point of the meditation. For example, with each inhale visualize a rose in its fullness, and with each exhale visualize the rose sealing into itself. Focus on letting go completely.
11. As you seal your meditation, observe any shifts in your body or mind.

5. New Moon Spirit Message

Intention

To draw your energy in, let go of the old and receive
insight on new beginnings and sources of inspiration
to support your current visions.

1. Have your journal, light a candle, and sit in silence for at least five minutes.
2. Allow your body to relax completely.

3 Ask yourself:

- What is rising in the form of opportunity, learning, and new beginnings at this time?
- What am I ready and willing to let go of?
- What positive words will support me through this lunar cycle?

4 Allow the moon to speak to you and listen for the direct call to action. Connect to your current life's dreams and prayers and call forth what will support you in realizing them.

5 When you are ready, write your message down, and place it on your altar or a place where you can reflect on it often.

Here is an example of a shorter and longer version of a new moon spirit message:

Shorter version

"I am vast and rooted all at once. My shape-shifting capacity allows me to diversify my portfolio and time travel into unexpected dimensions."

Longer Version

"I am vast and rooted all at once. My shape-shifting capacity allows me to diversify my portfolio and time travel into unexpected dimensions. I receive insights steeped in a cosmic kind of faith, my own inner knowing discerns what is illusion and what is truth. My breath takes me there. The quietude of my morning meditation, the uproar of my own scattered contents, this opposition also takes me there.

"I lay down the fragmented pieces, setting them free at last. I swoon at the great mysteries before me. Behind me the ancient incantations call. I receive insights and the direct call to action towards my current evolution. I liberate myself from past conditioning and limited body–mind loops, cycles, and patterns.

"I step into the circle of my power where the revealing of my truth becomes not only my destiny but my birthright. I marvel at the dark night sky, bathing in the iridescent halo of the moon soon to emerge. She whispers, 'welcome home, sweet one, this is the life that is waiting for you.'"

6. Full Moon Spirit Message

Intention

To ground your energy, align with the radiance
of the full moon, and receive an intuitive message
to support you in all areas of your life.

1 Have your journal ready, light your candle, and sit for at least five minutes in quiet reflection.
2 Ground your lower body, lift your upper body, and allow your breath to be full.
3 Ask yourself:

- What is my intuition saying to me at this time?
- What habitual patterns or past experiences am I ready to release?
- What will serve my higher self at this time?
- What boundaries and practices with nourish me and allow me to fulfill my work and my resting states at this time?

4 Feel the radiance of the moon's fullness, and let it channel through you.
5 Connect to your soul essence and allow your intentions and prayers to move in and out of you with ease and grace.
6 Call forth what you are truly ready to manifest.
7 When you are ready, write your message down, and place it on your altar or a place where you can reflect on it often.

Here is an example of a shorter and longer version of a new moon spirit message.

Shorter Version

"As I step inside the circle of gratitude, I no longer carry what burdens me.

"As I shed this outmoded layer of the past, I greet my intuition with a listening heart and an open mind. I accept the invitations and messages coming to me now. With divine timing on my side, I activate through my personal grounding and expanding. I stay steady and cosmic all at once."

Longer Version

"I step inside the circle of gratitude.

"As I count my blessings, I lay down the complexities that cloud my mind and armor my heart. I remember how to feel free. The moon's pull shakes my sensuality alive. My inner mystic is ready to be unleashed. The echo of my lunar howl reverberates across the valley. I know I am not alone. No longer do I play by the rules inside the labyrinth of my mind. I break free, bust down the doors of hardship, and I dance my wild dance.

"I cradle my inner child who longs for me to hold her, I walk hand in hand with the twin flame who is the brightest version of myself. I am my own twin flame. As I enter the supernatural portal inside this lunar house of spirit, I let down my guard and bask in her waters of illumination. She projects my shadows so I can see them for what they are. I cast a spell of goodness towards all living beings. A planetary evolution flashes before my eyes, my prayers for all set free, far and wide.

"Stardust encircles my heart, life's greatest mysteries funnel ancient wisdom to empower my mind, the earth's pulse channels through me, I am steady and cosmic all at once. As I wake from a full moon slumber I feel my cells freshly alchemized. I open my eyes to see a new dawn. My mind like a hawk, my lungs a field of wild flowers, my womb the bed of the ocean, my breasts the nectar inside the flowers, my spine the sap of the old growth cedars, my hands the warmth of the sun, my feet the salt of the earth. Inside the galactic wonder of the moon's core, I steep my soul awake."

7. Moon Bathing Ritual

Use your intuition as your guide. When the moon calls to you, follow her glow and bask in her luminous healing light.

I Find a comfortable and safe space outside where you can relax and have a clear view of the moon. If you can't get outside, sitting by a window with the lights turned off will allow the moon's illumination to stream through to you.

2 Connect with your breath, close your eyes, completely soften your body. On each exhale, imagine internal stressors leaving your body. On each inhale, invite in high vibration transmission and guidance—let the moon's light speak to you and envelop you.

3 Slow down your breath even more, breathe in for a count of four, hold your breath for a count of four, and exhale out your mouth as fully as you can.

4 Open your eyes and gaze at the moon. With each inhale, breathe the moon's glow into your whole body. With each exhale you may feel drawn to visualize specific stressors now leaving you—overwhelm, confusion, sadness, frustration, impatience, etc.

5 Allow your body to be a conduit of the moon's illumination.

6 Receive any feelings of awe and wonder that may come and welcome them. Bask in the moon's nourishing and nurturing glow.

7 Practice traditional moon gazing: focus your gaze on the center of the moon without blinking. Attempt to softly focus while keeping calm, and when your eyes water, simply close them.

8 While you are resting your eyes between gazing, visualize a moon's glow at the center of your forehead—your third eye seeing the internal image of the moon.

9 Open your eyes when you are ready, continue for as long as you feel relaxed and at ease. Observe how you feel.

10 Perhaps journal about any insights you received.

8. Altar Creation: Unleash Your Inner Wild Self

A grounding ritual to be done on the eve of the new moon or the full moon to connect to your intuition and set your spirit free.

Intention
To refresh and uplift your space with a collection of sentimental relics and fresh seasonal items. To reveal and embody your current emotions, mental processes, and spiritual awakenings.

Preparation

If you have access to the outdoors, gather fallen items: flower petals, leaves, branches, berries, etc. If you have your own garden, gather items that delight your senses. Source inspirational quotes, poems, images, treasures, crystals, oracle cards—all things that are symbolic of your past, present, and future self. Have a candle, cleansing scents, a bowl of water (tap or sourced naturally) and a journal ready. It may be helpful to have a large tray to create your altar upon.

This can be done indoors or outside.

1 Once you have everything you need, light your candle, burn incense or sage, or diffuse essential oils. Come into a meditative state and attune to your breath.

2 Call forth your personal intention to create an altar that will support your inner wild, creative, and sovereign self. There are no rules here.

3 Invite in your intuition and your compassionate guides.

4 If you are comfortable, converse with your guides and speak your questions, prayers, and requests for support out loud.

5 Share what you are ready to release in order to reclaim your creativity or state of flow in life.

6 State your current core values, for example: "I am committed to my creative process, I love myself unconditionally, I am a student of both light and shadow energies."

7 Call forth three ways in which you are committed to co-creating your life right now. For example, "I am committed to practicing self-love, trusting in divine timing, and listening for the messages currently entering my life."

8 Begin to create your altar from this space of clearing and freedom.

9 Without thinking, let it be abstract or patterned, literal or symbolic. Observe how the five elements merge and intertwine; let it be purely experiential and delightful.

10 When complete, observe your altar and journal about your experience.

11 Each morning for seven days, light the candle in your altar and bask in its creative energy. Be sure to tend your altar so that it stays fresh, clean, and vibrant until you make another one.

9. Movement Medicine: Let Your Rivers Flow

Intention
To release tension and find renewal.
Connect to the lunar rhythms and get wild!

1 Light a candle and play some music that will inspire you to move.
2 Release all of your expectations and self-conscious judgments of yourself.
3 Feel the beat of the drum and let your body move with the five elements:

Earth

Start with your feet and legs and let them find a grounding rhythm. Let each step, each movement release fear and embody freedom.

Water

Bring your awareness into your hips. Make large hip circles, rock your pelvis forward and back, side to side, shake your buttocks. Feel the sensuality of connecting to your sacred sexuality. Soften your womb, lower your abdominal area and lower back. Visualize dancing water, allow the cleansing rivers to move through your whole body. Become water.

Fire

Bring your awareness to your solar plexus and ignite your passion. Visualize the flame burning bright in your center and let this light stream out from your core essence to your skin. Move fast now; shake, kick, stomp, sing, get primal! Let go of looking good and being in control. Receive this transmission with your full attention. Some days you will need to move with great intensity to clear your energy channels, some days will be softer, more subtle.

Air

Bring your awareness to your lungs and your heart space, including your shoulders, arms, hands, throat and neck. Encourage movement patterns to flow through you the way the element of air surrounds all living things on this planet, like a soft breeze or a fierce wind. Let your heart be soothed by the swaying undulations, the rocking back and forth. Be vast like the clear blue sky. Let your arms and hands be receptive to the lunar and solar energies all around you. Sway, rock, undulate, release and return to the essence of compassion inside your heart—strong inside your lungs.

Ether
Welcome union within. Move your whole body now as it dances earth, air, fire, and water.

4 Become a conduit for spirit to move you —step out of ordinary time and step into the circle of spirit.
5 In this sacred space, release your thinking mind completely, and follow the true impulse inside each movement.
6 The element of ether will move you in unsuspected ways. Chop, flow, sway, kick, chant, breathe, pull, rock, expand, contract, sing at your highest pitch, moan at your lowest, follow the desire for repetitive movements to clear fragmented energy channels.
7 You may feel like you're being released, like a snake shedding skin. Get primal, make sense of nothing, and move through different realms and dimensions.
8 Go into the core of the earth, and find land in the starry night sky.
9 Go with the vision and the mission, and trust this is a healing process.
10 When you feel complete, find your way back to the earth and rest for long enough to feel calm, connected, and rejuvenated.
11 Visualize yourself resting inside the alchemy of the lunar rhythms and receive her wild feminine energy.
12 Journal about your experience. Was there a guiding message or a direct call to action? This mind–body movement journey is deeply healing and transformative. Trust what comes up and reflect upon how it resonates with your current life process.

10. New Moon Ritual: The Cosmic Reset

Intention
To welcome new beginnings in the form of attitudes, beliefs, intentions, visions, projects, relationships, and prayers. To perform a cosmic reset, to align with your inner life, and to receive nourishment for your divine feminine channels.

1 Set up your altar, light your candle, clear your space with fresh air or purifying scents, and sit in quiet reflection. Make a pot of soothing tea. If possible turn off all lights so the candle is the only light source.

2 Set your personal intention to align with your inner temple for reflection and reset, listening to the call of your divine feminine nature to soften.

3 Set your timer for at least 10 minutes and simply follow your breath. Bask in silence and the simplicity of your breath.

4 When your meditation is complete, begin to sip your tea, allow your divine feminine nature to soften and to become filled up with nourishment from the tea.

5 Begin to consciously call on your intuitive self and your supporting guides.

6 If you are comfortable, begin to speak out loud as if you are "checking in" with yourself and spirit.

7 Share what projects or visions are on the horizon. These can be symbolic, as in, "I am holding space for inner peace this lunar cycle," or literal: "I commit to completing a specific project over the next month."

8 Praying out loud in this way, connect with your intuitive nature. Call forth the support you need for your projects and visions. Ask for assistance in letting go of what no longer serves you. If you are doing this in a group, hold the intention that you are speaking to spirit while you are also being held in the safe container of your loved ones.

9 Sip tea and write down any visions, intentions, and prayers that come to you.

10 Go back into a silent meditation and visualize a dark cave in front of you. Enter the cave and sit by the fire.

11 Bask in the fire and receive any insights from your intuitive self about what will support your prayers and visions. Receive guidance from your guides.

12 As you commit your whole heart, mind, and body to this cycle of rejuvenation and new beginnings, stay open to receive a guiding mantra, a symbol, a landscape, or any other nurturing energies.

13 Close the sacred circle by thanking all those present, honoring the elements for their life-giving qualities. Place your hands upon your altar and give thanks for the spiritual devotion that leads you on this path of cosmic awakening.

14 Seal your ritual by journaling about your experience or continue your ritual into a creative pursuit.

15 Revisit your new moon intentions the next morning and put them in a place where you can revisit them often as inspiration during this lunar cycle.

11. New Moon Bath Ritual: Cleansing Your Spirit

Intention

To honor the new moon, the beginning of a new lunar cycle, by cleansing, charging and rejuvenating your whole system in a sacred bath.

1 Set your intentions to call forth the essence of renewal, new beginnings, and internal transformation.

2 Write down your intentions: What new beginnings are you envisioning in your life right now? What new projects do you have on the horizon? Journal about connecting within—what is in need of cleansing right now? What will support the balance between internal and external in your life?

3 As you run your sacred bath, add bath salts, fresh lavender and rosemary sprigs, flower petals, or any herbs and essential oils you are drawn to. Drop in your cleansed crystals for a powerful cleansing and charge. Light candles, turn off lights, play soothing music or bask in silence.

4 Consciously enter the bath, leaving all of your concerns behind you, holding the intention of renewal.

5 Relax your whole body, let go completely.

6 Begin to gather your intentions and speak them out loud if you are comfortable. For example: "I am ready to receive support at this time. Guide me on my path, send me omens and signs so I can receive the clarity, nourishment, and activation necessary to meet my highest self."

7 Repeat this affirmation three times: "I am open to new beginnings, I am renewed, I am nourished."

8 Take eight dunks, submerging your whole body, including you head, underwater. Each time you go under remember your new-moon affirmation.

9 Visualize stepping into a timeless state where the unseen realms are accessible; enter into the realm of possibility. Welcome change

and renewal as you stay open to the visions that may come like a flash.

10 Complete by getting out of the bath, putting warm layers on and lying down to rest. Embody this rejuvenating state completely.

11 Journal about your experience. Write out any insightful messages and place them on your altar.

12. Journal Prompts

- What needs to be nurtured in you at this time?
- How can you support your highest self more fully?
- What is ready to be cleansed?
- What is ready to come to life?
- What do you need to release during this cycle in your life?
- What is ready to come to completion or is there a new beginning on the horizon?
- What is your intuition sharing with you now?
- What will be your guiding affirmation at this time in your life?

Follow the lunar rhythms as your guide in the sky. Look up often.
Lay down the impossible burdens for they are too heavy to carry anymore.
Strengthen the muscles around the nest of your heart.
Your mind, celestial and earthen all at once.
Synchronicity strikes once again.
Awaken, pause, rest, and re-vision the vision.
The vast galaxies of all things possible await your courageous soul.
From sun to moon, warrior to mother, child to elder,
the archetypes encircle your bones.
Billions of years past, and billions of years to come.
You are stardust at the core.
Everything is connected—never forget.

EVOLUTIONARY PRACTICES OF THE MYSTIC

Be your own healer.
Pray daily and often.
Take your questions to your altar.
Counsel yourself the way a mystic would.
Your body as the channel, your heart vast, free,
and ever evolving.
Your faith is your superpower.
Go heal the world.

Chapter 8

Evolutionary Practices of the Mystic
Enhancing Your Personal Alchemy

INTEGRATION:
WEAVING THE SACRED INTO YOUR DAILY LIFE

A daily devotional practice steeped in self-love and connection to the natural world brings balance, depth, and joy to your life. You find unique pathways to awaken the best version of yourself. Every day you receive an opportunity to weave the sacred moments and practices into the rhythms of daily life. This becomes a conscious choice, an internal call that leads to a radical lifestyle shift. The soil within your spirit becomes abundant and fertile by attuning to an inquisitive mind, and a supple body; you begin to make choices that generate positivity over negativity. Through the practice of mind–body connectivity, the flow state makes you grounded and insightful all at once. Living with steady and conscious daily rituals imbues you with an energy larger than life's daily dramas. The stress of deadlines, decisions, projected outcomes, past attachments, imbalanced relationships, and reactive patterns falls away as you remember to practice your core values. When you practice honesty, intimacy, and solidarity with yourself, you naturally cultivate a life that allows you to be deeply honest and intimate with others.

Be in active conversation and intimate relationship with your soul. Discover what lights you up and brings you joy. Lean into these things, and find the rituals and practices that support their growth. The compassionate care you give yourself is the healing balm of our times. It will allow you to be in harmony with all aspects of your life, even during the most complex times. We are all connected to each other and to the natural elements we absorb every day.

Bring your attention to the resources that sustain you and this planet. Allow your daily existence to be an honoring of earth, air, fire, and water. Celebrate the moon, the sun and the ethereal energy that swirls and connects all of life together.

As you are sustained by these forces, the question is, what gift will you give in return? How will you stay open, honest, connected, and grounded? Will you no longer take for granted what you have? How can you disrupt the paradigm of mass consumption that keeps you wanting more material objects to feel good? When you slow down enough to get quiet, you can understand more fully how to manage your energy body. This is the art of integrating the numinous into daily life. The practice of discerning needs versus wants, of keeping your words and actions steady and honest—this is a sacred ritual in itself. Remember that when you evolve, you are contributing to the evolution of the planet.

The art of cultivating steady rituals is like weaving shimmery threads into the tapestry of your life. Lighting candles every morning as you sit in silence with your gratitudes and prayers ushers illumination and positivity into your day. The beauty of living through this ritualistic perspective lands you inside the comfort of your own skin. Meaningful, transformative, and intimately sacred experiences shift your focus away from the daily stressors and into inner space. Though the external stressors will continue to be there, you will feel supported by spirit, your intuition will grow, and you will live in joyful presence.

Each morning hold the intention that your life is a living, sacred ritual. Be curious about what gifts, symbols, or teachers may come to you today. Welcome the unknown. Free yourself from the mental loops that are negatively charged before you even begin your day. Ask for support every morning from spirit, and invite your compassionate guides to help you navigate both the days of hard work and the days of rest. Even the hardest of tasks can shift when we simply shift our attitude. And this process becomes efficient and effective when we can trust there is a higher power supporting us. If you are feeling resistance or inertia in caring for yourself or others ask yourself: "What is the deeper soulful message coming through at this time?

Where is the learning here? What can I let go of in order to remember the spiritual practice inside this moment?"

When you activate small daily rituals, they evolve and expand into soul-whispering connections. Your personal process deepens. Steady and simple rituals lead to expansive awakenings. The ripple effect of your personal and devotional work is the real game changer—not only will it alter your life, but it can significantly and positively alter the lives of others. Never under-estimate the power of the ripple effect. Being quiet enough in the mind to catch the way the wind touches the willow branch, to hear the wing of the eagle or the hummingbird, to see the tides shift before your eyes—it is in these moments you find your place in the world. By creating space for the unknown, by simply observing energy, you gain access to a world of mysti-cal happenings and divine timings. Your days begin to swell with symbol-ism, clues, and cues towards living your best life. Trusting this steady and mindful process will be what transforms the mundane tasks of everyday life into soulful living and loving.

THE JOURNEY:
DANCING INSIDE ALL THE REALMS

Life is a journey of initiations as you explore your human form on this evolving planet—heartbreak, soul loss, cosmic timings, creative explora-tions, witnessing a child being born or holding a loved one as they leave this world. Living inside the conscious sphere of life's exquisite and ephem-eral happenings is the path towards living fully awake. With every direc-tion taken, another mystery is revealed. Each life adventure guides you to your own becoming. No time is lost. No work is lost. No love is lost. Profound teachers encircle you, the guides come to you like a flash, the ancestors bring you messages in the least expected moments. Your muses are everywhere you go. Stay open, stay awake. When you forget, simply remember: You are not alone on this journey, you are supported.

Take each life experience as a teaching; gather them all in and discern their deeper message. Acknowledge the life-altering moments and people that have touched you and changed your life forever. Discern the stories that are no longer necessary to your growth and release them. Gather the wisdom teachings all around you; they are filled with goodness, truth, and beauty—let them live inside you. Welcome life's synchronicities and gather your soul family. Feel the depth of life's most cherished moments—the ones that take your breath away and stir your soul. This is the path to follow.

Do not fear the pause between what feels like a birth and what feels like a death. Death of the ego can take many forms: lack, scarcity, comparison, inertia, emptiness, unknowing. Be with them all. Use intuitive tools to seek the deeper meaning inside the story; no longer let them steal your light. Rebirth comes with a conscious and profound humility. Step into the unknown, bow to your teachers and guides, stay humble and true to your own intuitive power. Give yourself permission to be both terrified and liberated as you take the risks necessary to climb the mountain and share your soul's calling with the world. Dance this cosmic life dance through all of the realms from birth to death.

Time traveler, truth seeker—you are the midwife and the creator of your own life. To begin again is to know nothing. To know nothing is to be spacious enough to witness your own rebirthing into the next phase of personal evolution on this planet. To stay awake is to observe the death of your past and to stay focused on the maturation of your own mind–body process. Let yourself go to this dark place. Fall into a heap on top of that spirit mountain and rest for some time. Then pick yourself up and sort, sift, discern, burn, and synthesize all pieces ready to transform. And like the phoenix rising from the ashes, land at home inside this sacred body temple and begin anew. This is the place and space where you rise again. Crackling in the ancient embers, the heart stone speaks; the elder inside you is ready to share her wisdom. The transmuted relics of your own history can now be woven into the inner mystic of your holy body.

PARADIGM SHIFT: LIFE AS A TRAINING TOWARDS PRESENCE AND MIND–BODY AWAKENING

Once you place your faith and dedication in the mind–body-intuitive realms, you will never go back. The felt sense of connection will become so strong that you will no longer question the signs and symbols from your intuitive nature. You will feel guided by spirit. And there is more. This is not a passive role, it's an all-encompassing energy of reciprocity—when you place your attention on how energy moves and flows, energy comes back to support you.

Spirit works in the same way. When you begin to observe, listen, and activate your life with a deep, unconditional love for spirit and nature, they will come and join you in co-creating your life. The difference between being passively guided and actively guided is fundamental: you fully support and create the life you want by making choices according to your core beliefs, while feeling the nudges from spirit. Walk hand in hand with spirit and turn down the repetitive and limiting voices. Be as discerning as you are open; be as calm as you are wild. Co-create with vigor. Be attentive to present-moment details, and fill your mind–body channels with inner radiance on a daily basis. This is the paradigm shift: your life becomes a work in progress, an ongoing process toward present-moment awareness, a journey of awakening.

Life is a training towards understanding, cultivating, and following your own truth, building trust in your own inner knowing. By honoring change and possibility as a steady force, you build the inner listening required to trust the intuitive call to rest, pause, and take action. This becomes a felt sense when your inner systems organize and align into a state of flow. This flow state brings clarity and a deepening of personal core values. You can discern, in a flash, what feels right and what doesn't. And in turn, your capacity to share your most heartfelt desires and intuitive visions expands, bringing freedom over inner judgment and criticism.

Every day, we awaken to a world of possibility. Every day, we awaken to the potential for a new body and a new mind to emerge. Feel the goodness in you and count your blessings every morning. Call forth your gratitudes, light a candle, sip tea in the quietude of the early morning's light. Cast out your visions for your day; how do you want to walk into this day? See it, feel it, sense it by visualizing specific events in your day. If you anticipate any struggles or complexities, encircle them with a glow of possibility for goodness and right action.

Each morning as you wake, bless your loved ones, the earth, and yourself. Something wildly sacred happens when we consciously awaken with a pure, clean heart. Even if you didn't have the best sleep, feel tired or stressed—how can you greet yourself and your loved ones with loving awareness and open-ended possibility? This becomes an inner paradigm shift and a quiet felt sense. Instead of seeing what you don't have or feeling overwhelmed by what your day might bring, embrace yourself and your beloveds in a sacred space. Create room for energy to shift and for goodness to ripple out into the world.

As humans, we are naming and making machines. Why not train our naming and making around positive, higher vibrational energies? Instead of shooting arrows of projected illusions and lower motives, why not retrain your brain and your heart to embody universal life-force energy? Find the everyday pathways that imprint higher vibrational experiences rather than feeding the hungry lower vibrations. This is a powerful everyday ritual that will radically shift your life. Choose one activity a day that you know creates lasting joy and freedom and do it every day for seven days. Observe the effect it has on your life.

Developing intuition is always a work in progress; never assume it will stay active and alert. You must continue your daily rituals and soul-care practices in order for them to communicate with you. Let go of pleasing, proving, following, and posturing! Then you go so deep within your true nature that the pure essence of your authentic gifts emanates from you. This is the quest up the spirit mountain and down into the soul cave. Spirit calls you to tend your fires in both dimensions. Gather wood on a daily basis; let the sun's radiance merge into the field of your heart's most cherished prayers. Follow the moon's journey; she will keep you steady. Be a truth seeker, a love builder, and a soul weaver.

Hold the essence of grace and strength every step you take, and answer the call to be in service of the earth's glory. Tend to the winds of change, and feel the shape-shifting waters carry you into this present moment. Kiss the earth, touch the sky, lay down your selfish ways of consumption and ownership. Awaken to the stewardship of your own elemental body coming alive. This becomes a living practice, and it will allow your dreams to come alive.

Find solace in the natural world. This is where the magic is found. Practice non-judgment and choose love over fear. Refine your mind–body channels; make this a non-negotiable and wildly sacred daily event. Become deeply committed to your inner self so that you can look at yourself in the mirror with compassion and say "I love you," even on the toughest days. Build your discernment muscles just as much as you strengthen your core. Be constantly curious about your own process and acknowledge the flashes of intuition that bring you absolute clarity. Get to know those sensations so well that you can recognize when they are calling to you.

When you find yourself in a funk, let yourself go there. Breathe, dance, shake it out. Move your energy any way you can. Feel into your process, knowing that there is a greater message in it for you. Ask yourself often, "What can I learn? What is the deeper message coming through?" Feel into wholeness of the present moment while seeing with the eyes of spirit. Open your awareness to this paradigm shift. Practice patience, find counsel in good company with the ones you trust. Observe your inner motivations and call them out when they are not clear and pure. Everything is connected. What you feed your mind becomes your reality. What you allow to live on in the form of habits and thoughts, words and actions, becomes who you are. Refine your core values and call forth what you stand for. This is your invitation to think like a mystic. No longer invite low vibrational energies into your sacred forest.

Whatever your faith, culture, ancestry, lived experience, and belief systems are, are you ready and willing to commit to living as the best version of you? Not only for yourself, but to inspire others and contribute towards the planetary evolution for the betterment of the earth and humanity? An embodied spiritual path is one of connection with the natural world, one of awakening. It is placing utmost value on the art of living with an inner knowing that your good, conscious efforts will affect everything you touch and see.

As humans, we are deeply wired to find connection and seek true purpose in our lives. For you this may come through a career, a creative endeavor, or a deepening of family relations and friendship. The art of living and loving spiritually, with true purpose and fulfillment, becomes integrated within everyday life.

The connective integration gets interrupted when the mind spins with fear and the narrative of taking the wrong direction in life consumes you. Release the identity and fantasy you have around "readiness"—you will know when you are ready to go there. You will know when you are ready to meditate on a daily basis because you know how good it makes you feel. You will commit to writing your morning pages because it clears you mind. This inner feedback is your inner mystic nudging you onwards into the next phase of your own evolution.

SOURCING PERSONAL CAPACITY: COSMIC AND STEADY

When you open your awareness to a state of cosmic yet steady observation you move into the simple yet wildly auspicious place between rest and activation. Dwell inside this enigmatic pause when it arrives, and reflect on the medicine of your heart's calling. Always come back to your heart. It is here that the inner critic softens, your constant mind chatter decreases, and you befriend your heart's flame like a long-lost soul mate. As you lay down your past relics and enshrine them with your most spirited and intentional surrenders, a brave new realm emerges. The old fires have burned to ash. The new fire awaits you—the collective fire, where consciousness has shifted and hearts have become de-armored and liberated. You are not alone on this journey. Welcome others into your ceremony.

This initiation calls on you to be both brave and discerning, soft yet strong. Your past fears no longer rule you, their fires have burned long enough. And there you are, basking in the arms of the ancient ones, receiving wisdom from the future ones. Walk through the door. The intuitive whispers come to you in the night and touch your heart like a newborn in your arms. This is you birthing yourself alive. This is you becoming your own healer. This is you steady and cosmic all at once. This is you effecting positive change in the world—leading the youth, caring for elders, and inspiring your community towards seeing the simple beauty in all of life. The call of your own maturation in you is calling you to the fireside. Sip tea, chop wood, carry water, and be the lighthouse on your personal journey. Your evolution is the revolution. You are the shape-shifter, stone carver, thread spinner; you are the weaver, the farmer, the hunter, and the gatherer. Touch the earth, kiss the sky, feel the water, and build your fires.

Open yourself to the call of your own destiny. When the ancient ones call you to walk backwards to receive the most exquisite incarnation, accept the invitation. Lay down your fast paced, forward striving agenda. Your current journey may need rerouting—this will feel like you are walking backwards to receive insight. It may be time to slow down: bask in stillness to hear, see, feel, and sense what is emerging now. The collective heart will hold you to your highest. You are supported. You have already arrived. Your purpose is already known to you. Lay down your constant striving and your unquenchable thirst, and drink from the well of goodness and truth. Give your fears and worries to the wind. Arrange them with precious care as you say goodbye.

Go to the water and cleanse yourself of longing and attachments, and let the sun's glow fill you with the vibration of the ancient stars. No longer do you need to climb the endless ladder. Release the narrative that your greatest desires are out of your reach—for you have arrived.

Walk backwards to remember where you are going. Trust. Every single day anew.

THE CALL OF THE MYSTIC: PRACTICAL WISDOM

A mystical approach to life calls for surrender and contemplation leading to unity consciousness through the physical, mental, emotional, and spiritual channels—oneness with self and oneness with nature. A mystical attitude invites spiritual encounters and connections.

To live into this paradigm, you must believe in the possibility of attaining insight into the non-ordinary realms through the development of intuition. Trust in the unfolding of divine timing while accessing the sacred moments inside the mundane of everyday life. To believe in oneness with the natural world—using meditation, mind–body practices, and deep reverence for the beauty of the natural world—builds resilience, faith, and hope. These are far stronger than your personal limitations and fears. Through meditation and mind–body practices, your intuitive systems align and come alive. You can have a spiritual experience in the form of the human body.

Remaining Grounded as a Modern Mystic

The modern mystic sees love as the ultimate source of life. You acknowledge that the universe is infinite, complex, and mysterious. You are a student of life, honoring spirituality as a personal experience cultivated through dedicated mind–body practices, and embracing each stage of life as a lived experience towards personal evolution. The intuitive mystic holds a natural curiosity about the physical and spiritual realms and can relate to both while staying grounded in the present moment. You value ancient wisdom teachings where knowledge, language, and physical senses come alive with insight.

As a mystic, your intuition is both guide and teacher. The mystic has a developed and unshakeable belief in divine timing and trust in what the universe delivers. You find comfort in the unknown, yet you know when it's time to rest and when it's time to activate—this is one of the mystic's superpowers. With curiosity, the mystic initiates daily soul-care rituals and traditions that trigger growth and have a profound ripple effect on personal and spiritual evolution. This daily work becomes the art inside the ritual, finely crafted and attuned to expand and respond to your current lived experience.

Humble at the core, the modern mystic is more concerned with understanding and integrating emotions than engaging in power plays. The modern mystic is committed and dedicated to supporting all living things.

A mystic believes and trusts that the universe has a greater plan for positive planetary evolution. You are a contributor and a co-creator in this process through continued learning and releasing, through activating, and attuning to body–mind channels. Thus you welcome experiences of oneness. You care for your body like a finely tuned instrument, develop your mind with clearing practices, and work to refine and integrate your emotional energy in order to sense the exquisite divinity and cosmic happenings in every step you take.

THE QUEST OF THE MYSTIC

The modern mystic's quest is to be compassionate on all levels. To be wildly forgiving of your inner child lashing out, to laugh at your own idiosyncrasies, and to marvel at the wonder of the starry night sky. It is the call to awaken to the hawk messenger swooping before you, or how the stormy waters pulled the salted tears out of your heart. It is that moment when the colors in the trees shift before your eyes to send you a signal. Take all of this to heart. You are an intuitive, mystical, wildly loving, and imperfectly perfect work in progress. The path of liberation is woven into the marrow of your bones, and your mind is ready to make this shift. Give it permission. Cut the cords to your wounded warrior and step inside the cocoon of your own inner alchemy; this is your superpower now. And yes, it takes hard work, a daily practice, and a lifetime of compassion and forgiveness. And yes, it lives in you, it lives in your lover, your children, animals, and your family. It lives in the plants in your garden, the trees in the forest; it lives in the ocean and lakes and in the moon and the sun—all expressed in different ways. It is the universal life-force energy of kindness, compassion. The unshakeable knowledge that beauty and love live everywhere.

What do you do with the mind loops and repetitive thought processes that hold you back? Do you go to sleep? Do you choose to put the book down, turn the page, or stop the chapter from unfolding? This is the work: to acknowledge where you fall asleep, forget, and live a passive life. Not living in harmony and unity within your own being is to turn your back on your own evolution. And that is okay, because it becomes a choice. When you practice non-judgment, you can forgive yourself, let go, and begin again. Back to the breath, to the tea pot, to the nature walk, to the relationships—bringing your own heart and soul into everything you do. Nothing more, nothing less.

When you find yourself inside the dark night of the soul, how do you know things will change? Because they will. Because divine timing is on your side. Because you will grow tired of the dark lonely nights. Because you can receive support and guidance from your loved ones and from spirit. Once the bond is formed between you and your inner mystic, it won't be forgotten. You have reached a new level in your own evolution. Your inner mystic awakening is wildly personal and developed through consistent practice, personal responsibility, and following your heartfelt desires to understand the spiritual medium that brings you into a state of oneness. Follow the desire and release the outcome.

If personal and spiritual expression comes in the form of dancing, painting, writing, cooking, cross training, mountaineering, singing, counseling, weaving, or running marathons—then do it! It's not what you do, it's how you do it. Bring your conscious work into a fluid state—trust it, and become wildly embodied inside your craft. Find the outlet in which you can be free, fluid, peaceful, and completely at home in your own skin.

Untangle the knots of your unconscious negativity and low self-worth.
Disrupt the power-over syndrome.

Feed your inner child with the wild, soft,
sweetness of nectar-infused love.

Hand in hand, walk your younger self through the portal
of compassion out of abandonment.

Clean mind, pure heart, a fierce grace of letting go to remember.

Lay down your worries, toss your limited systems
like an offering to the fire.
Soothe your mind with an awakened promise
that you are deserving of a deeper love.

Re-dream the dream. Feel its glow like sunbeams infusing your bones.

This new world has already prepared for your mythic arrival.

THE PATH:
EMBODIED, INTEGRATED, ALIVE

Embodied

The mystic lives through an embodied energy where the physical, emotional, mental, and spiritual channels become aligned and work together. This becomes a daily practice—an intentional way of weaving the sacred into your daily life. Living with an anchored yet mindful presence lets you see beyond the pull and tug of your daily emotions. When you become aware of how your energy affects everyone else around you, you begin to receive the reflections of your own defense mechanisms and reactionary patterns. This then becomes the present-moment "accountability" feedback for you to pause before falling into the autopilot reactions of the past. Here you call yourself out with compassion and learn how to respond in a new way. Once you clean your own energy field, you no longer take everything so personally—because you yourself are living this reflective, intentional, and present-moment experience.

Trust that human emotions and minds are complex. By not taking everything so personally, you acknowledge there may be something you don't know that is causing the issue. It's not always about you.

Through personal accountability you also set clear boundaries, because you are no longer acting out of defense but out of inquiry and non-attachment. You learn how to build your listening and observing skills. The one deep breath you take instead of saying something harmful builds your body of intuitive resilience. This one simple breath can redirect limiting thoughts and patterns into a moment of awakening.

Your daily meditation practice, or mindful moments of stillness, calm, and quiet, expand your viewpoint. Through this perspective you are more likely to call yourself out when you are not being impeccable, and you can see it in others as well. This wisdom teaching comes through the practice of non-judgment, being mindful of words and thoughts, and taking action based on pure truth—not ulterior motives. Empowering your inner spirit through mindful state changes and activations is the practice and the medicine of the modern mystic.

Integrated

Inside the force field of your personal alchemy live the universal oppositional energies: darkness and light, waxing and waning, life and death, pause and activation, dreaming and realization. Each expression of opposition provides signs and symbols showing you how to utilize inner body awareness towards outer body expression. When you can stay in real time with the elements and how they support you, you can ebb and flow through life with grace, ease, and resilience. When you find yourself lost, confused, or overwhelmed, how do you come back home to integrate your experiences? Falling off center allows you to find your center. And this is the powerful moment of integration—when you can radically accept what the current situation is, not push it away or repress it, but hold it with unconditional curiosity. This inquiry creates space to process your emotions and eventually grants you clarity. When you can integrate the process of letting go more efficiently, you receive guidance through a deeper message coming through. Your visions can become your reality when you stay awake to your process.

Work with the limitations and blockages in your life in order to see more clearly where to focus your attention. For example, if you experience a constant belief of unworthiness inside a relationship, and this story continues to loop endlessly in your mind, you actually become a magnet for unhealthy (or non-existent) relationships. You will literally and symbolically understand that the death of your old habits, patterns, and mind loops is the path towards reclaiming wholeness. Where you once could not stand to look at yourself in the mirror, you will go to the mirror and see the beauty inside your soulful eyes. You will relish the radiance in your heart. You will begin to see the aura around your body glow. You will believe in the power of life's great mysteries, see them inside the wonders of nature, and allow them to live inside of you.

Herein lies the nectar of integration—when you allow your life experiences to elevate your personal evolution rather than damage it, you welcome your true essence and your highest self. By feeling the birth of your visions come alive in the dreamtime, you enable them to manifest in real time.

Alive

To live awake and present in this highly distracted, technological, and individualistic world requires a diligent practice of self-care. To embody and integrate the wisdom teachings of heart-centered living, you must hone your skills of compassion and forgiveness with yourself and others. To practice compassion is to recognize that each living energy has its own unique capacity, story, and desire for expression. In your deepest life partnerships, the work of compassion and forgiveness become perhaps the grandest work of your lifetime. When you become anchored into your own living body as a vessel of compassion and forgiveness through mindful, quiet moments, you build this capacity. You greet your loved ones each morning with a clean and clear love because you have done the work to see yourself with love. You hold space to forgive yourself. You simply apologize for your ill intent, you overcome your pride, and you become truthful with your intentions. You understand more readily that each person has their own unique way of processing information. The work is not always to understand, but to be compassionate to your own and each other's process.

The glowing candle reminds you to live in the way of beauty and illumination. As you gaze into the candle's flame, call forth your gratitudes. Visualize your inner radiance moving though your day with grace and flow, and let go of the external expectations and events that are simply out of your control.

To embody a living sense of wonder and curiosity feeds positive energy into every life cycle, stage, and situation. To see through the eyes and heart of a child is a true gift. The questions "What if?" and "Why?" become the bridge towards an integrated, embodied, and awakened presence. Why not ask these questions? Why assume you are right? Why do you believe the complex mind grooves that say you are not enough? This kind of mindful living takes daily commitment.

The space you create to truly inhabit your body with a conscious and clear mind will radically shift your life for the better. Ritual and creativity feed the curiosity of a beginner's mind that becomes the healing elixir of modern life. How can you lose yourself in a creative process and get to the state in which time stands still, the mental chatter quiets, and your fragmented and stress-based holding patterns begin to dissolve? Your breath becomes fluid, longer, deeper; your body softens; your mind expands into your heart. Spirit comes to you in these places of creativity and soulful connection. Spirit dances inside the realms of life's most wondrous ephemeral moments—the fleeting moments, not recorded, not repeated—pure presence embodied, awake and alive inside you. Let this be your inspiration and your guide towards living a full, whole, and present life.

The freedom trail awaits your return. The spirit house is ready for you to move into. Make a commitment on a daily basis to activate soul-care rituals that remind you of your worth, that teach you presence, and that inject you with a wild love and cosmic joy. Your spirit guides will give you a standing ovation. They are cheering for you, bravo! Encore! Again! They are right here with you, encouraging you to share your life's unique and wondrous mission in the world.

In a flash, recalibrate your body–mind–heart field.
Diversify your inner matrix.
Be a truth-seeking trailblazer.
Liberate yourself from external expectations.
For this one moment, no longer dwell in the past or future.
Frequently ask yourself "what if?" and "why?"
This conversation becomes the fuel to sculpt your current process.
Climbing spirit mountain is an artistic relationship.
Your heart-centered devotion is the path and the journey.

EVOLVE YOU, EVOLVE THE PLANET

To evolve into the next stage of your unfolding journey, you must attune to your current physical, emotional, mental, and spiritual capacities as a living, breathing energy. Through this personal inquiry into your own energy, you discover what needs tending. Your body–mind temple provides the sustenance, vigor, calm, and connection that allow you to stay present in your mercurial energy body.

The evolutionary path of the human psyche is to elevate the mind–body–spirit connection. As humans, we feel joy when we relate to others with love. We receive life-force energy when we spend time in nature's beauty. When we live in harmony with the five elements as our teachers, we find connection to something bigger than us. We tap into an alchemy that allows us to take deep, full breaths, we allow our perspective to shift, and we feel held and inspired through all of life's complexities. We trust that we are being supported by spirit. Our connections with other humans become deeply moving and meaningful when we are aligned ourselves. This path allows us to evolve. Each of us has come into this world with a unique energy to heal, learn, express, and evolve.

By following your passions and doing the work that truly lights you up, you do it not only for you, but for others. Your conscious work ripples out in wild, immeasurable ways.

When in doubt, remember that your words are like golden threads. What you speak inside your mind and out into the world can shift not only your life, but also inspire others to live out their dreams. Rise up when you catch a glimmer or a whisper of your truth speaking to you. Be brave, bold, and steady, and let spirit come into you like a flash of energy, taking your breath away. Spirit love has no conditions or rules, yet it is infused in respect for all living things on this earth. Spirit love is being at one with nature. Grow your body of spirit love, and good energy will encircle you and your loved ones. Spirit love for Mother Earth, for clean waterways, for clean air, and for the passion of your fire.

When spirit love is deeply integrated and embodied, it pushes you to take action for what you believe in; it shows you how to express it out into the world. Spirit love expands and ripples and rips through the places and spaces that need it the most. Once you embody this essence, it never dies. When others feel it, they naturally gravitate to its luminous light energy. Make spirit love your life's work. Steep it inside your body temple; feed it joy, creativity, and kindness. Practice joy over judgment, creativity over slumbering in the mundane, kindness over criticism.

Observe the surges of spirit-love energy—be love maker, bridge builder, spirit seeker. Plant your seeds of goodness and beauty every chance you get. Be one with the dark nights and dance with your shadows until they alchemize into compassion and understanding. Awaken your inner trail guide, the luminous healer within, the death doula, the midwife of life, the peacemaker, and the activist for social change. You are all of these things and more. You are a living, breathing, body of sacred timeless energy. The ancient ones, the elders, the future generations—they see you, they feel you, they walk with you.

Allow your brave eyes to see with this infinite, timeless love and channel your sacred tears to flow with ease and grace, for they are the salt of the earth. Praise your own spirit for its dedication to keeping going, and breathe life force into your own potent soul essence. This becomes the daily work of the modern mystic. Allow your intuition to be your guide. You no longer need validation to do this work. For if not you, then who? For if not now, then when?

Be the impassioned warrior for the betterment of humanity. This energy brings the vibrations of goodness, passion, and peace. You will feel good, nourished, and free in this mystical spirit-love presence. Everything and everyone around you will receive this numinous energy; its expansive and clear channels will feel good and right.

EMBRACE THE MYSTIC WAY

To embody the alchemical attitude of the mystic's way is the call of modern times. At this turning point in human evolution and consciousness, we are ready and equipped for this planetary shift. The current changes and uprisings in the world are calling us to wake up. You have the tools and the resources to practice mind–body connectivity; in truth, you were built for this reckoning. To express yourself freely and fully is the path of the living mystic. Share your reverent humility and fiery grace with the world. No longer slumber your days away; remember who you are and where you have come from. Recall your ancestors' journey and awaken to the healing that must come through you to liberate the coming generations. Walk backwards in order to remember. You have gone forwards long enough. The ancients are calling you home. Welcome yourself home.

In our modern world, everything, including change itself, is happening at a more rapid pace than ever. Combine this hyper convenient fast-food reality with a mix of climate crisis, existential threat, and the uprisings of humans all over the world (whose land, culture and people have been stolen from them). The longstanding paradigms of colonialism and power-over politics, religion, and war are currently being named for what they are and dismantled. Racism, sexism, patriarchy, colonialism, misogyny, and violence—this is a time of necessary uprising. In the current stage of planetary alchemy, the limiting ways of the past are dying, literally and symbolically.

Wear your heart on your sleeve for the good of humanity. Honor that the path of spirit has a thousand names, endless forms, lineages, and structures. For your own faith to be truly embodied, recognize it as the practice of being awake, aware, open, and embodied.

A new era has arrived. We are on the precipice of something never lived before. Our children's eyes are watching, and their ears are listening. Our elders have insight into this epic transformation. How will we walk into this new cycle of life, remembering the call of the mystics for soul liberation and collective awakening? At this precipice, we continue to find the good medicine for our times. This will light the fires of change and planetary evolution. We must carry the healing waters forward while shedding the toxic build-up of our past. As we clear the polluted waters inside our own vessels, we create space for change. We see with fresh eyes and we no longer pass on the pollution to the coming generations. Instead, we teach them how to grow food and survive in the wild. They need to know the land as well as they navigate technology. We must plant seeds of presence every step we take. We must pray for our loved ones to flourish, and we must pray for the earth to be replenished with goodness.

For this energetic and planetary shift in consciousness, what are you willing to do? How are you willing to change in order to live sustainably and have less impact on the earth? What responsibility will you take?

Gather by your sacred fire, witness the wood turn to ember and to ash. Feel the ashes in your hands, sense the ancients support your journey, and allow your own evolution to unfold.

Then pay it forward—become a humble channel for the simplest gestures for the song in the medicine flowers. Birth your inner mystic. Let the old ways die and slide off like a snake shedding its skin. This is how the mystic co-creates with the universe. Every day is a series of births and deaths. Living through all the realms—the highs and the lows—the mystic is armed with humor and heart, with levity and gravitas. The journey is timeless and infinite.

Life is a living ritual. Follow this path with a grounded body, an open mind, and a curious heart. Be ready and willing to merge into the timeless recall of the shooting stars, the pause in the owl's call, the shimmery sunlight sparkles on the lake in the late afternoon sun—this is how to fill the well of your own evolution. It's in the quiet, unexpected moments that the flashes and surges of spirit energy come through. A little goes a long way. Make room and space for this quiet in your daily living and loving.

The Mystic Code

Write sacred love notes and poetry to the divine. Cast your heartfelt, crystal-clear intentions out into the universe. Have a conversation with your highest self.

Pray out loud, and often. Co-create your reality with the support of universal life-force energy that lives all around you. Train your mind to be touched by the striking beauty of the natural world. Let it speak louder than the hardships of life.

Build an authentic relationship with the elements, the sun, and the moon. Synchronize your inner body with their cosmic rhythms. Let their essence become your muse and your teacher. Go beyond the mind chatter, and open your channels to receive messages from your guides. Commit to developing your intuition, and trust your gut. Keep your mind–body energy clean. Listen to the divine whispers that come through you like a flash—they have come for a reason. Observe energy as a practice. Immerse yourself in nature as a healing balm for your senses. Widen your lens in order to see from another perspective. Ask yourself the questions "What if?" and "Why?" often. Take things less personally, and belly laugh more often.

Dwell your consciousness in the mystical, mysterious, and wondrous places. Practice the art of non-attachment and letting go on a daily basis. Pay attention to how you wake up and go to bed—make it spiritual. Stay true to who you are and live out your core values. Observe when you are exaggerating the truth and reroute the pattern. Catch yourself when you are gossiping or speaking unkindly about others. Practice soulful kindness, humility, and compassion—unconditionally. Become a channel of oneness; call forward your prayers of love, truth, joy and peace for the collective. Every day, trust that your ripple effect makes mountains move and fields of the most exquisite wildflowers grow.

ELEMENTAL WISDOM: FIVE CYCLES OF AWARENESS INSIDE THE WHEEL OF LIFE

The rhythms of our daily activities can become a spiritual practice if we shift our consciousness from a state of negativity or dread to one of expansive acceptance and revered presence. This daily practice can be cherished in the rhythms of weaving the elements, the seasonal wheel of the year, the 29.5-day lunar cycle. You can honor your personal alchemy as a work of art. Allow your process to be one of conscious evolution—hold the intention that your energy is divine, and tend to it like the precious temple it is. The path of possibility and connection will open before you, both in the physical and spiritual planes, inside the literal and symbolic realms. Your energy body will come alive with reverence and commitment to loving and living your soul's passion. Through this process of illumination your dreams will unfold as your consciousness expands.

Awakening

Element: Air
Direction: East
Season: Spring Equinox
Body Channel: Heart
Essence: Sovereign Heart + Perspective

Honoring the rising sun in the east, welcome in the dawn of the new day. Awaken to the potential to move through your day with ease, grace, and clarity. As you light your morning candle, call forth your gratitudes and visualize glimmers of your day and how you want to show up inside them. Breathe in fresh air as if it holds the alchemy of joy and strength to follow your heartfelt desires. You begin anew each morning, like the scent of spring, the bulbs shooting from the earth, and the birdsong alive with joy. Give thanks to the sky realms, the winds of change at your back, and to the element of air for breathing into another day on this planet.

Call forth the visionary inside your heart. Gather your roots and your wings and set yourself free from what binds you. Plant your seeds into your heart; remember, you are a good person. Embrace your spirit with an unshakeable, non-negotiable and wild self-love. Call on your good ancestors and your compassionate guides. Ask for support as you journey through this cycle of your life. Pray out loud from the pulse of your heart, always be in conversation with it. Check in and honor what is coming through you. Pray out loud for the collective heart of the planet to awaken to a world where heart-led and soul-fed leadership consciously and collectively brings about positive change.

Give yourself permission to practice the art of forgiveness and compassion inside the realms of ordinary life. Through letting go of judgment of yourself and others, move through your day with the sweetness of nectar in your heart, the rooting of an ancient cedar tree, and the wings of an eagle. Give weight to your shifting perspective as it surges through you—this is the call of the mystic. Share your heart wisdom with honest humility and non-attachment. Give it freely and cleanly. The world is so ready to receive your honest heart wisdom!

Transformation Through Purification

Element: Fire
Direction: South
Season: Summer Solstice
Body Channel: Solar Plexus
Essence: Active Transformation + Pure Inner Power

Honoring the direction of south, greet the passion of your energy field knowing that you can purify yourself through mind–body practices. Your daily rituals will allow you to stay clear and clean in your authenticity. Welcome your teachers on a daily basis. They will come in your thoughts and habits, in your reactions and judgments of self and others. The messengers will come through your family, your work, and the planet at large.

Welcome the feelings of lack, unworthiness, and shame as the material through which you practice discernment and develop your authentic core beliefs. When your limiting core beliefs begin to dance inside your mind and swirl through your sacred body, interrupt the process. Pause, breathe deeply, and toss that outdated energy into the fire. Watch it transform before your eyes.

Feel the sacred refinement of your inner power at your solar plexus. Work with the element of fire to remind yourself of your inner power and strength. Light candles, make fires, feel the warmth of the sun's glow, and let them purify and transform you in a flash. Express your own abundance and inner power; celebrate and share it with the world.

Like the sun, burn bright. Give freely without expecting anything in return. When you are ready say goodbye to outmoded ways of living and being. You will know when the time is right; the call to take action will speak loudly enough that you will simply act. This is the foundation of reclaiming your true self and transforming your life.

Illumination and Flow

Element: Water
Direction: West
Season: Fall Equinox
Body Channel: Pelvis, hips, womb, lower abdomen
Essence: Flow + Intuitive Integration

Honoring the westerly winds of change, welcome your ability to flow, shape-shift, and work with your emotions on a daily basis. Allow water to remind you of how to dance inside your own fluidity. Let yourself be hydrated, soothed, refreshed, and rejuvenated by its healing properties. Water teaches you how to let go so that you can consciously welcome oppositional flows of energy. This connects you to your higher self. Remember that nothing is to be repressed or buried down in your emotional body. Speaking your truth to yourself and others, with compassion, gives you the permission to work through your current state. Spirit will endlessly support your process and your journey.

Water clears judgment of self and others so you can dive into your own highly creative, sensual, and pleasure-filled experiences. Ignite your own signature essence. This awakens your intuitive receptors. Your gut instincts come alive when you are well nourished— emotionally, physically, mentally, and spiritually.

As you move through your day, walk with beauty. See the illumination inside energy fields; trust in the positive insights and messages that light up your soul. Observe when guilt, fear, inertia, and stress take over your guts. This is a sign for you to pause, place your hands on your lower abdomen, and breathe deeply. Connect to what your stressors are, visualize them leaving your body, and let go of what you cannot control. Commit to what you can do to better your situation, and enter your flow state.

Drink a tall glass of water. Like the autumn leaves falling from the tree and regenerating the soil, trust in the letting go of your own triggers and stressors—they will give birth to illumination within you. Be like water— shape-shift into a new version of you.

Building Intuition and Tending to the Inner Life

Element: Earth
Direction: North
Season: Winter Equinox
Body Channel: Tailbone, pubic bone, sitting bones, legs, feet
Essence: Grounding + Honoring Abundance

Every step you take, honor the earth for her wild, rugged beauty and infinite abundance. Cast your gaze towards the north. Feel the mountain's strong presence, the vast plains, and the softness of the earth's delicate womb all within you. You are of this nature too; both soft and strong all at once. Honor the indigenous cultures that inhabited the land before you. Rekindle a connection to your ancestry and your chosen spiritual practices, faiths, and lineages. Commit to a daily practice that allows you to live inside the presence of real time. Find the techniques that light you up, give you clarity of mind, ground you in your body, and connect you to your intuition.

Believe in your ability to be steady and cosmic, to live fully present in the physical realms while being open to the unseen or spiritual realms. There you receive support and guidance. Then you can consciously discern between your critical mind tendencies and what your sixth sense wants to communicate with you.

Open your inner senses to see the visions, hear the whispers, and dream the dreams. For if you can't see it, you will not live it. Dance with the unknown, and welcome it in. Let your guides in; they are willing and ready to support you towards the best version of you—your highest self on this earthly plane.

Pray out loud and often. To live a spiritual life in human form is to honor each interaction, emotion, thought, experience, and event as a teaching. Be a student of life. Dance with curiosity and humility, and embrace your body temple with the warmth and nurturing of Mother Earth's most glorious beauty. No longer just see her beauty, *be* her beauty.

Unity: Integration + Embodiment

Element: Ether
Direction: Center
Symbol: Spiral
Body Channel: Throat, mind, and energy body
Essence: Space + Spiritual Embodiment

Honor the element of ether, which lives inside space, stillness, and all that contains and holds energy. This sacred element is found in your center. It encapsulates the gifts with which you were born, and its soul purpose is to align with your highest self. It is the space between your inhale and your exhale, the pause in your thoughts, your words, and your songs. The space where spirit holds the physical and where physical holds the spiritual. It dances with your feminine and your masculine mythology. It holds you and reminds you that you are a spiritual being, and that your intuitive nature, your ability to access the other realms and pray, has a ripple effect in the world.

Our prayers and heartfelt intentions hold weight. They effect change within us. Ether is the teacher of possibility, the miracle of life, and the tragedy of death. It is the messenger that calls us to the tea ceremony, the trailhead, the vision quest, the silent retreat, and the rite of passage that brings us to our knees in prayer. We feel it when we give birth to a child or a new paradigm within our soul; it holds a magnetic light, an unforgettable glowing and growing presence.

Ether holds an internal enigma. It is untouchable and cannot be named. It has a felt sense that inspires change, positivity, and deep imprints within the heart that will alter the course of your life. Ether exists everywhere. It grows inside a daily practice of trusting in the compassionate support from the unseen realms. It lives through your eyes as you walk in beauty and see the beauty all around you. Trust in the glimmers of light that cross your path, the animals that greet you on your journey, the omens in the shoot-ing stars, the glow of hope in the full moon's light, the ripple on the lake's surface, the wind that calls to you. Trust in these auspicious moments, which breed devotion over duty, love over fear, and clarity over confusion.

Build your capacity to attune to the cosmic glow that lives in the pause and the space between spaces. This will generate a field of possibility within your reality.

SPIRIT MOUNTAIN:
THE SACRED ART OF FINDING THE MIDDLE WAY

Being in any kind of relationship is a creative process, and with conscious effort it can become an intentional and cherished living art form. The creative journey of intimacy is vast, open, and process oriented; it can be applied in your relationship with yourself, with your loved ones, and with spirit.

Your ability to stay clearly attuned to the needs, wants, and desires of self or others is essential to the awakening process. When you turn towards judgment, defensiveness, and reactiveness, you lose clarity and connection. You find yourself in the weeds, deep in the murky waters, lost and no longer grounded. You build walls around yourself in order to grasp something familiar. You revert to your inner child. The moment you can honestly call yourself out and take personal responsibility for your actions is the moment of awakening and evolving. The work of building any form of sacred relationship is through listening, opening to the deeper teachings in the moment, and hearing the message from spirit that may want to come. Over time, the spiritual art forms and practices of prayer, meditation, nature infusion, and daily ritual become the ground for conscious relationship.

When you find yourself feeling imbalanced, when extreme feelings, thoughts, and actions overcome you, visualize a quiet country dirt road in front of you. Connect to your breath, soften, and see yourself simply walking down the middle of the road. Open your awareness to the horizon in the distance. Remember that you are supported by the elements, the directions, and the spiritual realms as you journey down this open road. Receive any feelings, intuitive messages or surges of insight that come through you. Is there a nourishing energy that will support you in this moment? Practice compassionate inquiry; be as spacious about your own perspective as you are to that of all living beings. This way of creative visualization and perceiving is both a practice and a tool that will support your spiritual and physical relationships. You give them space to breathe; you grant them your good energy rather than your reactionary or defensive energy. When you train yourself to stay out of judgment and move into discernment, you allow the practice of compassion to grow inside you. This leads you back into the awakening of your own personal maturation and development time and time again.

The art form of simply listening without formulating judgment inside your mind instantly widens your ability to see and perceive. The breath deepens, the body grounds; the defensive, hurt, angry inner child no longer takes over. This shift will alter the course of your life. This is both the moment of reckoning and the moment of returning to your higher self. It's learning to understand when your pride and ego strongholds you into believing your own ill-willed judgments. When you can't apologize because you are too proud, or when your ego can't acknowledge where you were acting out of personal integrity—you turn away from connection and inner guidance. This is true on all levels—the physical, emotional, mental, and spiritual.

You shut down and turn away from your own higher self. You get blindsided by judgments and bounced around by your own critical mind. You convince yourself of the limiting "I am always…, I am never…" statements. In this surge of a second, intuitive messages get lost and the middle way up spirit mountain is no longer visible. Herein lies the work. You must practice getting lost in order to find yourself again. When you practice the art of living and loving with an open ear and an unarmored heart, you get spacious and compassionate once again. The middle-way journey up spirit mountain reopens when judgmental behavior no longer defines you.

This is how to creatively work with daily rhythms and rituals as sacred art forms. You are the artist, creator, and sculptor. You become so skilled in the creative process of living and loving, of listening and observing, of supporting and receiving, that you find yourself more equipped for life's wild ride than ever before. Sometimes we just need to pause and listen in order to see the open road before us. The path of the middle way leads us towards greater connection and fulfillment on all levels. It's wildly invigorating.

Because you give yourself permission to fall off the path and go to the depths of the earth for healing, you get to travel to the stars for an illuminating transmission. And you always know where to land back home. The ritualist, the alchemist, the modern-day spirit seeker travels long distances down the dusty, sun drenched, middle road. You know the way, and when you find it, you will never question it again. It lives inside you. It is you. You are the living, breathing, wild spirit seeker/truth teller/mystic in training—creating the middle way.

THE COSMIC WEB: YOUR HEART IS YOUR MEDICINE

To live, be guided, and to lead from the awakened heart is to evolve your own consciousness. Through the dedicated practice of soul-care rituals you honor your higher self. Over time, and with true commitment and personal accountability, you release the deep-seated patterns of lack, scarcity, fear, mistrust, anger and guilt (to name a few). These must be acknowledged, recognized, and released for you to live from your own sovereign soul leadership. Through this process comes an opportunity to create a new mythology within your own consciousness and that of the collective. We live deeply within this wild, cosmic web of life, where everything is interconnected. As we begin to understand how the elements, the seasons, the directions, and our own personal alchemy contribute to our life's direction, we begin to sense how our own energy influences everything.

In feeling this web of interconnection, we also touch upon the literal/symbolic, ancient/contemporary sense that the art of embodied ritual exists when your inner alignment and your external expression harmonize. What you do in your own web affects the web of everyone and everything around you. When your consciousness evolves, you begin to clearly envision and feel how you can contribute to a new world order. You become more aware of human rights, climate change activism, and compassionate living and loving. You become an activist. Can you begin to sense how your own finely crafted and attuned heart-led leadership will contribute to the new world that is being born before our eyes?

What if our daily check-ins rekindled the mind–body wisdom that the collective heart paradigm is infinite, timeless, and steeped in the universal truths of love, joy, peace, and balance? In this golden era of convenience, technology, and free will, we have a great opportunity to heal from our past conditioning and karmic wounds. We have the intelligence, facts, resources, and heart to reach another level of consciousness. To journey deeper in our own freedom and joy, we must do the work to deepen honest self-reflection, anchored in the present moment reality and inspired by the rhythm and ritual of daily life. When we do the hard work of rerouting our mental wiring and become pure in our motivations, we align with the intelligence of the mind–body, which then allows the intuition and the spirit realms to be expressed through us.

Practice speaking truth over exaggeration. Express love beyond fear; live from devotion and commitment rather than duty and guilt. Build your heart relationship inside the sphere of goodness over co-dependency. Allow daily interactions to come from presence and wholeness rather than slumbered ego states of ignorance, power-over and lack of interest. No longer get consumed within your own self-serving bubble of ignorance. Become an earth-side angel; a good ancestor.

Harness, cultivate, integrate, and embody the sacred energy that exists everywhere. Train your inner eye to see beyond the mundane. See it inside your lover's eye and see it inside your own soul. Let this sacred illumination come alive.

Structure your daily life rhythm as a living ritual. The beauty of your own present mind and awakened heart is the greatest gift and contribution towards the cosmic web. Individually and collectively, spin the web daily; see it glisten, watch it break, weave it again. Observe how the web integrates your life events—both softly and with great strength—not only through you, but around you. This is the work. You are vast and dynamic, fierce and fluid, clear and mysterious. You find comfort in the dark, quiet, internal moments. You activate your heart's magic like the sun's warming glow and cast it out far and wide. Let your alchemy be a gift to the universe. Let it be an act of compassion. Be a heart medicine gardener, and watch your spirit flowers bloom and ripple in the minds and souls of many.

Share the wildflower bouquets of your soul with strangers, with your kindred, and with the ones you know are in need of love. This cosmic heart web grows like wildfire. It's infectious, magnetic, ephemeral, and cosmic. It lives inside the precious miracle of the life–death–rebirth cycle, where new beginnings merge into endings and in turn, rise into new beginnings.

Let the scent of the wild rose seep into your heart, feel the ocean water rinse you clean, receive the warmth of the sun's glow to soothe your fragmented mind, and taste the winds of change at your back. Trust that this miracle of life and death will shake your soul awake. Bear witness to it all. In a heartbeat, your mythology shifts for the good, and the ancient stars in your cells rekindle their flame. It is this kind of mythic potency that you get to experience when you trust in the divine timings, the signs, the symbols. Your teachers are around each corner. Stay open to altering the course of your life in a flash. This is how to clear your energy channels and be an earth-side angel. The mystical creature inside you births itself into the world. She arrives ready to thrive.

The evolutionary, cosmic, and ancient flow lives inside the elements. Trust this. Turn to this when you need to and dwell inside the spirit and science of your inner technology. In this cosmic heart web there will be a deep recognition that by making peace with your past—individually, collectively, and historically—you will be a good ancestor. The ancestral healing and honoring you do will inspire the coming generations to evolve, shape-shift, and become leaders of compassionate inquiry and authenticity.

To be a heart and soul trailblazer is to integrate your core beliefs, your physical presence, and your spiritual inquiry into practices on a daily basis. The artistry of embodied and integrated ritual forever alter the course of your life. When you awaken to the depth of your own healer, your own guide, your own inner student, you will never forget this medicine. Your mind lands inside your heart, and your heart shoots up to your mind and deep into the roots of the earth.

Embody the channel of earth to sky—sky to earth.
Imbue your mind and heart with this infinite alchemy.

Stay close to your heart and observe with a clear inner eye. Witness your ability to shift your own mythology. It comes from the heart—the feminine mythic superpower brings it all back to the heart. The quest of the modern mystic is to do the heart work to activate the soul's purpose. Rise up to evolve your heart's alchemy. You will never look back on your life and regret doing this powerful work.

The complexities inside your tricky mind will keep you working hard to be the peaceful warrior. Let this be the living content for you to work through and evolve from. Accept the invitation to work with your mind's loops and spirals with compassion, and remember they come through out of habit, past trauma, karmic layers, and ancestral experiences. When you are ready to untangle and heal from their patterns, you will do so.

Your daily conscious mind–body training and awakening become your everyday therapy. Be your own healer. Receive the mind counsel as it arrives. Be ready, for it will show up in the most unexpected times—both auspicious and mundane. Receive the messages as they arrive. Let go of whatever is not yours, have compassion, and trust you are taking another step in evolving your own consciousness.

You are exactly where you are supposed to be. One step closer to liberating your mind and unlocking your heart. One step towards your own becoming. One step sideways in your alchemical process. You are energy in motion. Dance with your own energy body to co-create and co-direct your life with spirit. You have arrived here in this chapter of your life to be strategic, resourceful, and raise your life-force vibration to evolve your consciousness. You are cosmic and steady. You cast your vision seeds out and watch them evolve.

The elements—air, fire, water, earth, and ether—become archetypal wisdom teachers. You dive deep into their universal life-force energies for ongoing guidance and to reveal the next steps of work on your journey. You stay steady and connected inside the wheel of the year, and the seasonal symbolism honors your current life process. The sun, moon, and stars are your teachers in the sky. Look up often and observe their changing states.

The daily practices you invite into your life must be grounding, inspirational, and liberating. Find a way to channel the creative process to invite joy. You protect your own energy field by setting strong boundaries. Not buying into the materialistic, capitalist mindset will free you from being a victim to the high demands of productivity and convenience. Return to the slower pace whenever possible. Find the pause in the pause. Go inside when spirit calls you to, and share your gifts with the world when you are ready.

The whole world awaits your mystical, heart-led, evolutionary thinking, feeling, and being. The journey is abundant inside the process, and the process is endless inside the journey. What a gift it is to hold your life in the realms of body to mind to spirit, as earth to fire to water to air is to ether. A timeless, infinite swirl of depth, wisdom, and heart awaits you—every single day. Be the love channel of devotion over the channel of duty. Each step on this journey—backwards, forwards, sideways—reminds you that wholeness and presence take you to the depths of life's most soul-stirring awakenings.

Come to the temple door. Set your tired cloaks free, burn away the karmic residue that grips your heart and numbs your mind. The sun burns bright here, the altars are set, the incantations are calling you home. Banish the urge to only please others, write soulful poems to yourself, share your garden harvest with your neighbors. Drop to your knees in honor of the honey bees—the pollinators are of the mystic way. Honor the farmers who grow your sustenance. Be a protectress of the waters, for they nourish your soul. Grow your earth-angel capacity through daily prayer and compassionate action. Become a devotee of soul care, and inspire others to rest and pause and renew once again. For this path of the mystic is not for the faint of heart. It requires conscious rest, non-negotiable self-care, and a devotion that pulls you stronger than life's ongoing dramas.

Walk in beauty. Allow the light of the sun's reflection to encircle you. Receive the messengers and the messages; there is goodness, depth, and cosmic presence everywhere. Take them to heart. Stay grounded, calm, and steady in everyday life. Feel the surge of illuminated energy moving through you. Sometimes it feels like a wild wave, sometimes subtle like a rose petal floating to the ground. These surges are visceral. Let them affect you—you will feel them inside your body. Begin to train yourself to notice them. Feel how light forces pervade darkness and obstacles. Weave this felt sense into the daily rhythm of everyday life. Let it stop you in your tracks. Create space to be astonished by wondrous moments of luminous energy.

Come to your altar with the seeds of discernment, intuitive reflection, right action, and divine timing. Do your spirit work for yourself and for our youth. Through your actions, show them the way of compassion and honesty. Above all, show them how to walk hand in hand with spirit. Remind them that there is a bigger force at play. Show them how to make earth altars and teach them how to give blessings through their hearts and hands. For they are the change makers of the future. Encourage them to be exactly who they are; teach them that they are more than enough. No longer over-praise them for a false sense of security. Ask them questions, often, and read to them about the heroines and heroes who did good work. Awaken them to living with a heart full of gratitude; give them a tool kit of resourcefulness so they can survive in the wild. Release them from the firm grip of your own needs and wants, your projections and reflections. Do this for your elders, for your ancestors, and for the unborn generations to come. Take action for the betterment of humanity and the earth. Trust that you are a part of this evolving legacy. Your intentional goodness will extend further than you can conceive.

The inner mystic comes alive when the beauty you see in the world becomes grander than the devastation. When love speaks louder than violence. Armed with a bouquet of wild flowers in her heart, her language codes universal truths. Her cells are marked by the star-kissed webs of the ancient mystics. She speaks star, planet, galaxy, moon; she speaks sun, and wind, and fire. She lives inside the wild roses, the rivers, oceans, and waterfalls. She falls to her knees to pray; not for her own desires, but for the evolution of the planet and for the antiquated wisdom to not be lost. She reclaims the ancient codes, she frees karmic wounds, soothes the inner child when she cries, and she tends the forest through the raven's eye. Earth keeper, wind dancer, water walker, fire keeper, and energy medicine maker—this is the call of the mystic. He lives you in. She lives in you. They live through you. No longer forget to reclaim your beauty, goodness, and truth. Be the messenger of hope, the planter of dreams, the soul shaker of destiny, the change maker of love over fear.

My soul's mission, uniquely crafted, speaks an unspoken heart tongue.
I hold nothing back, I release limitations, and I surrender to the outcome.
Like a huntress, I follow the fresh tracks of opportunity before me.
Inside the sphere of the unknown, a vast world awaits.
And I know, somewhere there is magic to be found.
As I bring my visions to life, I answer the call to be here and
to do what I am meant to do.
My soul shakes awake.
I alchemize, synchronize, and ritualize the sacred pieces of my life altar.
The stories speak of a thousand lives back and a thousand lives forward.
And here I am, listening all the while.
The song of the mystic whispers, welcome home sweet one, welcome home.

Rituals for Mystical and Spiritual Integration

Learn how to activate sacred, ritualistic and transformative practices within the daily weave of life. Unearth your inner mystic through breath, prayer, visualization, journal prompts and activating a steady spiritual space. Ignite inner power and purpose, align with the chamber of your soul, and become the creator of your embodied dream life.

1. Prayer to Invoke Sacred Space

This prayer can be used to open or close a solo or group ceremony. You can turn your body to face each direction as you speak. You can also write your own prayer to call in the elements in a way that feels resonant with you.

Call to the east,
The place of the rising sun.
Welcome winds of new beginnings.
Winged perceiver, fly high.
Shift my perspective.
Activate my heart visionary.
Call to the south,
Gather the wood.
Light the fires.
Embers burn bright.
Compassionate guides arrive.
Remind me. Alchemize me.
Transform me.
Call to the west,
Mountain top waters journey.
Wild rivers, cold lakes, salted oceans.
A confluence of remembering.
Fluid grace.
I am in the Flow.
Call to the north, the earth cries,
The ancestors speak.
Gather stones, concentric circles form the path.
Listen, watch, learn, fall, take a chance.
Find the center within the center.
The space within the space.
Hear the call, wake up.
Mend, patch, and weave.
Luminous one—carry the wisdom forward.

2. Breath Work: Collective Heart Pulse Breath

Intention
To awaken the energy field, release stress, and breathe your heart alive.

1 Find a comfortable seat, draw your awareness inwards, and soften your
whole body.

2 Begin to slow down your breath to a count of six on the inhale and six on the exhale. Repeat for at least 12 breath cycles.

3 Switch your breath rhythm: Take two quick inhales through the nose, hold your breath, and take one long exhale out the mouth.

4 Repeat for at least 12 rounds.

5 Shift your breath rhythm to five short inhales—count them on your fingers. Then hold your breath for as long as you can, pull your navel toward your spine, and bow your chin to you heart. Exhale out your mouth, making any sound that feels energizing and clearing.

- Directly and clearly visualize your breath entering the center of your heart. Call forth your ability to self-love, and send a prayer of compassion and healing to the collective.
- As you hold your breath, draw your navel in and shoot your core essence up to your heart.
- When you exhale, visualize your compassionate and loving spirit streaming out your back and front body.
- Repeat for six rounds.

6 Observe any symbols, shapes, light tracers, memories, or affirmations that come forward.

7 Sit for two minutes in silent meditation. Let your heart expand and integrate into your whole body.

8 Come back into your body and the present moment. Observe or record any insights or shifts experienced.

3. Visualization: Mystic Heart

Intention
To integrate both grounding and rising energies to awaken
and explore the mystic wisdom inside your heart.

I Find a comfortable seat where you can be quiet for at least 10 minutes.

2 Visualize yourself in a landscape that makes you feel calm and peaceful. Observe what is growing there; connect to the elements. Integrate the colors, sounds, scents, and shapes of your surroundings.

3 Sense the roots of a tree. Now visualize yourself connecting to these roots from the bowl of your pelvis, deep down into the earth. This is your source of grounded nourishment.

4 Take in the texture, shape, and tone of the roots.

5 Bring your awareness to your navel and begin to lengthen your spine.

6 Imagine beads of light spiraling inside and around your spinal column, through the back of your neck, inside the center of your brain, and out the top of your head towards the stars.

7 Make a visual connection from your navel through your crown to the stars—see the star formations above you. This will naturally lift and lengthen your spine.

8 Go back to your roots and reverse the order: as the roots draw down they also begin to come up, entwining your legs, encasing your torso until they reach your lungs and heart. Imagine the roots are feeding your heart's most brilliant capacity to love.

9 Return to the starry night sky and allow the illumination of the stars to stream down into your heart.

10 Imagine your heart and lungs now filled with millions of stars. See the stars and the roots intermingling through your whole body.

11 Receive any symbols or messages from your mystic heart—the elder in your heart. What advice would support the evolution of your current heart consciousness?

12 Listen for a call to action or a call to stillness. Record your insights.

13 Place both hands upon your heart and give thanks for another day to live and love on this planet.

14 Journal about your experience for two minutes.

4. Meditation: Soul Chamber

Intention
To reclaim your sacred space, your sense of self,
and to rebalance your nervous system.

1 Find a comfortable seat or lie down. Wrap a blanket around you, and make sure you are warm enough.

2 Begin to consciously attune to your breath.

3 When you are ready, allow your inhale to become a channel of
   illumination, like the sun, and breathe it in fully.

4 With each exhale, simply soften into your own skin, and let go completely.

5 Visualize yourself entering your soul chamber. Here you ingest, receive,
   and digest the highest frequency of pure energy. Allow yourself to enter
   a zone that is so deeply nourishing that each inhale is the nectar that
   infuses your soul with goodness, beauty, and truth. This is your own
   spirit energy, like a butterfly cocoon.

6 With each exhale continue to soften, let go again and again. Let go so
   much that stress, imbalance, and fatigue simply fall off you. Shed the
   continued layers of outmoded ways with each exhalation. Fill the edges
   of your soul chamber with your personal radiance, balance,
   and harmony.

7 Let each inhale peacefully fill your soul chamber with illumination.

8 Seal your meditation with the color that you most resonate with— and
   visualize your soul chamber filled with this healing color.

5. Visualization Journey:
Awaken Your Inner Mystic, Reclaim Your Soul Purpose

Intention
To attune to your inner compass and welcome
your intuitive power. To activate and illuminate your
higher self and shed what no longer serves you.

Supplies
You'll need paper, colored pencils or paint, a candle, altar items,
your journal, music, open space, and a blanket.

I Light a candle, cleanse your space with fresh air, incense, or plant or
   essential oils that make you feel at home in yourself.

2 Make an altar that incorporates anything you are currently working
   with—words, images, stones, plants, simplicity, complexity—this is a
   healing in itself.

3 Sit in a quiet space for at least two minutes. Let yourself go completely;
   breathe deeply.

4 Visualize a body of water in front of you. Look into the water's reflection and welcome your inner mystic. Attune to your higher self, honoring all the work coming to you: the emotions, the words, the task list and all of the unknowns.

5 Call forth what you are inviting into your life and what you are releasing at this time—every worry, concern, stressor—let it go for now.

6 Begin to map out your heartfelt intentions inside the directions of the compass, in your own creative way. For each direction: Write it out, sketch, sing, dance, pray, love. Let it be a mind–spirit–soul mapping exercise. What are you ready to invite in? Where do you need to release?

East

Call forward your heart visionary, the element of air. What message is there here for you? What is your heart ready to feel and share?

South

The element of fire. Welcome in your honest, humble and clear inner power. What does it have to share with you? Write it out, call it forward. What is ready to be processed, burned, and transformed out of you?

West

The element of water. Express your connection to water, fluidity, and staying connected to your emotions as your superpower. Your guides will call your attention in the least unsuspecting moments. Allow yourself to feel the spark of the inner mystic's call.

North

Call in your connection to Mother Earth, and weave the golden threads of your ancestors forward. Welcome in your grounding and your soul's mission.

Ether

Call forward your highest self. Honor from your quiet moments to your most expressive moments—honor your range. Let it be free and intentional.

7 As you sketch, write, and make symbols of where you are now and where you are going, begin to formulate which path, direction, or commitment feels most aligned with your higher self.

8 If your best self was to look down at you in this moment, what would it say? What would be the call to action?

9 Once your map is sketched or formulated, place it on your altar and gaze into it. Let any deeper meaning and messaging come through you at this time.

10 Seal the sacred space all around you by honoring the directions, their meanings, and your messengers.

11 Journal your reactions, write a poem, or share your soul mission with your best friend.

6. Empower Your Spiritual Voice, Embody Your Mystic Beauty

Intention
To let go of the roles you play out in everyday life, clear channels from lack to love, and liberate your spiritual voice for intuitive embodiment and mystical beauty.

Purpose
To empower and channel your spiritual embodiment in order to receive messages, healings, and calls to action to live your fullest, most joyous life.

Supplies
Altar items to represent the elements earth, air, fire, water, and ether. A journal, a candle, incense, herbs, or essential oils to purify the air, a space to move freely, and access to an outdoor space if possible.

1 Sit in silence, let go of any roles and responsibilities. Breathe calmly for at least two to five minutes, visualize yourself free of any attachments.

2 Place one hand on your heart, and one hand on your navel. Welcome in your spiritual voice and the expression of your inner mystic.

3 Invoke sacred space by fanning essential oils, herbs, or incense. Open the windows to allow any negative energies to be released.

4 Invite your compassionate guides to support you and welcome your own spiritual essence to be fully expressed.

5 Journal the following prompts.

The beauty I see in my heart is _____

The beauty I see in my releasing is _____

The beauty I see in my current transformation is _____

The beauty I see in my ability to flow is _____

The beauty I see in my grounded self is _____

The beauty I see in my spiritual expression is _____

The beauty I see in the world is _____

The beauty I see in personal alchemy is _____

6 Create an altar based on your intuitive creative impulse. Receive inspiration from the above journal prompts, along with the sacred items in your home.

7 Light a candle on your altar and begin to pray/channel out loud the journal questions above. Then call forward your gratitude and your soul's desires, speak for the healing of the world, and allow your inner mystic to be expressed through you freely.

8 Embody what comes forward: emotions, expressions, movements, and desires. Do not hold anything back.

9 Stand up before your altar and begin a movement journey. Dance, move, or jog on the spot for five to 10 minutes without stopping. Let your breath and voice be free. Hold the intention of birthing your inner mystic alive.

10 Return to your altar, place your hands in the center of it, your inner mystic may want to sing, speak, or pray once again.

11 Find stillness, receive the ritual healing, and observe any intuitive flashes or sensations in your body.

12 Choose any altar items that are ready to be given as gifts back to nature. It is a gift of reciprocity, an acknowledgment and commitment to your spiritual self and to your environment.

13 Seal in sacred space by honoring your spiritual voice in the world while acknowledging your compassionate guides. Allow words, prayers, or songs to flow through you.

7. Journal Prompts

- List your top core values and write them into a soul mission statement. Use the first person to craft this piece. ("My core values are…" or "I believe in…")
- If you were a mythical creature, what would you be? Why?
- What wisdom would your inner mystic share with the world right now?
- What advice would you give your younger self?
- How does this advice apply to your current life journey?
- What have been your most profound life-altering experiences? How did they shift your consciousness or belief systems? What message or core value did you integrate from each experience?
- What daily practices connect you to living the best version of yourself?
- What soul-care rituals and daily practices keep your heart awake, expansive, and warm?
- Write a soul mantra or code of ethics to your inner mystic. Weave in what lights you up, what makes you unique, strong, creative, and spirited. Like a soul love letter, begin each sentence with "The beauty I see in you is…"

Spirit is calling.
A sense of another presence, a scent, a sound, a vision flashed.
The numinous speaks louder than the mundane.
Listen. Pause. Reset.
Where am I?
Who am I now?

In the company of otherworldly kinship,
unravel your best-kept secrets.
Lay down your most precious relics.
Somewhere between slumbered states,
your electric nature awakens.

This becoming suits you,
fits like a glove, merges into the marrow of your heart of hearts.
Pulse. Boom. Beat. Skip. Quiver. Shake me awake.
Oh, to know this great mystery we call life!

Source neither mastered nor coded,
neither lost nor found.
Pure. Untouchable. Sensory.
Infinite energy in its purest form.
No ending. No beginning.
Cosmic, ephemeral, unconditional.

Answer the call, spirit always holds you in your highest.

Rose scent forever in my heart,
I am lifted up by the salted ocean, cleansed.

The warmth of the sun's glow soothes my fragmented mind.
The winds of change push at my back,
this miracle of life to birth to death shakes my soul awake.
And I bear witness to it all—imprinted like an ancient star in my heart,
deep in the well of my bones.

In a flash I recall that unforgettable moment when my mythology
shifted for the good, everything seemed different.
My mythic creature—potent, open, and ready to express its
timeless song to the ancient cedars—birthed itself alive.

And in this awakening, I remember that there is a grand power in
staying true to my own pure and shape-shifting channel of energy.

Navigating the divine timings, the signs and symbols,
this ritual life keeps me steady and cosmic.
I dance wildly with the soul of the earth.
I pray daily for the good of humanity and all living beings.

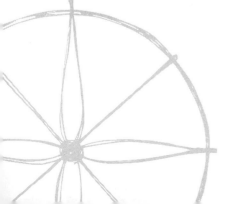

EPILOGUE

To embody the art of ritual inside the weave of daily life is to craft your existence through the union of body–mind–heart–spirit. The body is the channel, the mind is the canvas, the heart is the nest, and the spirit body is the sphere encircling your personal alchemy. The dance between surrender and activation is the greatest dance in life. When you hold reverence for the dynamic and cosmic rhythms inside every living thing, you fully embrace this great mystery. While you can never assume you know what is happening on a cosmic level, you can align your own channels by activating practices that you intuitively and inherently know are good for the soul.

Observing the rhythms and rituals with consciousness in your daily life allows you to balance the polarities of work and play, joy and grief, beginnings and endings. As you merge with the universal life-force and the powerful archetypes of the sun and moon and the five elements, you develop your capacity to heal. Your personal alchemy evolves rapidly. And when in doubt, when life gets hard and the inner critic takes you for a ride, you bring your inquiries to your altar with discernment and a heart full of compassion.

Life is full of surprises! When you trust that you are supported, when you show up and do your spirit work every single day, you receive powerful clarity on your next steps. Feed the forests, oceans, and lakes with your intentional and sacred surrenders—time and time again. As you release the inner tensions, you allow the outer complexities to fall away, if only for a moment. And it is in this sacred pause that the body remembers, the mind clears, and the heart comes alive.

Research the rituals and traditions of your ancestors. Get to know your family tree. Gather images and make an ancestral altar. Glean the gold from your family lineage, welcome what resonates and discern what does not—there is healing in this process. With reverence and respect, also study the rituals of other cultures that light you up. Find the teachers and teachings that inspire you. Learn the traditions that allow you to ground, evolve, explore, and become the best version of you.

Gather in community with like-minded folk, let the simple joy of everyday conversation warm your inner fire. And when everything becomes overwhelming, soften your grip. With humility, become a beginner on this planet once again. Trust in the unknown, and welcome the winds of change all around you. Let this be the journey and the steady, cosmic deepening within you.

Cherish your mornings and your evenings with sacred moments. Light candles, create altars and sanctuaries in your home that reflect your co-creation with spirit. Beginning and ending your days in sacredness will bring stability and balance to how you rest and how you activate. Be willing to rise and sleep with the sun's rhythm.

Open your own energy field to merge with your natural surroundings; touch the earth, kiss the sky. Transform your mind–body state when needed. Discover the freedom that lies inside your unique creative expressions—artistic, physical, emotional, or intellectual—and practice them ceremonially.

Allow change, opposition, and challenging times to be what they are. Have your support systems in place, and show up for yourself through your soul-care regime. Ride your habitual patterns like waves. Observe when guilt, shame, lack, fear, or unworthiness begin to swirl inside you. Greet them like the impeccable warrior you are, and celebrate your awareness before these emotions take over. See your emotions for what they are. Rise up, meet them squarely, name them, and begin again, with your body–heart–mind steeped in compassion.

Embrace yourself in a wild, untamable force field of unwavering love. Swim in a stream of self-forgiveness, compassion, and awakened consciousness. Get curious and intimate with what truly lights you up. Create ways to shape-shift within—this is what your spirit longs for. And when you tend to your inner garden, no longer repressing or bypassing its true desires, you set yourself free of hardships and a worldly weight that no longer needs to sit on your shoulders.

Welcome your grandmothers, grandfathers, aunties, uncles, and cousins—both blood and spiritual—invite them to warm their hands by your fire, and listen to them with a wide-open mind–heart. Around every city corner, trailhead, cafe, ocean walk, there is yet another teacher, a muse, a reflection showing you another experience of embodiment on this planet.

Walk hand in hand with your own spirit. Let your heart be your twin flame, and welcome this blessed life journey as the dimensional, sacred, deep, loving, and joyful experience it is. Remember to walk backwards at times in order to remember—to re-route, find another way. There you can truly hear the call of your intuitive nature beyond the critic inside the trickster mind.

Call on your compassionate guides, invite them to tea. Welcome their goodness into your own heart and give yourself the gift of quietude in the early dawn light. For the simple and still moments of letting go, clear the path for freedom to grow within your energy body like wildflowers on a mountain top. Like stardust coming alive within your cells to infuse you with an ancient serum of worldly, timeless wisdom.

The whole of your life is like a call and response song. All the colors, shapes, pathways, portals, and dimensions whisper to you when you are ready. The work is to discern the random and cyclical thoughts over the honest moments of epiphany. You go on your own unique journey, up the mountain peak, down the dusty country road, over the superhighway where the pace is faster than light. You gather your basket full of healing tools, inner resources, relationship lessons, and heart-infused symbols. Your inner mystic is equipped for this.

Each cycle in your life leads to the next, and when you birth your alchemist alive, no longer do you live your life half asleep—no longer do you feed negativity and toxicity into our circles of existence. You become awake, aligned, and fueled by the universal truths of goodness and compassion. An inner beauty streams through you, touching the hearts of strangers on your path, healing yourself, your family, and your communities, enlivening your experience through your own channeled goodness and truth.

Your work now is to listen fully, rest deeply, commit to what lights you up. You activate the vision when your desire becomes louder than your inner critic. To the very core of the earth and up to the stars you go— sometimes walking backwards to remember your goodness, beauty and truth, sometimes spiraling into the swirl of ethereal mystery.

Show up for yourself every day in one small way, do the work you need to do. No longer feed the lower vibrations. Instead, awaken your inner mystic powers through your heart-led, rock steady, earth loving and wild warrior ways. The world is ready to hear you, see you, accept you, and witness you in your highest.

Celebrate the evolution of your most free, grounded, joyous and authentic self. Inside of you is everything you need. Your earth angels and guides are here, cheering your brave heart onwards, giving you standing ovations for the journey. All the while, you learn, you find your way home, and you open to love time and time again.

I drank the moon
last night.
One massive gulp.
Instantly,
she tore me apart.
A timeless swirl of darkness
engulfed me.
And I awoke, and I awoke.
Gathering. Mending. Weaving.
My contents back together.
Stories, songs,
the ancient-ness
of my bones. Of my bones.
The ancestors called.
It's time.
The revolution is now.
Sifting fossils. Mixing sand. Bird call. Leaf fall.
Lightning flash. Star smash.
I left it there in a heap.
And the wildflowers burst through the earth.
Hungry for the sun.

Overview of Rituals

Chapter 7
The Moon's Cycle: Ancient Wisdom for Transformation and Renewal
Rituals to Align and Source Pure Energy from the Moon

Chapter 8
Evolutionary Practices of the Mystic: Enhancing Your Personal Alchemy
Rituals for Mystical and Spiritual Integration

Recommended Reading

Barks, Coleman. *The Essential Rumi*. New York: HarperCollins, 1995.

Blackwood, Danielle. *The Twelve Faces of the Goddess: Transform Your Life with Astrology, Magick, and the Sacred Feminine*. Woodbury, Minnesota: Llewellyn Publications, 2018.

Brown, Brené. *Braving the Wilderness: The Quest for True Belonging and the Courage to Stand Alone*. New York: Random House, 2017.

Desikachar, t.k.V. *The Heart of Yoga: Developing a Personal Practice*. Rochester, Vermont: Inner Traditions, 1995.

Dispenza, Joe. *Becoming Supernatural: How Common People Are Doing the Uncommon*. New York: Hay House, 2017.

Estés, Clarissa Pinkola. *Women Who Run with the Wolves*. New York: Ballantine Books, 1992.

Gibran, Kahlil. *The Prophet*. New York: Quality Paperback Book Club, 1995.

Ingerman, Sandra. *Walking in the Light: The Everyday Empowerment of a Shamanic Life*. Boulder, Colorado: Sounds True, 2014.

Judith, Anodea. *Wheels of Life: A User's Guide to the Chakra System*. Woodbury, Minnesota: Llewellyn Publications, 2009.

Kempton, Sally. *Awakening Shakti: The Transformative Power of the Goddesses of Yoga*. Boulder, Colorado: Sounds True, 2013.

Kimmerer, Robin Wall. *Braiding Sweetgrass: Indigenous Wisdom, Scientific Knowledge, and the Teachings of Plants*. Minnesota: Milkweed Editions, 2013.

Mate, Gabor, M.D. *When the Body Says No: The Cost of Hidden Stress*. Toronto: Vintage Canada, 2004.

Myss, Caroline. *Anatomy of the Spirit: The Seven Stages of Power and Healing*. New York: Three Rivers Press, 1996.

Oliver, Mary. *Devotions: The Selected Poems of Mary Oliver*. New York: Penguin, 2017.

Roach, Geshe Michael and Christie McNally. *The Essential Yoga Sutra: Ancient Wisdom for Your Yoga*. New York: Three Leaves Press, July 2005.

Roth, Gabrielle. *Maps to Ecstasy: A Healing Journey for the Untamed Heart*. California: New World Library, 1998.

Ruiz, Don Miguel. *The Four Agreements: A Toltec Wisdom Book*. California: Amber-Allen Publishing, 1997.

Starr, Mirabai. *Wild Mercy: Living the Fierce and Tender Wisdom of the Women Mystics.* Boulder, Colorado: Sounds True, 2019.

Syedullah, Jasmine, Lama Rod Owens, and Angel Kyodo Williams. *Radical Dharma: Talking Race, Love, and Liberation.* Berkeley, California: North Atlantic Books, 2016.

Tippett, Krista. *Becoming Wise: An Inquiry into the Mystery and Art of Living.* New York: Penguin Press, 2016.

Wilcox, Joan Parisi. *Master of the Living Energy: The Mystical World of the Q'ero of Peru.* Vermont: Inner Traditions, 1999.

Wohlleben, Peter. *The Hidden Life of Trees: What They Feel, How They Communicate.* Canada: Greystone Books in Partnership with David Suzuki, 2016.

Index

About the Author

Photo by Kornelia Kulbackie

Mara Branscombe is a mother, writer, yogi, artist, teacher, mindfulness leader, ceremonialist and spiritual coach. She is passionate about weaving the art of mindfulness, self-care, creativity, mind–body practices, and earth-based rituals into her life and work, and she has been leading community ceremony since 2000.

An adventurous spirit, Mara has sailed across the Atlantic Ocean, trekked across the Himalayas, studied yoga in India, planted trees in Canada's north, lived off the grid in a remote cabin in the woods, worked as a Waldorf (Steiner School) teacher, and then found her passion for dance and choreography. All the while yoga, meditation, mysticism and ritual have been at the heart of Mara's journey. Her trainings in the Incan Shaman lineage and the Pagan tradition have greatly inspired her life's work of earth-based, ceremonial, intentional, and heart-centered living and loving.

Mara currently lives in Vancouver, Canada with her husband and two daughters.

For more information visit: **www.marabranscombe.com**

FINDHORN PRESS

Life-Changing Books

Learn more about us and our books at
www.findhornpress.com

For information on the Findhorn Foundation:
www.findhorn.org